VISIONARY
PRAGMATIST

SIR
VINCENT
RAVEN

North Eastern Railway
Locomotive Engineer

VISIONARY PRAGMATIST

SIR VINCENT RAVEN

North Eastern Railway
Locomotive Engineer

ANDREW EVERETT MA

TEMPUS

First published 2006

Tempus Publishing Limited
The Mill, Brimscombe Port,
Stroud, Gloucestershire, GL5 2QG
www.tempus-publishing.com

British Library Cataloguing in Publication Data.
A catalogue record for this book is available from the British Library.

ISBN 0 7524 3924 3

Typesetting and origination by Tempus Publishing Limited
Printed in Great Britain

CONTENTS

INTRODUCTION

When *The Railway Magazine* of January 2000 published the results of its Millennium Poll, Sir Vincent Raven gained forty-second place, along with Thomas Newcomen and Arthur Peppercorn. He, like them, usually merits little more than a brief mention in railway history books, yet in many ways he was much more than a typical man of his time. In appearance, he bears quite a striking resemblance to his contemporaries in music, Sir Hubert Parry and Sir Edward Elgar (1857–1934), the latter being Raven's almost exact contemporary. Ironically, like Parry, Raven lost out to a younger and more famous successor, namely Herbert Nigel Gresley (ranked third in the Millennium Poll). There is a solidity and style about the work of both the older men, which came to be eclipsed in the public mind by the more famous creations of the younger men. This is an attempt at a reappraisal.

Much of Raven's steam and electric locomotive-building activity has been charted in a piecemeal pattern without seeking to make a cohesive biographical narrative of it or place it in the context of his life and times except briefly, tentatively and unsatisfactorily in obituaries and in other incomplete digests about him, such as the 'candidate circulars' for Institution of Mechanical Engineers (IMechE) and Institution of Civil Engineers (ICE).

The title of the book, *Visionary Pragmatist*, was chosen because Raven used the North Eastern Railway Co. (NER) frameworks to develop his career in quite a traditional and practical way both as a junior and senior company servant. Yet he became convinced at the end that rail electrification was the most practical way forward for the future, being both a complementary and an alternative means to the development of steam rail locomotion.

Facts about his own family both before and after his lifetime are sparse. Raven, like other railway notables in the last years of the nineteenth century, had a clerical father. His wife and his five brothers and four sisters all remain shadowy figures with only a few facts known. His two sons, and his grandson and granddaughter, Michael Litchfield and Mary Gifford Taylor, emerge a little more from the shadows as does his daughter, Edith Guendolen, because of her relationship to Edward Thompson. While there is much discoverable material about what he did, especially about his locomotives and how successful they were deemed to be and dates available about his professional, civic and committee life, it has been much more difficult to learn about what kind of the character the man was, whether as pupil, apprentice, husband, father, friend, engineering colleague, successful engineer and senior manager in a profitable company or as elder statesman knowing about railway matters. Raven's extant writings, the conference papers and reports for NER, plus newspaper reports of what he said, are couched in language carefully worked out for the occasion and only give occasional glimmers of what motivated him at work.

His life falls into seven distinct phases. Firstly, there is his childhood and schooling. This leads naturally to a second phase – his choice of apprenticeship. Here, Raven seems to have decided early on his own career pattern rather than that of his father's family, going to Cambridge University. Instead, he chose an apprenticeship in a career in engineering with the railways of the North East of England. A third phase followed with his early career as employee of the firm. It included his marriage and fatherhood as well as his climb up the ranks under four different locomotive superintendents, gradually moving to the forefront of a design-and-build team.

A fourth phase is marked by his becoming chief mechanical engineer and his further moves into the civic life of Darlington and the marriages of his daughters. This period was interrupted by a fifth phase as a result of the First World War, namely his work for the Ministry of Munitions and the Admiralty. He now exceeded the social achievements of his Raven ancestors and that of his children and grandchildren in gaining a knighthood, very much as a result of his own efforts.

A return to NER and a dedication to electrifying the railways and developing his *Pacific* characterises a sixth phase – his last three years with NER. A seventh and final phase is ushered in by his retirement from NER, which left him time to become both a railway guru as well as an electrification Cassandra, to do a lot of committee work, investigations and subsequent reports. It is a story of a largely self-educated man making the most of his talents in a chosen field of activity.

How he related to the many people, who met him over the years can be inferred fitfully from the evidence available. His religious and political opinions and his social objectives are not easy to uncover. For instance, his membership at the local Masonic Lodge probably served as a vehicle for meeting local people of consequence or influence. His church attendance was for main life events, rather than devotion, although there is a deep underlying honesty in his approach to his work and to how he related to others.

The family tree material has been gleaned from a variety of sources, e.g. from the International Genealogical Index, Cambridge University Alumni and Registrar General's Office – Free Births, Marriages and Death Project and War Graves Commission For consistency, the variants of his wife's forename of Gifford and her surname Crichton, e.g. Giffard or Chrichton, have not been used.

Family trees and tables included in the book have been drawn up by the author. Photographs taken by the author show what is currently available from Raven's time, while archive photographs come from as near contemporary material as possible.

ACKNOWLEDGEMENTS

Thanks to Lorraine and Madie of North Road Study Centre in Darlington; to the many library staffs of the universities of Newcastle and Northumbria libraries, to Newcastle Discovery (Tyne and Wear Archive Service), Durham Record Office, the National Archives (UK) and New South Wales (NSW) National Archives and NSW Government Library; of the Public Libraries at Darlington, Oswestry, York, Gateshead, Newcastle in UK and Blacktown and Baulkwell Hills (NSW) for their help to me; to the Public Libraries staff at Felixstowe, Winchester and Basingstoke for their help by phone and letter; to staff of the National Railway Museum at York for their time and help in gaining access to their archival collections, to the archivists of ICE, IMechE and Institution of Electrical Engineers (IEE) for their positive help with their material both by post and personally; to the two librarians of Aldenham School for the book on the school and further Raven family information, to the archivists at Polam School, Darlington, and of Uppingham School, Rutland; to Mrs Myers, the president of Darlington Townswomen's Guild; to the owner of Old Hall, Hurworth; to the secretaries of Felixstowe Ferry and Lydney Hall Golf Clubs for their helpful suggestions; to Roger AC Hennessey and other members of the Stephenson Locomotive Society; to Geoffrey Hughes and members of the Gresley Society; to members of the Railway Correspondence and Travel Society and to Chris Wolstenholmes, librarian, and to many other members of North Eastern Railway Association for their encouragement; to Ross Verdich and members of the Australian Railway History Society in Sydney and Newcastle (NSW); to a large number of other railway and history societies I have contacted and spoken to about Raven for their encouragement and suggestions; to descendants of Raven's family still living for their interest, courtesy and correspondence; to Malcolm Middleton for information on Alpine Cottage and Bowls Club; to my son Paul and daughter Catherine for their encouragement and advice; and lastly, to my wife Mary, for her patience and support during the writing of this book.

ABBREVIATIONS

AGM	Annual General Meeting
ARLE	Association of Railway Locomotive Engineers
ASRS	Amalgamated Society of Railway Servants
CE	Chief Engineer
CME	Chief Mechanical Engineer
CR	Caledonian Railway
EBR	East Bengal Railway
EIR	East India Railway
EE	Electrical Engineer
GCR	Great Central Railway
GER	Great Eastern Railway
GIPR	Great Indian Peninsular Railway
GM	General Manager
GNR	Great Northern Railway
GS&WR	Great South & Western Railway
GWR	Great Western Railway
H&BR	Hull & Barnsley Railway
ICE	Institution of Civil Engineers
IEE	Institution of Electrical Engineers
IMechE	Institution of Mechanical Engineers
LB&SCR	London Brighton & South Coast Railway
LN	Leeds Northern Railway
L&NER	London & North Eastern Railway
L&NWR	London & North Western Railway
LS	Locomotive Superintendent
L&SWR	London & South Western Railway
L&YR	Lancashire & Yorkshire Railway
M&M	Merz & McLellan
MR	Midland Railway
NBR	North British Railway
NECIE&S	North East Coast Institution of Engineers and Shipbuilders
NER	North Eastern Railway
	National Archives former Public Record Office (PRO)
RCA	Railway Companies Association
RE	Royal Engineers
ROD	Railway Operating Department

SD&R	Stockton & Darlington Railway
SE&CR	South East & Chatham Railway
SR	Southern Railway
WBR	West Bengal Railway
YN&BR	York, Newcastle & Berwick Railway
Y&NMR	York & North Midland Railway

Note on locomotive wheel arrangement

The usual number format denoting wheel arrangement for steam locomotives is followed, namely 'leading wheels'–'driving wheels' (second set of driving wheels, if applicable) – 'trailing wheels', e.g. 4-8-2, or 4-6-6-4. Labels commonly used for certain types of wheel arrangement are also used in the text, e.g. *Atlantics* = 4-4-2, *Pacifics* = 4-6-2 and *Baltics* = 4-6-4. For electric locomotives, the mixed number/letter (the latter being used for driving wheels only) format is used, e.g. 2-C-C-2.

I

FAMILY BACKGROUND AND EARLY LIFE (1858–1875)

Over many centuries, branches of the Raven family have become widespread throughout England and in Northern Europe, even if not very numerous. Revd Vincent's branch came originally from Norwich. Raven's great-great-grandfather was Henry Raven of Norwich, who married Sarah Baldwin at St Giles, Norwich, in 1781. His son, Henry Baldwin (noted as working at the Treasury), was baptised in St Peter Mancroft, Norwich, on 2 December 1781. He eventually moved to London. There he married Mary Ann Litchfield (whence came Raven's middle name). She was from a London family (her father's name was Vincent). Henry died in December 1872 aged about ninety-one. There were three children of the marriage, Revd Vincent (Sir Vincent's father), Sarah Baldwin and Revd James Dillon. The two sons both went to Cambridge University and then followed a clerical career.

James Dillon, the younger son, was born on 12 November 1823. He followed a similar career to Vincent as a priest of the Church of England. After attending St Peter's Grammar School, Pimlico, London, he matriculated at Michaelmas in 1838, entered St John's College, Cambridge, on 18 January 1839, and quickly transferred on 21 January to Magdalen, where his brother was completing his MA. Graduating as a BA in 1842, he was ordained deacon in Chester on 18 December, working in a number of places, including as a curate at St Mary's Bolton, Lancashire, from 1842–1824. After ordination in 1844 and gaining his MA at Magdalen in 1845, he worked in the Home Counties. After 1858, he lived at St John's Lodge, St John's Road, Eastbourne, and was living there in 1881[1] with his wife, Mary Anne (born in 1830). He had moved to several rural parishes in Home Counties from 1852–1858, finally settling at Eastbourne as a clergyman. There were no children at home in 1881 (if any had been born to the couple). However, he was a clergyman without a benefice, making his living as a schoolmaster to ten boys between the ages of seven and eleven from the northern Home Counties and Midlands. James Dillon later lived elsewhere on the south coast, dying at Shanklin on the Isle of Wight on 24 March 1900.

Sarah Baldwin was born at Cadogan Square, London, on 24 November 1922, but remained single; after Revd Vincent's death, Anne Rainbow went to live with her sister-in-law in Chelsea.[2]

Vincent, the older brother, was educated at King College, London. On 23 April 1833, he matriculated, joining Magdalen College, one of the smaller Cambridge Colleges in Michaelmas 1833 as 'sizar'. Linked originally with East Anglian abbeys, Magdalen is one of the more ancient university foundations, dating back to the 1470s. Its most famous past alumnus was Samuel Pepys.

Vincent went on to obtain his BA (10th Wrangler) in 1836, becoming a fellow the same year. As a fellow, he is likely to have had contact with nineteen-year-old Charles Kingsley,

Magdalen's most celebrated nineteenth-century alumnus, who came to Magdalen in 1838. Raven was ordained deacon at nearby Ely and priest of the Church of England in 1839, becoming an MA at Magdalene in 1840. He then served as curate in London from 1840–1843, returning to the academic life at Cambridge, becoming dean at Magdalen between 1844 and 1846. He took up the post of tutor between 1846 and 1853, serving as president from 1850–1853. As the tutorship at Magdalen was a bachelor one, Revd Vincent Raven had had to resign his fellowship and tutor's post when he decided to marry in 1853 Anne Jemima Rainbow, daughter of John Rainbow (a variant of Raimbaud) from London. He was fortunate that Magdalen could provide him with a benefice, that of the rector of All Saint's, Great Fransham. It meant that he returned to the county from which his father's family had come.

Great Fransham is a small, very scattered village, lying in fields in the open North Norfolk countryside. Despite hedges and trees, it is open to winds and rain, especially in winter. It lies about six miles east–north–east of Swaffham, down a lane a mile from the King's Lynn to Norwich road, eventually petering out after the station building. It had 391 inhabitants in the 1841 Census and had only relatively recently been connected to the King's Lynn and East Dereham Railway, built from 1846–1848 by a station to the north of the village. By 1854, it was served by four passenger trains and one goods train each way daily, despite having only seventy-four houses, a reduction to a population of 319.

The church of All Saints is rather piecemeal in style and run down in appearance, and has some Perpendicular features with a south arcade of four bays and a square tower with a short spire; its nave was restored in 1878, during Raven's time as rector.[3]

The Rectory lies a few hundred yards from the church. It is approached by a short drive to the two-storeyed house. It has a Georgian front and door case, added in the early 1800s to an earlier farmhouse with its lower ceilings and crossbeams, still to be seen in kitchen, larders and storage rooms to the rear. Being in the gift of Magdalen College, it had sixty-three acres of glebe and a yearly rent of £552 in lieu of tithes. Charles Reynolds, the previous rector, had built a school, which continued to be chiefly supported by Revd Raven.[4]

All Saints, Great Fransham, where Raven's father was rector from 1854–1887.

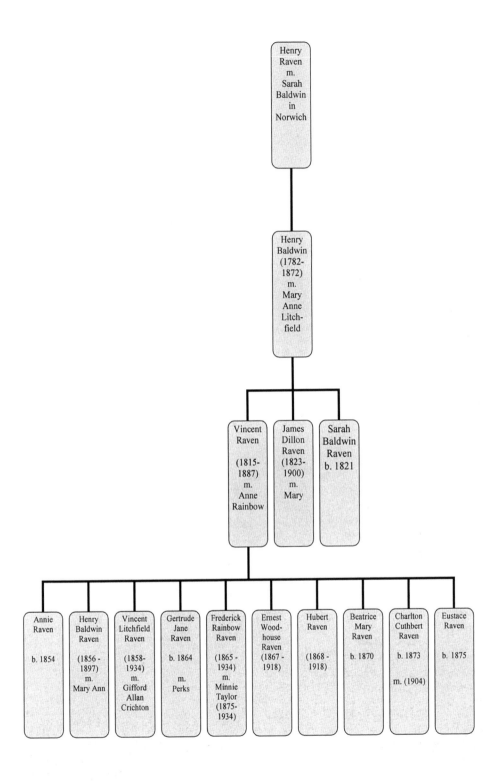

Henry
Raven
m.
Sarah
Baldwin
in
Norwich

Henry
Baldwin
(1782-
1872)
m.
Mary
Anne
Litch-
field

Vincent
Raven

(1815-
1887)
m.
Anne
Rainbow

James
Dillon
Raven
(1823-
1900)
m.
Mary

Sarah
Baldwin
Raven
b. 1821

Annie
Raven

b. 1854

Henry
Baldwin
Raven

(1856 -
1897)
m.
Mary Ann

Vincent
Litchfield
Raven

(1858-
1934)
m.
Gifford
Allan
Crichton

Gertrude
Jane
Raven

b. 1864

m.
Perks

Frederick
Rainbow
Raven

(1865 -
1934)
m.
Minnie
Taylor
(1875-
1934)

Ernest
Wood-
house
Raven
(1867 -
1918)

Hubert
Raven

(1868 -
1918)

Beatrice
Mary
Raven

b. 1870

Charlton
Cuthbert
Raven

b. 1873

m. (1904)

Eustace
Raven

b. 1875

Raven's ancestors and siblings.

The Rectory where Raven and his six brothers and three sisters were born.

Arms of the Worshipful Co. of Brewers, whose Trust Fund has supported Aldenham School since 1576. They share the same motto.

As a couple, the Ravens were prolific, producing seven sons and three daughters all born at the Rectory Besides the family, the Rectory supported a governess for the children, a cook and a housemaid. Apart from his domestic role as paterfamilias Revd Vincent, his spiritual duties as rural parson and educational ones as supporter of the local school and its teachers, he spent his leisure time in providing his church with a finely carved and detailed pew bench, lectern and altar table in a quite elaborate ecclesiological Puginesque style, rather at variance with Low Church practice. During the autumn of 1887, Gertrude Jane married Arthur Perks in the area. When RevdVincent died on 12 December 1887, the rest of the family had moved elsewhere out of Norfolk.[5]

Raven himself was born on 3 December 1858.[6] Following upper- and middle-class custom, Vincent was sent to preparatory boarding school at Brighton, probably when he was about seven years old. He may have had some contact with his uncle in nearby Eastbourne during that time. He then followed his older brother to Aldenham School in Hertfordshire from 1872 to 1876.

Henry Baldwin, Raven's oldest brother, was born on 17 March 1856. Five of the brothers, Henry Baldwin, Raven himself, Hubert, Ernest Woodhouse and Frederick Rainbow were all educated at Aldenham School, Hertfordshire, from 1872 to 1881. Henry Baldwin was there from 1870 to 1876. He was a good enough sportsman to play on the school football and cricket eleven in 1876.

Aldenham was a good private grammar school, where the spirit was High Tory and solidly traditional Church of England. It is sited about five miles south-west of St Albans, where it had originally been set up in 1549, having been endowed by Richard Platt, a Freeman of the Brewer's Co. It had lingered on through three centuries until taken in hand by new headmaster Alfred Leeman in 1843. It normally had about seventy-two pupils with a class

Aldenham School buildings in 1867, viewed from Alfred Leeman, the headmaster's, garden.

average of twelve. Fees from 1873 were £15 to £25 a year for tuition, with boarding fees not exceeding, £65.[7] Sons of the middle-class men, such as clergy, doctors, lawyers and farmers, would come from as far away as Ireland Northumberland, Kent and Cornwall to a school where the food was adequate, but home comforts rather rudimentary.[8]

Alfred Leeman was headmaster, a Cambridge man to the core, who actively recruited other Cambridge graduates to his staff, and also anticipated that his more able pupils would gain entrance to Cambridge and graduate there. Born in London on 14 December 1816, Leeman had attended Louth School, and matriculated in 1835 for Cambridge, gaining his BA in 1839 and MA in 1842. It is possible he met Revd Vincent and Revd James Raven there. Leeman was ordained deacon at Winchester on 11 July 1841, but did not immediately continue into Church of England priesthood. Instead he took up a career in education for the next forty-two years. A second master at Oakham School from 1839–1841, he became headmaster at St Paul's School, Southsea, in 1841–1843, before moving to Aldenham, remaining there until 1876 during which time he set it on its feet. Revd Vincent Raven may have come to know of Leeman's reputation as headmaster at Aldenham.

Of average height and thickset, and not very careful about his dress, Leeman had dark greying hair and whiskers, which framed a red face. Despite his easy manner, keen sense of humour and mild eccentricity, he showed that he was no mere figurehead. He could be very vocal in his representations to the governors about the well-being of both staff and boys. He taught the senior pupils of the school Latin and Greek. The pupils, who called him 'the Gaffer' did Horace's Odes and Satires and a Greek play using cribs, year in and out.[9] He patrolled the school in carpet slippers, wearing a tall hat, accompanied by his little dog 'Tan', who sometimes barked to give the lads warning of the Gaffer's approach, if they had not heard him humming to himself and so were caught in doing something they should not have been doing. Punishment was swiftly meted out with the cane he carried.[10][11]

Presumably Raven started at Aldenham in January 1872,[12] the year being divided into two halves – a term about twenty-five to twenty-six weeks from January to June with an Easter break of seven to ten days (except for those who lived 100–200 miles from home, who continued to board) – and a twenty-week term from August to December. Prior to starting the school, there was an old ritual of inspection by the school governors to undergo for all prospective pupils (including Henry and his brother Vincent and later his other brothers). They were required to attend Old Hall of the Worshipful Co. of Brewers, Aldermanbury, near Moorgate. The candidates were asked one or two questions, given a glass with port in it and a big sweet bun, after which they were approved as pupils.[13] A pupil could be paid for totally privately or possibly be a *foundationer*. A proportion of the boys were partly funded by the Brewer's Co., those from the local parish of Aldenham or sons of the Freemen of the Brewer's Co. for which parents could pay £20 to become freemen.

The school was in the grammar school tradition, preparing its graduate material pupils for going on to Cambridge, the likely perceived goal for the Raven's boys both at home and at school. Indeed, fostering a 'Cambridge' atmosphere was part of Leeman's educational plan, a scheme he furthered by appointing young Cambridge graduates to his teaching staff.

There was 'Mac', i.e. Herbert James McGill, whose classes read Vergil and Xenophon, but who was a keen naturalist; 'Robar', i.e. Charles Robert, a kindly, genial man, taught the junior classes and did elementary work in general. 'Both McGill and Roberts were painstaking and energetic, and did their best to instil scholarship into us… and R. Stevelly, who ground Mathematics into us all… The Mathematical instruction was invariably of high class, and well carried out.'[14] Apart from learning to read and write good English, Raven probably benefited most from this teacher. Monsieur Quesnel came in to teach French and Messrs Gilbert and Lupton, music and drawing. The two worst features of the school according to the accounts were the dull food (although this was relieved by what a boy had in his own tuck-box, such as Fry's Cocoa and home-made jam) and above all, the quite execrable state of the toilets.

As can be seen, the curriculum was narrowly academic. Science subjects, the mechanical skills and the higher mathematics to promote them at an advanced level were missing. In this respect, the education Raven received was of little use to a future railway engineer, although typical enough for its time. A report from the Schools Inquiry Commission of 1869 noted that the instruction at the school presented was Classical: no scholars learn bookkeeping, mensuration, physics, chemistry or natural history.[15] It would take some time after Leeman retired and the older Raven boys had left before these were introduced into Aldenham's curriculum.

Raven and his brothers followed a daily timetable, which operated most week days, but was suspended on Sundays, where there was attendance at local church. Prayers were said in the morning and early afternoon or in school if the weather was too bad. On 5 November, Guy Fawkes' Day, there was a school holiday.

Times	Activity
6.30	Rise (2 hours allowed for dressing)
7.00	Roll call
7.00 – 8.00	Lessons
8.00	Breakfast, i.e. bread, butter and tea
9.00 – 10.50	Lessons, introduced by daily prayers
11.00 – 12.00	Lessons, followed by a hasty game of cricket
1.30	Dinner of meat, potatoes, served with beer, then pudding or cheese
2.00 – 4.00	Lessons (except for Wednesdays and Saturdays)
5.00	Tea (with bread and butter)
6.00 – 7.00	Lessons – prep(aration), finished with prayers
7.30	Supper as for breakfast
Later for seniors	Supper of bread, cheese and beer

Daily timetable at Aldenham School, 1870s.

Aldenham, in the light of Raven's future career, would continue to give him a surface polish and self-confidence, an ability to write clear correct English and at least a start in mathematical principles. From the point of view of religious belief, Raven would not be notable as a devout member of the Church of England, but later seem to attend more as a part of social custom, for instance for his own marriage and that of his children. With regard to railways, he could well have read about such matters at home and school, but his formal education did not give him a theoretical or practical basis for an engineering career with a railway company. Both Raven and his brother Henry left Aldenham in 1876.

The time spent here stood his brother Henry in better stead. A good enough sportsman to play on the school football and cricket eleven in 1876 (there is no mention of Raven himself being picked), he left Aldenham, having possibly gained an Exhibition grant of £40 from the school, and followed the footsteps of his father, uncle, other Aldenham teachers and pupils by going to Sydney College, Cambridge, in 1880. He was resident at 25 Doughty Street, St Pancras, in 1881, lodging with an elderly couple, Robert and Sarah Price, possibly on Easter holiday or on some kind of work experience there before graduating as a BA in 1883. He became a solicitor with Hare & Co., the firm of solicitors to the 'Treasury', where his namesake grandfather had worked. Henry was an Associate Member of the IMechE from 1886–1894. He was appointed as Master of the Supreme Court in 1897, but died at the early age of forty-one on 25 August 1897 at Kew.

Later, from 1879 to 1881, three younger brothers, Ernest Woodhouse, Frederick Rainbow and Hubert also attended the school. They very likely took their older brother Vincent's lead, when they turned to engineering, civil in their case. In 1877, Leeman had been replaced by another 'Cambridge' man, John Kennedy. He revised and developed the curriculum quite drastically and provided a curriculum more appropriate for engineering.

1 3 April 1881 Census
2 She stayed with her brother on the night of 1881 Census, but in the 1901 Census she and her sister-in law were living together
3 Pevsner, Nikolaus, 1962, *The Buildings of England: North-West and South Norfolk*, Penguin Books, p.177
4 White, Francis, 1854, *History, Gazetteer and Directory of Norfolk*, p.789
5 There were no members of this branch of the Ravens in Great Fransham rectory or indeed in Norfolk at the time of the 1891 Census
6 Raven's birth year is 1858, not 1859, as he states clearly in the Candidates Circular for Associate in 1898 and later Full Membership of Institution of Civil Engineers (ICE) in 1910
7 Evans R.J., *The History of Aldenham School 1599-1969*, Old Aldenhamian Society, p.102
8 Evans R.J., *vide supra*, p.119
9 Evans R.J., *vide supra* from account of his time at Aldenham from 1873-1879 by Richard White, p.121.
10 In Evans, R.J., *vide supra*, from an account of his time at Aldenham (1862-1867) by D.F. de l'H. Ranking, p.108
11 Evans R.J., *vide supra*, p.126.
12 The ICE candidate's circular in September 1910, written by Raven, clearly states that he was at Aldenham from 1872 to 1876, i.e. from age thirteen to eighteen
13 Evans R.J., *vide supra*, p.119
14 Evans R.J., *vide supra*, p.121
15 Evans R.J., *vide supra*, p.94

II

STARTING WITH THE
NORTH EASTERN RAILWAY
(1875–1882)

By the 1870s, careers, other than the traditional professions of law, the Church, the armed services on land or sea and medicine, were being increasingly developed to include service to the rapidly growing industrial/commercial sectors of Victorian life. Such careers arose partly as a response to commercial pressures from industry, who sought more efficient and cheaper systems of producing goods and partly as a human response to the discovery of an increasing variety of practical applications of science to everyday life. Engineering moved from being mainly an artisan occupation earlier in the century to becoming more and more a middle-class career. This is manifested by the number of clergymen's sons, like Raven, who, with their talents and moral background, came forward find new careers, for instance, in railway engineering. At the very least, an engineering career provided a steady, if unspectacular, means of earning a living with the added bonus of a comfortable social and domestic lifestyle. Many engineers, financiers and others in trade were, as a consequence, seeking recognition through their professional associations.

There was a connection between the Brewer's Co. and the Midland Railway, making it more understandable if Raven had gone to Midland Railway (MR) at Derby for his apprenticeship rather than to North Eastern Railway (NER) at Gateshead. 'Premium' apprenticeships with qualified engineers had to be paid for, usually by the parents of some benefactor and Gateshead was probably more within Revd Vincent's financial means rather than having to pay university fees and provide him with upkeep. After all, there would be another five younger boys to see to.

It is possible that Raven's choice may signify the acting out of some form of teenage rebellion against a path which family and school may have mapped out for him. The imminent Stockton & Darlington Railway (S&DR) Golden Jubilee celebrations of the founding in September 1875 may have been a final spur in making Raven's decision about career and where he would pursue it. Whatever the truth, his father must at least have acquiesced and agreed to support his decision and pay his fees of about £50 p.a. His successful completion of apprenticeship could well have made it easier for his younger brothers Frederick and Hubert in their turn to take up apprenticeships as civil engineers around the time he qualified as a railway engineer.

His father would have made an approach, including a personal letter of introduction, to Edward Fletcher, locomotive superintendent (LS) to the NER. This resulted in Raven being engaged as a 'premium' apprentice with an agreement to pay the requisite fee to the engineer to cover the time the youth spent with him. As he received the premium himself, it was one of the 'perks' of the job.

Raven left Aldenham probably at the Easter break of 1875, to serve a 'pupilage' from May 1875 to 1880 with the NER Co. The 'pupilage' took place at the NER Greensfield

Arms of the Noth Eastern Railway Co., showing the arms of the three original companies, which amalgamated in 1854.

Works on the south bank of the river Tyne in Gateshead. He probably initially worked as a potboy in a kind of 'work experience' until his apprenticeship proper started in late 1875 or early 1876. He was fortunate in his choice of master and this could well have helped him to settle as Fletcher's character was warm and somewhat like his former headmaster, Alfred Leeman.

Edward Fletcher, born in Redewater on 26 April 1807 to Alan and Ann Fletcher, was baptised on 4 May the same year in the Scotch Presbyterian Chapel in Birdhopecraig, Rochester (the Roman *Bremenium*) in the north of Northumberland, very close to the Scottish border. In 1825, he was apprenticed to George Stephenson and thereafter spent most of his life involved with the railways in the North East. He married a Miss Fedarb and had two daughters and a son by her. He worked for the York Newcastle & Berwick Railway (YN&BR) at their workshops at Greenesfield. The YN&B merged with the York and North Midland & Leeds Northern Railways to become the NER in 1854.

Fletcher lived across the lane in nearby Greenesfield House. His policy as LS was to preside paternalistically over the workshops of the constituent companies of the NER, working on ideas for more efficient and larger goods and passenger locomotives within the limits of the technology available to him. A photograph of him in later life shows a portly man, with a full greying beard looking out with a benign mild fatherly expression. Fletcher was responsible under Henry Tennant for the NER Co.'s GM from 1871–1891. Between them, they gave the company much stability during all the mergers and their after-effects.

Fletcher, although paternalistic and to some extent autocratic, was able to listen to his men, being usually open to new suggestions. For instance, in 1873, the NER engine drivers petitioned him to make the block system of signalling more regular and efficient. He made sure it was done. Despite his new designs being standardised to a great extent during the 1870s, he did not insist rigidly on a company style, corporate image or standardisation of parts, but

Above: Greenesfield Works, Gateshead, in 1864. Little changed until after the Second World War.

Right: Edward Fletcher, Raven's mentor during his 'premium' apprenticeship.

allowed different locomotive building shops at Gateshead, York and Leeds some leeway with details of design and livery.

On arriving at Gateshead, Raven must have found the town and the workplace at least somewhat daunting. The depot itself was large and was due to be extended in 1877. The town itself around the river was depressing and industrially urban despite being surrounded by open countryside and villages. He had to learn how to cope with the typical rough and tumble of a Geordie place of work. Coming from the rural gentility of a Norfolk rectory and the comparative refinement of a small exclusive public school in a rural setting, he with his southern speech, his middle-class approach and manners must have been appeared as alien to the his workmates as theirs did to him. The difficulty of understanding the Geordie dialect with its unique accent, archaic diction and obscure vocabulary from both his boss or 'gaffer' and his workmates, not to mention their rougher manners, and the sheer number of people in such an industrial urban setting must have presented a challenge initially. He probably lodged somewhere in Gateshead or in Newcastle, as the NER possessed no housing for staff in the area.

From 1876–1878, Raven, as part of his five-year apprenticeship under Fletcher's supervision, underwent a comprehensive training programme in all aspects of the NER's engineering work at Greenesfield Works. The site consisted of a massive rectangular building (the original Gateshead Station and Terminus) housing large workshops, which by 1865 had five turntables with eighteen roads for locomotives. To gain practical 'hands-on' experience, Raven spent a fifty-three-hour week passing through the company's various workshops. His reward was 5s a week. He learned what a locomotive was by firing, maintaining and driving it on both day and night shifts. In his second year he received 10s a week plus overtime, followed by 5s increments each year until he qualified. Later, from 1878 to 1880, he went on to work in the drawing office. He would, at this stage of his apprenticeship, learn much about practical engineering, by making technical drawings of items of transport stock, carriages, goods wagons and other apparatus, but most of all about locomotives, especially Fletcher's class '901' 2-4-0 passenger and his class '398' goods 0-6-0 locomotives, built from 1872 onwards. The latter's profile has similarities to the contemporary LNWR 0-6-0's potent influence over much railway design, at home and abroad in the Empire.

This experience would have provided him with much to think upon, learn from and store up for the future. Theoretical work was coupled with the practical knowledge and the skills, which he was able to gain from the 'track-side'. This meant observing, working and communicating with various grades of workmen, who handed on to him the accumulated fruits of their own experience. Raven, no doubt, was eager to supplement this by studying the underlying theory and practice of mathematics and physics, especially mechanics and electricity.

As will be seen from his later reports and actions, Raven was acutely observant, with a good memory for any details he had seen and for methods he had been impressed by. He learned to gain control of his environment. While seemingly not very imaginative, he not only possessed a powerful intelligence, but an ability to concentrate on matters in hand. These characteristics were a part of a natural endowment, sharpened by a determination to come to terms with any opportunities, which a railway environment of the time could provide for him. This process of learning helped to integrate his approach to his work. It lasted throughout his working life and continued well after his official retirement. He now lodged with a Mr and Mrs Swallow and their young daughter at 81 Wharncliffe Street, Elswick. This was a terraced row of houses running down to the famous Scotswood Road standing above the large railway goods sidings, west of Central Station. He may have lodged there for the whole period from arriving on Tyneside until his marriage.[2]

Once he left his apprenticeship, likely to have been the end of 1880, he was to gain employment as a junior engineer for one of the best run railway companies in Britain. The company he now worked for, the NER, like all railway companies, had been inaugurated

901, the 1872 prototype of Fletcher's 2-4-0 express passenger locomotives. Note the open work splashers.

327, one of Fletcher's class '398' 0-6-0, built in 1879.

by statute, in the case of NER on 31 July 1854.[3] 'The NER was a well co-ordinated organisation... strong enough financially to provide a really good service, and to be cooperative towards any other railway, which wished to use its tracks.' The NER became a very great railway.[4]

While carrying increasing numbers of both passengers and goods as its lines spread out further into the areas more remote from the Tyne, Wear, Tees, Yorkshire and Humber conurbations, NER gained the majority of revenue from its mineral traffic. This was conveyed from the Pennine hinterlands of County Durham, the Cleveland Hills of North Yorkshire and much of Northumberland to a chain of ports on the East Coast, whose docks increasingly came into NER ownership. In turn, raw materials and other commodities were conveyed there to be processed. The railways became for the nineteenth century what the internal combustion engine would become for the twentieth. This provided a powerful spin off in its stimulation of the consumer market on a much wider scale, not only encouraging travel and holiday taking, but also increasing pressure to bring and distribute goods more and more quickly from sites of production of food or artefacts to a public eager to have them. It also gave a better means of national and international communication, especially through the carriage of the Royal Mail by rail.

By the time that Raven had started with the NER, it had gained a virtual monopoly over passenger, goods and mineral traffic in a region, roughly co-terminus with the Anglo-

Saxon kingdom of Northumbria. It had about 1,500 miles of track, a mainline from Leeds to Berwick, via York, Darlington and Newcastle, with other important loops like Northallerton to Newcastle, via Hartlepool and Sunderland or branch lines sometimes as long as sixty miles, like that from Darlington to Tebay, sometimes a few miles long that to Masham.

Throughout its existence as a company, NER continued to work to secure the boundaries of its compact territory by preventing serious incursions and hence loss of control of its passenger and freight sand mineral traffic movements. The main rivals between Humber and Tweed were absorbed slowly but surely by the beginning of the twentieth century (save the redoubtable Hull and Barnsley Railway along its southern flank, which from 1914 worked jointly with NER and was absorbed by it prior to 1923 grouping in 1922). After the initial amalgamations of 1854, it steadily absorbed other local railways: SDR and its locomotive workshops at Darlington in 1861, the Newcastle & Carlisle in 1862 and the Blyth & Tyne in 1864. It repelled those seeking to make inroads into its territory; especially the powerful LNWR from the west of the Pennines with its proposed North of England Union project aimed at joining up with the West Hartlepool Harbour & Railway Co., by its proposal to build a Wensleydale line to join the MR Carlisle & Settle line branch by Hawes or a proposed Newcastle & Derwent Valley Railway scheme to enable LNWR gain freight carrying access to Newcastle.

To the south, NER relations with GNR were generally harmonious and workmanlike, but to the north, relations with NBR were more ambivalent. NER had to construct its Alnmouth to Coldstream branch to block NBR scheming to find an alternative route from Edinburgh to Newcastle In reality, the NBR in the longer term, lost out to the NER, which out-manoeuvred it. In return for granting NBR running powers from Hexham to Newcastle, NER gained the power to haul the infinitely more prestigious East Coast expresses from Berwick into Edinburgh Waverley. This concession in fact made GNR and NER the main operators from London to Edinburgh in the Rail Races to the North in 1888 and 1895.

The NER's main operational drawback was that it had no rail access of its own to London, but it made up for this because it was able to charge the lowest railway passenger fares and yet consistently yield the highest dividends, when compared with other British railway companies.[5] This payment of good dividends to shareholders over the years remained even after investment had fallen off after the turn of the century and the company experienced an annual deficit.

The directors, being local men, ensured that ports, steel works and especially coal mines had feeder lines from their own businesses to the NER, often with rail systems of their own, led to NER metals. Kirby[6] estimated that County Durham alone had a minimum of 5,000 miles of track, as well as direct access to their own port facilities in some cases. The Londonderry Railway was a good example of this independence, although it was eventually absorbed by NER in 1900.

Like all contemporary British railway companies, NER had three distinct sections, namely the Board of directors, its executive officers and its workforce. Each section existed in a clear hierarchical order.

The NER Board consisted of seventeen directors, from whom was drawn a chairman and secretary.[7] Ultimately, the Board was answerable to the shareholders, who expected a good dividend in return for their investments. The NER seldom disappointed them. Directors, such as David Dale, James Kitson and Lothian Bell, to give characteristic examples, were appointed to the Board not only to promote the interests of NER, but their own as well, closely involved as they were with the running of different industrial interests, particularly from coal mining, steel-making concerns and the docks on the coast, all of which could benefit from local and regional railway development.

Furthermore, as part of the S&DR legacy, many NER directors and senior officers were Quakers, a Christian denomination noted for its humanitarian philosophy and long history of tolerance of others. They included members of the Pease family, Lothian Bell and David

Dale on the Board of directors; Henry Tennant as the general manager (GM); from 1883, the two Worsdell brothers and later their nephew, Arthur Collinson in the LS's office and their sons also moved into middle management; in the engineering department, there were the Cudworth's. Later, Ralph Wedgwood came from the famous pottery family to join the GM's office. Their tolerant attitudes and business acumen enabled the NER as a company to have a view of its workforce as human beings.

This attitude was revealed when, as a means of self-protection tinctured with a measure of common self-interest, the individual railway companies formed themselves into a group during 1868–1870 called the Railway Companies Association (RCA). Their aim was to defend their collective interests, gain trade concessions with other companies and in some respects standardise practice, in such matters for instance as braking or in conduct industrial relations. The NER differed at times from other members of the RCA, especially about ways of dealing positively with its workforce as it favoured arbitration. This willingness to arbitrate undoubtedly arose from the Quaker influence on the Board. Tolerance, combined with a beneficent rationalism, made the NER eager to promote good relations with the workforce, a stance not always recognised for what it was by more militant Trade Union members. Yet, NER was decidedly ahead of its time since most contemporary railway companies refused to acknowledge the rights of railway workers and their Unions. The industrial disputes at the turn of the nineteenth and twentieth centuries which afflicted the railways caused much trouble to the NER and constituted a not altogether fair reward for their attempts to work with the men and their Unions.

The senior officers of the Executive comprised various experts in engineering, financial, organisational and administrative fields. They were responsible under the Board of directors for the smooth running of their department's business from day to day and year to year within the company. The Board, in return, closely regulated their activity. All departments were closely tiered and run in a strict hierarchical order, but the ambitious person with ability, who knew in what direction his future lay, could use the structure to his advantage and gain promotion. Indeed, the officers themselves sought to become increasingly professionalised. This showed in their desire for more training, increased use of graduates and by the need to join professional bodies. For instance, engineers had access to the different levels of membership of one or more three key Institutions of Civil (1836), Mechanical (1847), and Electrical (1871) Engineering. Over the years Raven came to join all three. These professional institutions gave support to a member's personal development professionally, without being political in the way that RCA and the ASRS would be. In many sectors of the NER, through appointments of able men of experience in management and engineering from other companies, a wealth of knowledge and practical skills were gained. In turn, movements to other companies exerted an influence over their development too. Often there was rivalry between them, but there was also a degree of co-operation especially in the locomotive, carriage and wagon building fields.

The role of senior officers outside the workplace was a continuation of further company influence. By taking an active part in various benevolent societies for rail employees, they exercised a paternal interest in the well-being of their employees. As might have been anticipated, the societies were usually organised hierarchically, but were run by their members with patronage, presidency and senior positions given to senior members of the company's Executive. Examples were Literary Institutes, Brass Bands, Assembly Rooms, Temperance Associations and Athletic Clubs. These institutions continued well into the LNER era and beyond. They were seen as part of contemporary efforts to improve the wider physical, cultural and moral well-being of the workforce, an early form of benevolent social welfare. Another aspect of this was the introduction of NER Pension Fund for the company's employees of all grades, a scheme that Raven is likely to have subscribed to, ensuring some level of financial security for him as for other employees both during employment and after retirement as well as an incentive to stay in employment.

The last component of the company was the workforce. This made up the solid foundation of NER, as it did for other companies, having more personnel than the other two sections of NER. It was accountable to whichever executive officers were in charge of them in a detailed structure of authority. It was the NER's human driving force, whether porters, locomotive drivers or clerks in the wages department, and so on. It was provided by members of the various societies, promoted for their 'good' outside the workplace.

The workforce constituted the membership of the Associated Society of Railway Servants (ASRS). Following on from the Trade Union Act of 1871, ASRS was founded with the financial assistance of four Liberal MPs and with Parliamentary backing. Its aims were to harmonise relations between workforce and management, avoid striking and defend the workforce against injustice. It sought to obtain a ten-hour day and an extra day's pay for eight hours' overtime or Sunday working and to set up funds for benefits for those emigrating, the elderly and disabled.[8] [9] From 1890, the General Rail Workers' Union (GRWU) represented those working in and around railway workshops – the porters, the vanmen, the rulleymen – which the ASRS had not gained as members.

The secret ballot for Union action was introduced instead of the more open public vote the year afterwards. The NER Board showed a consistent will to work with the ASRS. Witness their joint concern regarding safety on the railways, especially where it concerned employees. With the co-operation of the NER, the ASRS staged an exhibition of automatic and other coupling devices, improved brakes and improved lighting for goods yards. It agreed to try out between 1871–1874, the Westinghouse braking system, as many other railways were doing in its response to safety requirements. This system did not become standard until after 1889.

Rail companies were, of course, major employers at local and national levels, providing much needed work and career opportunities in both town and country, especially in the great new industrial conurbations being built. Workforces, as a result, could wield considerable power if they wished. They were worked on by company officials through political agitation or sense of grievance (or both) at what was perceived to be inept man management; action concerning real or exaggerated grievances could bring the rail system to a complete halt. Unfortunately, by the end of the century and continuing right up to First World War and well beyond it, the power of the workforce was not always used wisely by the leaders of the Unions. Strikes and other industrial action meant considerable loss of revenue to railway companies, their shareholders and customers, as well as hardship to the strike-bound workforce and their families. Interestingly, much of the dealings in times of industrial unrest were in true hierarchical manner with members of the Executive at first, rather than directly with the chairman or directors of the Board, who often only intervened at a later stage in the dispute.

Regarding the role of the locomotive superintendents, this was becoming increasingly enlarged as a result of the expansion of company interests. As was to be expected, it encompassed the design, supervision of building and ongoing running maintenance (and modification, if deemed necessary) of steam locomotives, railway carriages and wagons. After its renaming in 1902 as chief mechanical engineer (CME), the role covered any mechanical feature and came to include NER dockyards, shipping and both passenger and freight road vehicles.

Steam locomotives are essentially robust and simple pieces of machinery, needing proper maintenance, including the renewal of the boiler and other working parts to have almost indefinite lives, if they are not worked too hard. In such circumstances, the average age of the locomotive stock overall rose because it was often more economic to maintain and modify older locomotives and put them on secondary duties than to replace them completely.[10] The Board of directors could initiate, for example, the development of a new locomotive so as to produce economies in running costs or to beat rivals with the speed of a new passenger service, or increase the volume of goods traffic it could handle. It might even decide, as it did in 1876, to appoint a locomotive committee, accountable to the chief engineer, consisting of the locomotive superintendent and his assistants, George Graham, the LS for the Southern

Division, William Snaith, locomotive accountant, and William Younghusband, the Darlington North Road Works manager. The detailed results of the decision-making were then handled by the company's executive officers as departmental heads, of which the CME was one. It was the CME who was delegated to keep the railway system running. This responsibility included budgeting within that department.

All departments had staff roles well defined from senior to junior. For instance, rather than the CME alone producing new locomotive designs, he worked closely with such key senior associates as chief draughtsman and chief engineer through any ideas he had for innovation of development. Once the main features and components of a design were agreed, the whole would be broken down into tasks suitable to a more junior level, where the junior would have some experience working with and designing a specific part, for instance, bearings. In the reverse direction, ideas had to go up the system, should some engineering feature, like compounding or superheating, be considered. A case would need to be made to the Board for final approval of the scheme. Once approval was given, the head of department and his team would be left to get on with it, while keeping the Board informed of progress, as thought appropriate.

However, it was the workforce themselves who had to operate the end product of the locomotive and rolling stock system. They had to fire and run the locomotives and marshal the rolling stock. On occasion, if the atmosphere lent itself to expressing it, they could clearly indicate their feelings about firing, steaming or the normal or abnormal wear and tear to such items as bearings, axles, pistons and so on, and therefore could bring pressure to bear on developments in design. When they were not listened to or felt aggrieved, industrial strife could be the result, however benign the NER Board was in intention.

Communication up and down the system was provided by a series of usually generalised orders from the Board, which were then broken down into finer detail in the form of rules and regulations by individual heads of departments, sometimes in concert or alone where it concerned specific groups or individuals. These provided a series of guidelines, enshrining the company's philosophy in a quite subtle way, especially when viewed in retrospect. It complemented the hierarchical structure. While capable of change from below, it was essentially was a top-down approach. Individual departmental heads could give more or less freedom for their staff. It was in challenging this top-down approach that the Unions, especially ASRS, backed the workforce in asking for better pay and conditions, endeavouring not always fairly, justly or legally to make the voice of the workforce heard.

Fletcher's avuncular rather charismatic style concealed slow moves by him to draw the disparate constituent elements of the company together into more cohesive work centres. For instance, each of the workshops of the constituent companies had continued to work as before amalgamation. The former YNB and LN continued to produce and repair locomotives and YNM carriage and wagons at York. Fletcher set about focussing building and repair of locomotives on two main sites, Darlington and Gateshead, with carriage works at York and wagon works both at Shildon and York. The locomotive repair shop at Stockton was closed in 1878 and 250 men transferred to Darlington; similarly, that at York for former LN stock was closed in 1879, and Leeds some time in early 1880s. Shildon closed under McDonnell in 1883. All these changes were carried out without difficulty from the 'men'

Apart from the apprenticeship training in Fletcher's office, it is not clear how Raven acquired his increasingly considerable theoretical knowledge. Besides having access to the *Engineer*, published for the engineering professions since 1855, he is most likely to have supplemented his widening 'on-the-spot' practical experience with attendance at the School of Science and Art, founded by Dr John Hunter Rutherford in 1877 in Corporation Street, a ten-minute walk from his Wharncliffe Street lodgings in Newcastle, where, added to the usual arts subjects, there was a goodly array of scientific topics on the curriculum: chemistry, physics, biology, mathematics, metallurgy, the principles of mining, mineralogy, nautical astronomy and machine drawing.[11]

Gateshead NER Literary Institute, Hudson Street, off High Level Bridge, adjacent to Greenesfield works. Raven was involved with it from the 1880s to his retirement.

Raven probably attended other schools or institutes set up for working men to extend his theoretical knowledge, the most likely being Gateshead NER Literary Institute, particularly in the light of his long association with it afterwards. It had been originally formed in 1854. A committee to run it was formed in 1876 and from 1889 it moved to new premises on Hudson Street at the Gateshead end of the High Level Bridge. The Gateshead Institute was one of a number of such institutes under the NER banner. Others were at Shildon (opened 1833), Darlington (opened 1858), Sunderland (opened 1893) and York. They were partly financed by the local authority and offered Science and Art classes and some technical classes. Gateshead's library steadily increased over the years to 12,000 volumes.[12] He is likely to have gone to hear John Theodore Merz at Armstrong College in Newcastle, then the University of Durham Department of Science, instituted like Rutherford in the 1870s.

Raven's apprenticeship was over by the end of 1880, but he stayed on of course as a wage earner, eventually becoming salaried. He would spend most of the rest of his life working his way up the promotional ladder, until he reached the pinnacle of CME within the company.[13] In this he followed his early mentor, Fletcher. This type of lifetime commitment to one company was rather unusual. A more usual career path was to complete an apprenticeship, gain a little experience elsewhere, for example with another British or Irish company, and travel abroad to the United States, the Continent or the Empire, particularly India or Australia, or to the Orient to widen knowledge and skills and to test application and endurance. Staying put did not seem to have disadvantaged Raven in any way. His way of widening his experience in his later years, apart gaining knowledge 'on the job', was from reading and attending lectures, later going to Germany and the United States to widen his experience by observation and detailed reporting and application, where he deemed it appropriate, of practice seen.

At this first stage his career, from 1881 to 1888, Raven was a locomotive fireman and then became foreman in the Gateshead workshops. He moved up to inspector grade in charge of the Northern District with responsibility for the running and repair of 200 engines. In this post, which gave him further valuable practical experience and insight into the working of the system, Raven could not help but observe the effect of management decisions on the way men worked as well as the increasing militancy of the workforce. How much he planned his career is not evident, but its progress was steady, being a mixture of continuous learning, establishing his reliability as well as his growing ability to manage well whatever enterprise he was given. Most of all, his loyalty to NER was shown by his remaining with the company throughout his working life and made him an obvious choice for promotion.

As will be seen, Raven was closely involved with it over his many years of service with NER, probably initially as a student member, but rising from committee member via being vice president and president (and treasurer), much as Wilson Worsdell had done before him, to being given appointment as one of its honorary life presidents. Raven continued to work under Edward Fletcher, until Fletcher gave NER his letter of resignation in May 1882, to take effect from 31 October 1882 with a pension of £1,200 p.a.

1 Candidates Circular for election as Associate Member of ICE, 14 March 1898, p.36

2 3 April 1881 Census

3 17 & 18 Victoria (local and personal)

4 Pratt Edwin A., 1912, A *History of Inland Transport and Communication in England*, Kegan Paul, Trench, Trübner and Co. Ltd, p.287

5 Vaughan Adrian, 1997, *Railwaymen, Politics & Money*, John Murray, p.134

6 Lewis M.J.T., The railway in industry, p.86–7 in Ambler R.W. (editor), 1999, *The History and Practice of Britain's Railway*, A New Research Agenda, Ashgate

7 Kirby M.W., 'Railway development and the role of the state' p.26–27 in Ambler R.W. (editor), 1999, *The History and Practice of Britain's Railway*, A New Research Agenda, Ashgate

8 Vaughan Adrian, 1997, *Railwaymen, Politics & Money*, John Murray, p.253

9 Clegg H.A., Fox, Alan & Thompson A.F. 1964, *A History of British Trade Unions since 1889*, vol.1 1889-1914, Oxford University Press p.232

10 Bonavia Michael R., 1981, *Railway Policy between the Wars*, Manchester University Press, p.89. Although writing about LNER policy in the mid-war period, the quotation is valid for NER throughout Raven's work time with the company

11 Note on 1877 curriculum in *Handbook for the opening of Extension to Rutherford College of Technology and the Claude Gibb Hall of Residence*, Newcastle on Friday 27 November 1953

12 Manders F.W.D., 1973, *A History of Gateshead*, Gateshead Corporation, p.259

13 Candidates Circular for election as Associate Member of ICE, 14 March 1898, p.36

III

PROGRESSING IN HIS CAREER
(1882–1893)

Fletcher's successor at Gateshead, Alexander McDonnell, was an upper-middle-class Irishman, born on 18 December 1829 in Dublin (he died on 4 December at Holyhead). An Honours graduate in 1851 from Dublin University, he had gone to work on the English/Welsh borders for the Newport, Abergavenny & Hereford Railway, a company developed by LNWR from 1858 to exploit coal movement from border coalfields to the south coast of South Wales. McDonnell moved on to Ottoman Empire (now Romania) as LS in the early days of the Danube & Black Sea Railway after the line from the sea port of Constanta was opened inland to Cernavoda on the Danube. He went to the GW&SR works at Inchicore, eight years after its opening as LS in 1864. Aided by the Englishmen, John Audley Frederick Aspinall (of later L&YR fame and McDonnell's successor at GSWR) and Henry Alfred Ivatt (of later GNR fame), he had worked to improve quality and introduce standardisation of parts with success, because of his administrative ability. Remaining there for eighteen years, he was appointed as LS to NER from July 1882 at a starting salary of £1,600 p.a. There was thus a three-month overlap between appointment of Fletcher and McDonnell. He was thus more controlling and corporate-minded than Fletcher, but a photograph of him around this time shows a bearded face with an enquiring, if rather anxious, expression.

From the first month of his appointment, he was involved with the introduction and later implementation of revised and modified pay structures, which had received the backing of the then Board chairman, Mr John Dent Dent, at the 48 Board Meeting held at the De Grey Rooms, York, on 9 February 1883, seemed to go well.

One of the first administrative actions that he carried out was to undertake a review of the NER's engineering workshops, reporting to the NER Board in July 1883. The Greenesfield complex had some machinery which needed repair; that in Percy Main, Hartlepool and Middlesbrough was not in good repair either. He advised an immediate tender to get engineers to look at the repairs to be done, yet pointing out that as most of the machinery involved had now been overtaken by more modern versions, it was a bit of an idle exercise and that replacement with modern equipment would be more to the point. He won the day.

The main works at Greenesfield were further rebuilt and extended as well as being re-equipped with machinery of the latest and improved types, all at a cost of nearly £20,000. It received six rope-driven cranes and a vertical wall engine to supply power repair tools. Steel was now becoming the metal of choice. Track also was increasingly made from steel rather than iron. Steel plates were now substituted for Yorkshire iron on locomotives, once special gas-furnaces for annealing these plates being installed. Steel castings rather than iron for the centre of wheels, fire-box roof bars and reversing gears were now used.[2] Hydraulic machinery for flanging purposes rather than doing it by hand was chosen because it was found to be

Alexander McDonnell, the second LS
Raven worked for from 1882–1884.

a cheaper method of working. Moreover, it housed other resources besides the engineering, having on site a stationery store and printing workshops as well as a general store (i.e. presumably for railway spares).

The works at York received between £11,100 and £12,000 of investment for tools and workshops, but the lion's share of £24,000 went to the works at Darlington where there was room for expansion, a portent of the future as well as pursuing more vigorously the earlier moves towards centralisation which Fletcher had begun. Darlington thus gained in October 1884 two new erecting shops and a new forge, and a through road was opened. There were, by the end of 1884, three important 50-ton overhead travelling cranes, costing £2,790 as well as a quantity of lathes, machines for planing, slotting, milling, drilling, screwing and boring. McDonnell affected such improvements that the costs for new locomotives and their ongoing maintenance fell over the next years quite noticeably – a sound investment.

He next turned to locomotives. Crewe had much influence over NER design from this time on until the late 1890s. McDonnell had already established a number of standard designs for neat-looking 0-6-2Ts, 4-4-0s (called 'Kerry' bogies) and 0-6-0s for GW&SR, each one designed specifically for its purpose with a distinctive company style, derived initially from those of Ramsbottom at the LN&WR. He and Webb provided a powerful seminal influence on both design and function to many future railways. Had McDonnell stayed longer, he would have undoubtedly developed a greater range of locomotives than actually came about, if what he achieved at GS&WR is a bench mark.

Previously, the style of locomotives had been bought in, derived from whichever engineering building works had gained the contract, rather than from any choice made by the company. This occurred in NER as it had in GW&SR, partly due to the number of amalgamations that had occurred. Indeed, the works at Gateshead, Darlington, York and Leeds continued to reflect the different local design policies and liveries of their original constituent companies. Over a period of eighteen months, McDonnell introduced a level of interchange-ability of parts between the classes of new engines he had designed, an important innovation to be much used in the future.

Mr McDonnell's administration was too short to do much in reducing the numerous varieties of engine on the North Eastern Railway system.[3]

Nonetheless, he made a start with two new types of locomotive in all probability intended to be the first in a series of locomotives fitted to the needs of the NER. In appearance, wheel arrangement and usefulness, they were remarkably similar to the broader-gauge ones he had built earlier for GW&SR. The first were 0-6-0s and despite initial hostility to them from train crews, became popular and reliable engines, numbering forty-eight in all. The second ones, 4-4-0s, were built for express passenger use. The men of NER liked neither the idea

Above and below: One of McDonnell's class '52' 4-4-0s with original chimney boiler and cab.

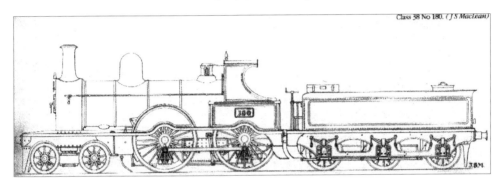

of bogies nor the left-hand drive, which McDonnell introduced. NER was just beginning to gear up to the demands for increasing speed and heavier loads; this meant bigger engines, with greater adhesion in order, for instance to pull mainline express engines smoothly and safely. Despite the elegant lines of McDonnell's engines, their boilers were too small and hence were underpowered. What worked in a more easy-going Ireland did not suffice on the mainland with its ethos of more competitive money making and accommodating an increasingly militant Union-influenced workforce.

As before in Inchicore, one of his more permanent legacies to NER was his ability to choose men of quality. He appointed Wilson Worsdell as his assistant and Walter Mackersie Smith as chief draughtsman to support locomotive development, and as his assistant a man equally valuable in the longer term, George Heppell, who continued to work on engine design until 1919, taking Smith' position over in 1906. In many ways, the pair made developments over the years possible, helping to produce a string of elegantly proportioned locomotives running from McDonnell's 4-4-0s to Raven's class 'T3' 0-8-0s. There was David Bain, who went on to design carriages for NER and like Smith's son moved on to Midland Railway (MR).

There were two areas of interest, which McDonnell had taken up in discussions at the Institutions. One was concerning braking systems on carriages and goods stock in which Raven took part in investigating. The concern arose out of need for both staff and passenger safety. McDonnell had been involved with this at the GS&WR. He had visited the Königliche Bayerische Staatseisenbahn in 1871–1872, as part of his investigation of turf-burning locomotives. It is likely that he talked and saw Heberlein's system of braking, while there. Ropes were attached via pulleys to roofs or through large stanchions above open wagons to apply the brakes, essentially a similar system to one patented by Newall for the LN&WR in 1853. Aspinall, after leaving the LN&WR, had indeed worked on two patented systems for GS&WR from 1876 with McDonnell's approval, a vacuum system and an automatic system derived from work he had done before 1876 with LNWR. NER slowly introduced the Westinghouse system as noted above. The second contemporary issue was about compounding, so much in the air at this period, which McDonnell's successor T.W. Worsdell would introduce to NER.[4]

Sadly, the tensions between McDonnell and the workforce occurred. They seemed to occur as much from his decisions and firmness in dealing with them as from the increasing militancy of the ASRS at this time. On the technical side the drivers resented left-handed driving, removal of Fletcher's exhaust cocks and the substitution of his own admittedly better-looking chimneys for the original stove pipes provided for Fletcher '901'. The drivers became convinced that the changes McDonnell had introduced now interfered with the efficient steaming of the engines. Whatever dissatisfactions the men had were worked on by an increasing militant stance from ASRS. Nor did the Board back him, anxious about the cost of changes he was introducing.

Further attempts to regulate pay and time worked were proposed so that from 1 September 1884, all men and boys should be paid at the rate of sixty hours per week, but had to be withdrawn on 24 August 1884. In many ways McDonnell became the 'Aunt Sally' of the company, for the workmen. Everything wrong or perceived to be so was attributed to him. Even words he said were used and exaggerated and then broadcast. His manner was more forthright and his speech 'foreign' when compared to Fletcher. Despite all his efforts on the company's behalf, McDonnell did not stay much longer, as he resigned on 19 September 1884, after protests about his changes to Fletcher's locomotives. The directors decided to pay him until 1 November and give him a gratuity of £300

How Raven felt toward McDonnell is not known,[5] but his later attitudes would show him to have learned much from McDonnell's predicament. Certainly, much of the working philosophy about standardisation of parts and of company design and notions of efficiency tied to modernisation of stock, which the Worsdell brothers and Raven came to demonstrate later, could well have had their source here. The pay and work time issues were addressed in the new year of 1885, when a notice went out from 6 January 1885. The response to increased time and a reduction in rates for Sunday was for the men at the Gateshead railway workshops to go on strike for several days, work being resumed when the notice was withdrawn. In an attempt to avoid this kind of dispute in the future, the so-called Darlington Programme was proposed, guaranteeing a ten-hour overtime at time and a quarter with a different rate for Sunday working, all rather similar to McDonnell's proposals of 1883. A national All Grades set of proposals of October 1886 was made, again similar, but following a meeting of chairmen of the Board and general managers at Euston.

Raven, following convention, married Gifford Allan Crichton, a daughter of a professional man. Raven had probably met Scottish-born John Walter Crichton, variously described as merchant, agent, metal broker and partner with Richard Cail, of the Walker Alkali Co. He had married Emma Elizabeth Brinton of Whickham in July 1858. By 1873, members of the Crichtons lived at 44 Bewick Road,[6] Gateshead, a substantial terrace house, up the hill from Greenesfield. Their daughter, Gifford Allan, born in 1859, lived with her parents and Crichton's mother, another Gifford Allan, born in 1798 but now a widow.[7] The Crichtons were a family of professional people for over a century in Leith, Midlothian, e.g. Crichton's father had been a shipping agent there and his great-grandfather Alexander a family solicitor, and so the Union was acceptable within the lower middle-class conventions of the time. On 15 February 1883, Revd Vincent Raven, presumably with Annie his wife and the three younger children, came north to marry Raven and Gifford at the elegant Victorian Gothic church of St Stephen's C/E church, Low Elswick, Newcastle, close to where Raven lodged and attended the Freemason's Lodge.

The couple went to live in the eastern part of Newcastle at 18 Heaton Road, in a plain but functional terrace house, about 150 yards from Heaton Railway and Carriage Works. While Gifford remains a shadowy figure, she provided Raven with a stable family background, from which he operated seemingly trouble free over the years. She only begins to appear with him at his public appearances later in his career. There their first child, a girl named Constance Gifford, usually called Connie, was born in autumn 1883.

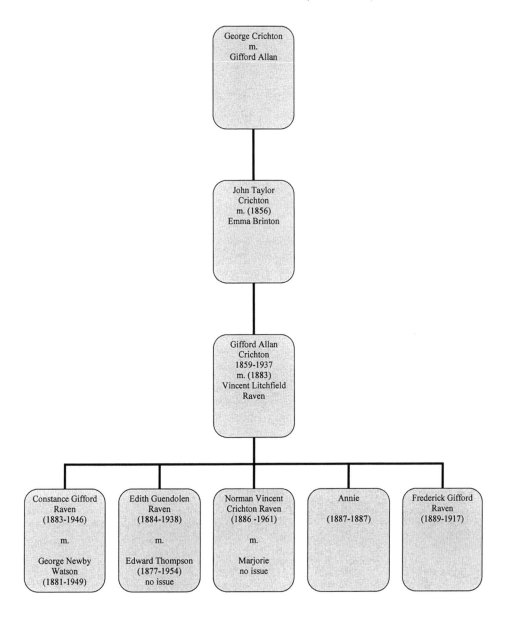

Sir Vincent Raven's children and some of Lady Raven's antecedents.

Raven does not seem to have engaged in any civic activities while in Gateshead, except to join the Freemasons. In 1883, a number of NER staff listed as 'engineers' were proposed as lodge members with the 1427 Percy Lodge, which met at Masonic Hall, Maple Street, Newcastle upon Tyne, founded in 1872 (significantly close to where he lodged in Elswick). Following normal procedures, Alfred Faulkner Ball was first seconded and proposed (16 January 1883), then balloted as a member of the Lodge (20 February), initiated as an Entered Apprentice and passed as a fellow of the Craft (20 March) and finally raised to Master on 17 April. Raven was probably proposed by Ball (they remained in contact for many years), then balloted for and initiated. He was passed as a fellow on 15 May, raised to Master on

Left: St Stephen's C/E church, High Elswick, where the Ravens were married (the tower is all that remains now).

Below: The first house the Ravens lived in at 18 Heaton Road, Newcastle (now Newcastle Flooring Co. as can be seen), but close to NER sheds at Heaton.

Percy Masonic Lodge, Newcastle, of which Raven was a member from 1883–1893, close to where he lodged in Wharncliffe Street, Elswick.

13 June, signing the Grand Lodge Certificate on 21 August 1883.[8] He attended enough meetings to remain a Master until 1893.

The next child was Edith Guendolen, usually called Guen, born at Home Villa, Kell's Lane, Low Fell, Gateshead, in late 1884, where they must have moved to in 1884. He was able to afford an artisan's terrace house, which was close to the horse trams which travelled from the town centre.

Henry Tennant, despite being general manager since 1871, now assumed the locomotive superintendent's role in the interregnum setting up another locomotive committee with himself as chairman. The need was for better passenger engines. The committee approved the introduction of Tennant's sturdy 2-4-0s built during the period June to September 1885. Darlington produced the first one as a prototype, successfully testing the 'waters' as it were, with No.1463. In three months they had produced ten other new locomotives, while Gateshead had produced a further nine. These new locomotives proved popular with the men who drove them. The committee carried on until Thomas William Worsdell (known as 'T.W.'), yet another Quaker, was appointed. Tennant was given £250 to distribute to the officials that had helped on the locomotive committee, while Tennant himself received £500 as a personal gratuity.

T.W. had worked first as a pupil before becoming a master mechanic at the USA at Pennsylvania Railroad's Altoona works. Different to most USA railroad workshops, which

Thomas William Worsdell, the 'compound' man, Raven's third LS from 1886–1890.

only did repairs and maintenance, Altona had begun locomotive production from 1866. This led to parts like boilers becoming standardised and hence interchangeable as McDonnell his predecessor had wanted.[9]

Returning to Britain, he went to the LNWR works at Crewe under Webb, becoming yet another man influenced by Crewe to work for NER. He introduced more spacious cabs with side windows as well as mechanical improvements. He co-operated with August von Borries, who was based at the Schichau-Werke for locomotives at Elbling, East Prussia, for the Hanover section of Prussian State Railways and who came on a visit to Great Britain and the USA. T.W. used 2-cylinder dual-pressure (one high and one low) compounds, applied to differing wheel arrangements, such as his 0-6-2Ts.[10] He went as LS to GER at Stratford from 1881–1885, being notable there more as an administrator than a locomotive designer. He was appointed at a NER Board of directors' meeting on 17 April 1885 as the next locomotive superintendent. He took up his post on 1 September at a salary of £3,000 p.a., twice the salary paid to him by GER.

Wilson Worsdell had followed his brother to Altoona and had been with LNWR, before transferring before his brother to the NER as an assistant mechanical engineer to McDonnell in March 1883. Like his immediate predecessor McDonnell and obviously benefiting from what he had learned about US railroads at Altoona, he continued the process of standardisation at the company's four workshops. T.W. promoted his brother Wilson within a month of taking office in October 1885 to the post of assistant locomotive superintendent of the Northern Division at £1,200 p.a.

T.W. continued to be a fervent advocate of compounding, also developing an automatic intercepting steam valve, which allowed the engine to use the low-pressure cylinder on starting but switched to the high-pressure cylinder once pressure had been raised. By using increased boiler size and power raised to 175hp he slightly spuriously showed the superiority of these new engines to the simple boilered ones of a mere 140hp. He also introduced double-sided windows for locomotive cabs, which the men appreciated. This was possibly explains why, when introducing the above changes, which included a re-introduction of bogies for his 'F' class 4-4-0s, they were all accepted by the workforce without quibble. He built 269 2-cylinder compounds in total. T.W. began by producing a neat 2-4-2T, which emerged from Gateshead in March 1886. From September 1886, he also introduced a new class 'C1' of 2-cylinder compound goods engines. By the next year working on a new express locomotive, T.W. produced a powerful 2-4-0, class 'D' No.1324 which was exhibited it at the Newcastle-upon-Tyne 1887 Jubilee Exhibition, alongside *Locomotion* – presumably as examples of ancient and modern rail traction at that time. One of his later sturdy and elegant class 'F' 4-4-0s would attain a consistent speed, just below 60mph in the 1888 Rail Race. Wilson Worsdell probably provided some of the input in the production and design of his brother's output. His photograph reveals a bearded man, this time with an appraising and more detached expression.

In such an atmosphere of enquiry and development, Raven's interest grew in what was happening in other countries, especially the USA, as a more senior engineer could well have found its beginnings in hearing of the experiences and lessons learnt from the Worsdell brothers there. NER would increasingly look to USA for inspiration as to the way forward for both steam and electric locomotives.

Meanwhile, at home in Low Fell, the Ravens had a son, Norman Vincent Crichton, the first of two, born on 14 April 1886 in Gateshead. Raven was also promoted again. By July 1887, a third daughter, named Annie, was born, but died after a few weeks of life. Raven took over from Wilson Worsdell in October 1886, as assistant LS of the Northern Division at a salary of £600 p.a. (George Graham became LS for Southern Division at £700 p.a.) Wilson worked with T.W. on designs to develop members of Fletcher's class '901', giving them a longer wheel base, because of rebuilding with larger boilers, larger cylinders, splashers and a Worsdell conical chimney, all of which improved the looks of the original. As he was able to afford better accommodation, the Raven family moved west and nearer Greenesfield to 2 Mardale Parade, Rectory Lane, just over brow of Bensham Hill.

Dr John Hunter Rutherford opened in 1886 the first temporary premises of Rutherford College of Technology in Diana Street. It housed with a Metallurgical and a Chemical Laboratory, where Practical Metallurgy and Iron and Steel Manufacture were taught and a 'Fuel' Course, by City and Guilds of London Institute, could be gained; there was a revival of classes in Telegraphy and a move to cover more electrical engineering. This important

T.W. Worsdell's 2-cylinder compound goods class 'C' 0-6-0.

Above: T.W. Worsdell's prototype 'compound' 2-4-0 passenger locomotive, No.1324, in November 1886. Note the generous cab on both locomotives, both above and on the previous page.

Left: Wilson Worsdell, Raven's fourth LS from 1890–1910.

development could well be the source of Raven's increasing interest in the theory and practice of applying electricity to railway practice. Learned speakers coming to the Gateshead NER Literary Institute and preparation for his associate membership of IMechE plus his reading on the subject could have added useful supplements to his learning.

Possibly as a result of his regular attendance at the lectures given there and his rising position in the management at Greenesfield, Raven eventually became a committee member of the Gateshead Institute. Three types of meeting were held as customary. There were regular monthly business meetings, especially the acquisition of new books for the library. To these, were added special ad-hoc meetings, for instance on 19 September about the opening of the new premises of the Institute on 22 October to celebrate the event, when Raven was asked to find artistes for a concert in T.W.'s honour. Raven would sometimes act as chair to either type of the meeting, e.g. special meeting on 6 December 1889. Lastly there was a more formal half-yearly meeting, which reviewed the progress of the last six months and elected new committee members and so on. Such a role would mark the start of the widening the sphere of his influence. It was limited as yet, as at work, he needed to devote himself to gaining experience and to studying, if he was going to further his career.

On the domestic front as a married man and eventual father of four, he had other responsibilities as the decade neared its close. A second son, Frederick Gifford, was born in summer 1889 to the Ravens. Raven now had become a committee member of the NER Literary Institute, his post being confirmed again and again over the years, until he became a vice-president. On 10 January 1890, arbitration between the company and the workforce averted a strike.

T.W. resigned though ill health caused by asthma and this was accepted by the NER Board of directors on 19 September 1890, taking effect from 31 September with salary paid until the end of the year. He remained as consulting engineer to NER for £1,000 p.a. for next two years.

T.W.'s brother Wilson now took over as LS from 1 October 1890 at a starting salary of £1,100 p.a.[10] Unlike his brother, Wilson sported only a long drooping moustache spreading to the side of his chin in his portrait, a sign of changing 'tastes' in the amount of facial hair left on the face; his expression is quite forthright. Wilson Worsdell had really little inclination for administration, recognising that ability to organise was Raven's forté. He also, as has and will be been seen, not only allowed, but positively encouraged, Raven's enterprise in new areas. Worsdell was a first-rate mechanical engineer; for instance, he superseded his brother's use of Joy radial valves in his locomotives, by replacing them with Stephenson's link motion and slide valves, a practice which lasted well into Raven's era. However, by standing above the day-to-day work of his department, leaving the general administration and locomotive running to Raven and the detail of his design to Smith (the chief draughtsman), Wordsell was able to keep the whole rapidly changing picture in perspective.[11]

He was also fortunate in receiving continuing managerial support from George Stegmann Gibb, following the latter's appointment in 1891 as general manager, after Henry Tennant retired on 30 April 1891. Gibb, born in Aberdeen, had been appointed solicitor to the company from 1882.[12] Open to new ideas, he set about reorganising and revitalising the whole administration of NER, which continued to benefit from it over the years.

Tennant had provided sound foundations for the NER, but the company needed a man like Gibb with the flair to lead it into many new developments. For instance, while all railway companies collected statistics, NER, as it progressed, introduced the gathering of more sophisticated and meaningful data. This, in turn, assisted the decision making and became an important feature of the role of executives in whatever aspects of the company's business for which they were responsible. This was particularly so after the appointment of George Gibb as GM. He was influenced by current theories of transport accounting, promulgated by such distinguished academics as Sir William Mitchell Asworth. This led Gibb to introduce the practice of operating statistics, including ton/mileages. This would still be in the air when Gibb went to visit the US in 1902, where the latest Industrial

George Stegman Gibb, NER Co.
solicitor from 1883–1890, GM
from 1890–1906.

theory, the work study methods of Frederick Windsor Taylor in 'scientific management'
of industrial enterprises, was being actively promulgated. Gibb was astute in encouraging
and recruiting men of ability to NER. These included later Ralph Lewis Wedgwood, who
started the traffic apprenticeship scheme, and became chief general goods manager by 1911,
later becoming later chief general manager to the LNER; and thus of great influence in the
future at national level; Eric Campbell Geddes, who joined NER in 1904 and was noted
for his management ability and statistical analysis, although his vigour would not always be
popular; John George Beharrell, an able statistician who worked closely with Geddes as his
financial advisor during and after the First World War, and lastly Frank Pick who would later
become a notable traffic development officer for the London Underground Railways.

Gibb was not averse to gaining the permission of the Board for travelling abroad or letting
other executives to travel to gain new ideas in running the service and view contemporary
practice elsewhere. Consequently, a number of the NER senior staff crossed the Atlantic and
brought back a variety of engineering, building and financial and administrative ideas and
reports on practice as it was being developed in especially the eastern seaboard states of USA.
On return, the experiences gained were at least discussed and new systems implemented.[13]
This putting of theory into practice would seem another facet of self-education absorbed by
Raven. Raven, in the papers on engineering and other matters he gave to various audiences
throughout his working life, continually used tables of figures collated and contrasted as part
of scientific evidence to reinforce a closely reasoned text. He was thus able, when the time
came, to produce far-sighted schemes based on sound statistics and logic while also pursuing
economic prudence. By 1904, Gibb had received a knighthood, leaving NER in 1905 to join
the Metropolitan District Railway.

Raven, for the time being, worked under Mr George Graham, now being promoted to
assistant chief locomotive superintendent.

Walter Mackersie Smith, NER chief draughtsman from 1883–1906.

By 1891, the Raven family had moved further up the hill south to a more upmarket house on Coatsworth Road at 2 Cambridge Terrace, a mere two streets away from his father-in-law. Still standing, it is a large family house with a similar terrace facing.[14] The property consisted of a parlour, dining room, kitchen, three or four bedrooms and an attic with rooms for a resident female domestic and a nurse (possibly a 'nanny' for the children or more specially for Guen). Guen's sudden demise after scarlet fever in 1938 means she had possibly suffered an attack of it in childhood, followed by rheumatic fever, which would have permanently damaged the mitral valves in the left side of her heart. In the light of Annie's early death, the Ravens may have felt she needed particular care. On the night of the 1891 Census, both Constance and her cousin Anne J. Crichton were staying with her grandparents on Bewick Road.

Things did not always run smoothly for NER as an employer: witness a strike by the engineers in 1892, which affected not only organisation of running goods and mineral traffic, but reduced receipts and dividends. Because Wordsell was good at delegating, Raven as middle manager gained both valuable experience and self-confidence, thus repaying Wilson Worsdell's trust in him. As a means of gaining some professional recognition, Raven chose to consolidate his status as an engineer by becoming a member of the Institution of Mechanical Engineers. At a meeting of IMechE on 1 August 1893 at Middlesbrough Town Hall, Raven was elected with fifteen others as a member of the Institution. He was seconded by John A.F. Aspinall, LS of L&YR. He was eligible, being ten years older than the minimum requirement for a working engineer, i.e. twenty-four years of age (it was eighteen years of age for graduates). His brother, Henry Baldwin, who was listed as an Associate of the Institution from 1886, worked for Messrs Hare & Co., Temple Chambers, Temple Avenue, London. Presumably his firm provided some sort of legal advice to the Institution.[15]

Cambridge Terrace, off
Coatsworth Road, the Ravens'
last residence in Gateshead.

This gaining of more professional status no doubt helped the next stage of his career, his promotion to chief assistant locomotive superintendent by Worsdell in October 1893, having supervision of all the Workshops and the outside Running Department with the Dock and Warehouse machinery in the Locomotive Department.[16]

This marked his accession to next level of management. He would be involved not only with keeping locomotives running throughout the system, but further special projects as well, thus further widening his experience. At a meeting of the Locomotive and Stores Committee, chaired by Lothian Bell, on 5 October, Wilson Worsdell had been asked to produce a report on compounding. He quickly delegated this special assignment to Raven and Ramsey Kendall (previously chief test inspector but also from October 1893 promoted to Darlington works manager).

During October, as Raven's log-book attests, he set out on a project to collect and collate the required information about what T.W.'s 'compounds' and other locomotives were capable of doing. He organised it like a military manoeuvre. After planning out what he wanted, he called inspectors to ensure that they were to travel on the footplate of the engines under trial (mainline goods and mineral) which were to have the same amount of coal (the afternoon of Friday 13 October). Next day (14 October), he allocated one man to see the coal weighed at Gateshead for engine use. From next Monday (16 October) the other inspectors were to ride on the footplate of ten express passenger (most likely north-running) locomotives, ten on south running mainline goods locomotives, ten on trains from Tyne Dock (most likely mineral) and

Wilson Worsdell's 2-cylinder express passenger class 'M' 4-4-0s.

ten south-running express engines. Arthur Cowie Stamer (later to be Raven's assistant) was detailed to find out cost of repairs, while another was to compile the consumption of ten compounds from 1887 to 1892. Thus a wide variety of types is included, reading like a muster of the previous twenty years or so of locomotive building ranging from S & DR no.1205 0-6-0 from 1874, Fletcher's goods '398' 0-6-0s from years 1878/81/82/, McDonnell's goods class '59' 0-6-0's of 1884, Tennant express passenger class '1463' 2-4-0s from 1885, T.W.'s passenger class 'J' 4-2-2 of 1889/90 and goods class 'C/C1' 0-6-0s of 86/87/90/91/92 and express passenger 2-4-0s to the latest 2-cylinder compounds – Wilson Worsdell's new express passengers class 'M' 4-4-0s, put into service earlier in the year 1893.

Raven himself went from York to Newcastle behind No.1459. He notes that, despite a strong wind, the engines steamed well but primed a little. The return journey on 1524 was similar; he notes that cut-off did not sound very distinct and that he felt the blast-pipe not to be exactly right. By Tuesday (17 October), he decided to add six old engines on the Tebay-Bishop Auckland run. On the 22nd he was down at Tyne Dock and on the 24th at Sunderland, and on the 25th Blaydon, at Hartlepool, where drivers comment on their good running on the road and at shunting (some remark they are markedly slower at this) and use less oil, but were poorer at starting off or going up inclines and have some limitations in taking loads larger than thirty wagons and are bad at stopping. One foreman notes that how well they work depends on the abilities of the driver in handling them. This comment is a good defence of the possible best way of running Raven's *Pacifics* later.[17] This project meant that Raven missed the inauguration of the Wear Valley Extension Railway on 25 October 1893.

A month later, in November 1893, their findings were published in a confidential report for the committee, rather laboriously entitled 'Report with reference to the Working of Compound Engines compared with Working of other Classes of Engines on the North Eastern Railway'. Having finished their collation of material, the authors produced charts, tabling the work done over the previous twenty-four years to 10 June 1893 by passenger, good and mineral locomotives, designed by Fletcher, MacDonnell and T.W. Worsdell. They had examined miles done, coal used, the cost of coal and oil used and the cost of repairs per 1,000 miles after either being built or rebuilt, in various locations, mainline, for example, fairly flat and cross country, i.e. with more difficult gradients in and across the Pennines. The two authors queried the efficacy of compounding, opting for superheating instead in their final summary.

The compound engines are fine once fairly away with a load in ordinary circumstances, but for shunting a train, they are very much inferior to the ordinary engine. On this question we should point out that at large Goods Yards, pilot engines of the simple type do all the marshalling of trains, the train engine being little used for this purpose, so that it is the pick-up trains which conspicuously bring the slow and difficult shunting into notice. In using the term 'difficult', it meant that engines of this class cannot be moved a short distance with any amount of accuracy, thus rendering (where obliged to be resorted to) pole or chain shunting a matter of considerable delicacy. Engine drivers generally prefer compound engines for through goods traffic, but consider them unhandy and slow for other purposes. Those in charge of mineral traffic inform us that the simple engine for their purpose is much to be preferred, and on certain occasions it has been necessary to reduce the load on account of engines being signal stopped on heavy gradients.

Domestically, the result of this promotion meant a move in late 1893 to Darlington for Raven and his family. Darlington was then an increasingly industrial township, but still continued to play its older role of country town, having 40,000 inhabitants. Raven and his wife would spend the next thirty years of their life there, coming to play an increasing part in its industrial, social, educational and civic life, while Connie was to remain in Darlington and Guen was destined to commute up and down the mainline, spending time in York, Doncaster and only eventually back in Darlington.

1 Mulligan, Fergus, 1990, *One Hundred and Fifty Years of Irish Railways*, Appletree Press, p.64

2 Wheeler's Directory 1894, p.988

3 Maclean, *The Locomotives of the North Eastern Railway, 1854-1903*, p.61

4 Grafton Peter, March 2005, Sir Vincent Raven and the North Eastern Railway, Oakwood Press, p.29. Grafton raises the interesting point of Raven's investigation braking systems. However, the experimenters he cites worked only with brake systems for coaches or goods wagons, not locomotives, e.g. with LN&WR, firemen operated the clumsy Newall system from the 1850s, Tyrell, Clark and Webb devised chain brakes, Sanders and Hardy vacuum brakes and Heberlein cable brakes for Konigliche Bayeerische Staatseisenbahn. To this list could have been added Eames' system for Baldwin locomotives on tour from the US in 1881

5 Oswald Nock, in *The Locomotives of the North Eastern Railway*, portrays Fletcher as a hail-fellow-well-met Geordie and McDonnell as difficult aristocratic Irish autocrat, opinions which have become accepted as a norm and which Grafton, in his *Sir Vincent Raven and the North Eastern Railway*, merely echoes. Neither author provides sources for their opinions. Fletcher, in fact, was an iron hand in a velvet glove as indicated in the text above and already moving towards standardisation. McDonnell continued to do what he had already done on a smaller scale at Inchicore, but did not reckon that an 1884 deficit in returns and increased local rail Union activity in the workforce would have their effects on his plans, as the local newspapers of the time attest. Nevertheless, his mission remained influential if essentially incomplete

6 Kelly's Directory for Durham, Gateshead entries, 1868, 1871–1872 and 1873

7 1881 and 1891 Census returns for Gateshead

8 Four more NER engineers were proposed, the first, William Benjamin Bellenonce of Cockfield Terrace, Gateshead, was proposed on 17 April, then Walter Elliott Nicholson (of 5 St Thomas Crescent, Newcastle) was proposed on 18 September, Charles Leslie Ryder (of Fern Avenue, Gateshead) was proposed on 18 December and lastly, Thomas William Brown (of 12 Gainsborough Grove, Newcastle) was balloted for on 15 May 1884. Information given by Ken Atkinson of Percy Lodge, 25 August 2002

9 Pennysylvania Railroad (1846–1968) – one of the great American railroads with more than 10,000 miles of track, serving about half the US population living in north-eastern seaboard, northern border and mid-western states with goods, minaeral and passenger trains

10 Reprints from *Engineer and Engineering*, June 1887. The whole matter of compounding is explored and analysed in detail in Addyman J., Grocock M.R., Horsman G. and Teasdale J.G., May 2005, 'Express Steam Locomotives on the NER: Compound Working of Steam locomotives', p.40-42, and 'The Locomotives of Class D', p.43-53, vol.44, no.178, *North Eastern Express*

11 Hoole Ken, 1967, *North Road Locomotive Works 1863–1966*, Roundhouse Books, p.68

12 Nock Oswald S. 1954, *The Locomotives of the North Eastern Railway*, Ian Allan London, p.84

13 Hoole Ken, 1967 reprint by Augustus M. Kelley, New York, 1967, of William Weaver Tomlinson, 1914, *North Eastern Railway: its rise and development*, new notes, corrections and updating by K. Hoole

14 Committee members were elected every six months, so Raven must have been elected in December 1888, if before. The records are patchy, those found so far are for 1889–1890, 1904, 1911, 1915–1916, 1927

15 1891 Census

15 Proceedings of the IMechE, 1 August 1893

16 Candidates Circular for election as Associate Member of ICE, 14 March 1898, p.36

17 Dates in brackets are Raven's logbook/diary entries

IV

MOVE TO DARLINGTON
(1893–1901)

The NER offices for Darlington (originally those of the S&DR) were on Northgate, several hundred yards into the town from the North Road Station and Works. Raven travelled back to Gateshead, or to anywhere else, with a staff pass, as necessary. Although initially his address was merely a work one, NER Locomotive Works, North Road, his new home was across the road from them at Alpine Cottage, Whessoe Street, Darlington, close to the large NER goods yard. It was a large house with extensive grounds.[1] Raven employed a resident nurse, cook and domestic and maids who came in to work. During the 1900s, the Ravens held balls on Friday nights, with the guests arriving in hackneys.[2] This marked a move towards a more active social life, but it was only later, when CME, that Raven sought more directly civic roles. He also became involved with the revitalising of the Darlington NER Railway Institute, working with his former Low Fell neighbour Ramsay Kendall, locomotive works manager, to reopen and renovate it. Initially the membership was 110 but it soon increased to 430, eventually rising to 630. By 1907–1908, AGM had 14,390 books available for members in its library. The chairman was Mr Arthur Pease.

In December 1893, Raven transferred to 1379 Marquis of Ripon Lodge of Freemasons in Darlington, it being noted that he had been a past Master at Percy Lodge in Newcastle. The Darlington Lodge, known as The Engineers' Lodge, met on the first Friday of every month (July, August and September excepted) at the Freemasons Hall (a former Baptist chapel) on Archer Street, close to where the new Technical College was built in 1896. This ensured he met other professionals within local society circles in Darlington. Such links smoothed his access to professional and civic life. He attended May and June meetings of 1894 as a visitor, being proposed on 1 November as a joining member by Dr George Middlemiss, one of the town's doctors, with Sir Thomas Putnam, managing director of Darlington Forge, seconding him. Raven continued to attend meeting several times a year, although he missed all meetings in 1897 and from 1900–1903. This did not stop him on re-attendance in 1904–1905 from becoming junior warden (February 1905) and then senior warden (March 1906).

At this time, his attention was focussed very much on his career and on his young family and their education. All four surviving children were given private education. The girls, Connie and Guen, both attended at Polam Hall, a Quaker school for girls. Connie left there in 1902; as a nineteen year old she went to the Evendine Court School, Colwall Green, a domestic science school opened in 1896 on the Herefordshire side of Malvern.[3] Among other skills acquired, she gained certificates in dressmaking and housekeeping, making a good enough impression to be asked to stay on as a pupil teacher. On her return to Darlington, she and Guen took up active membership of Polam School's Old Scholar's Association. Later, Connie continued interest as a subscriber of the magazine.

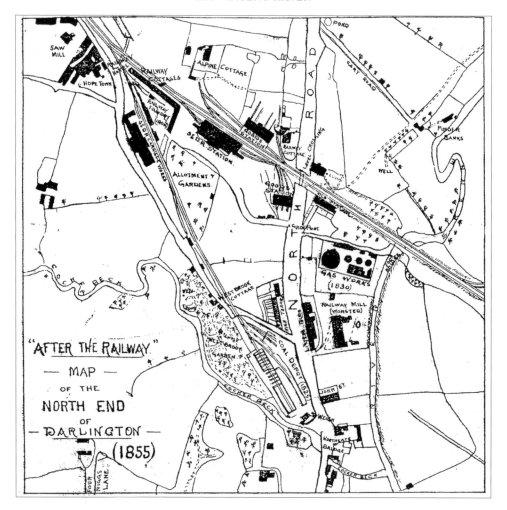

Because the Ravens still had a nurse living in the household, it is possible that she was still there to look after Guen. Norman became a pupil at Darlington Grammar School on gaining its Bellases Entrance Scholarship, which awarded free tuition fees for a year in 1895. Once there he gained a second prize for Excellence in his first year, 1896.[4] He was in Rutland, at Uppingham, from 1900 to 1904, while Frederick became a pupil at The Mount Board School in Northallerton and then followed Norman to Uppingham for a year from 1903–1904.[5]

After the work on compounding, he started another new project, this time with Charlie Baister, a long-term associate of Raven's. Baister was born in 1855 in Darlington. He began his apprenticeship at the former S&D North Road Works there in 1869, and stayed on until 1876 when he left to broaden his experience over the next few years in both general and marine engineering. He first worked to nearby Middlesbrough, West Hartlepool and Stockton. Then after a brief period with SECR, he went abroad on a tramp steamer to ports in the Near East, travelling via the Dardanelles to Constantinople.

He returned to Darlington in 1881, to live with his widowed mother, Anne, at 24 Raby Street. He became night foreman at Heaton Junction in 1884 under George Kendal. Promoted again in 1886 to locomotive foreman at Stockton, he went to Percy Main in April 1893 as district locomotive foreman at Hull, but in December 1893, with all his practical experience proving quickly to be of use, he returned to Darlington as assistant to Raven. They quickly set to work on a new safety measure.

Opposite: Map of the north end of Darlington in 1855.

Left: Polam School for Girls, Grange Road, Darlington, founded as a Quaker establishment in 1854.

Left: Darlington Literary Institute.

Below: Charlie Baister, Raven's colleague and friend, was co-worker on fog signalling.

Left: Marquis of Ripon Lodge, Archer Street, Darlington of which Raven was a member from 1893–1906.

The two of them designed a mechanical line side signal, which gave drivers a whistle as an audible warning in their cab when the weather was foggy. From 4 November 1894, it was first installed at Merrybent Junction between Bank Top and Piercebridge on the Darlington–Barnard Castle line and at the Shildon tunnel. The system was introduced more widely in 1896. By 1901, it had been installed from Darlington South Junction to Poppleton Junction at

Ground-level view of fog-signalling apparatus.

York. A further section was put in place from Forest Hall to Alnmouth. All in all, there were eventually 243 sites for the apparatus and all engines, except shunters were fitted. By 1919, those fitted with the apparatus totalled 1,488.

There were two parts to the apparatus – a ground unit between the rails and an alerting unit in the cab. The unit on the ground connected to the signal wire with a balance weight to make it move, should the wire break. It was attached to both distant and stop signals. It consisted of a rod going under the rail, with two trip arms attached to accommodate locomotives running either boiler or tender/bunker first. At first, the arms were fashioned in an inverted U-shape, but later a forged T-bar was used. The unit stood out above rail level, when in 'warning' position. If the signal was 'clear' the unit's arms were lowered and missed contact with the section in the locomotive. The locomotive unit had a vertical striking rod with a rounded bottom edge, protruding down through the cab floor. This hit the ground unit, if it was up in the 'warning' position. The striking rod in the cab worked a valve which let boiler steam into a dedicated whistle, which gave a warning that the signal was at danger. The whistle blew until the striking rod was reset. The locomotives fitted with steam brake made only the whistle operate, but with those with Westinghouse air brakes, the compressed air supply could also apply brakes. It was a notable success and a landmark in making railway practice safe. In 1903, only five failures of the system were noted.

Raven now started to investigate the adaptation of the application of electrical power for a variety of uses. The earliest indication of his interest came from the Traffic Committee, in 1894, when Raven was on the Electric Light Committee for Tyne Dock. He must have studied both theoretical material from a number of sources such as the proceedings of the institutions he belonged to and research and experimental material from German, French and other continental and American sources, as well as the ability to put that material to practical application. This was manifest in his application of electro-hydraulic principles to dock cranes and then in his improving safety through electrification of his fog-warning apparatus.

Raven thus took advantage of Worsdell's reliance on him, responding to special enterprises given to him within a teamwork model of management. This lesson in running a department in all likelihood derived from McDonnell's influence. It would not to be lost on Raven himself, when CME. Worsdell was seemingly content to be a very active participant in the design-and-build team, as well as being its figurehead. As the junior in the team, Raven would learn from Heppel and Smith.

The Smiths, Walter Mackersie and son John William, were two of the ablest men ever to work for the NER. A Scotsman, the older Smith was born at Newport on-Tay on the south bank of the firth of Tay, opposite Dundee in 1842 (then called Ferryport-on-Craig prior to the building of the rail and road bridges). He served his general engineering apprenticeship in Glasgow, joining the Glasgow & Edinburgh Railway, which had Samuel Waite Johnson as its LS. When Johnson moved to the GER at Stratford in 1866, Smith went there. At thirty-two, Smith was appointed carriage and wagon superintendent to the Japanese Imperial Railways, laying out workshops, machinery and running sheds. On his return to England in 1883, he came to NER as chief draughtsman, under Alexander McDonnell, as noted.[6] John William, born in 1866, was educated both in Dundee and in Newcastle, entering into the Works Drawing Office at Greenesfield, as Raven had done earlier.[7]

Because of a number of fractures occurring in slide valves at the time, Walter Smith, using a design he had been working on for a while, began straightaway to test the worth of freely operating piston valves on a Fletcher 2-4-0 of 1880, No.340. Its success and reduction of fuel consumption led him to produce an improved version.

Worsdell was happy to leave Smith and the team the freedom to work out his own solutions to engineering problems. Smith still had contact with his old mentor Johnson, who now had transferred to the MR. As a result there was a consistent dialogue between MR and NER at the time about compounding and engine performance. Smith senior's photographic portrait shows a man with a thick dark beard and moustache, hairier than the 'Imperial', but shaved to the sides of his chin. His expression finds him looking away from the camera with an intent, if somewhat wary, expression.

His son, meanwhile, had spent some time with NER, but then went off to Derby works of MR under Johnson, as his father had earlier. Like his father, he was appointed chief locomotive draughtsman there, designing Johnson's two famous 3-cylinder compound 4-4-0s, later in autumn 1905 working with Richard M. Deeley on a further ten engines. After this he went to the smaller Great Central Railway to work with Robinson as his Gorton works manager, not finally retiring well into LNER days in 1932. Another NER escapee, as it were, to Great Central Railway (GCR) was Henry Worsdell, a nephew of the Worsdell's brother, who worked at York carriage works, joining Robinson's team at GCR in 1902 as chief assistant in the carriage and wagon department at Dukinfield. Worsdell, in concert with Smith and increasingly after 1893 Raven, would go on to produce locomotives remarkably consistent in design and function, which enjoyed in most cases a life of up to fifty working years or more. This was a joint legacy to the NER, particularly important to north-eastern industry and passengers.

Worsdell now started to introduce a wide variety of locomotive types. His purpose was to respond to the company's need for larger, more efficient, engines as well as moving towards a notable company style. The result was a fleet of large, increasingly effective, steam engines of elegant proportions and consistent reliability for NER. He increased cylinder size and provided larger heating surface from larger boilers. He started in 1892 by introducing further developments of 4-4-0s, which derived from an enlarged version of his brother's class 'F' class, the class 'M', which had 7ft 1in. driving wheels. Class 'Q1' 4-4-0s followed in1896 with 7ft 7in driving wheels (claimed to be the world's largest) and lastly class 'Q' in 1899, with 7ft 1in driving wheels. With an even larger locomotive in 1899, he pioneered the introduction of a 4-6-0 – the first express passenger engine of this wheel arrangement in the British Isles – class 'S'. Later he went on to introduce to the company, after visiting the USA, another new wheel arrangement – the 4-4-2 or *Atlantic* with his class 'V' in 1903 and later class 'V1' in 1910. Taken as a whole, the designs of all his locomotives were notable for their clean lines, with external fittings kept to a minimum within the frames.

GM Gibb's major drive for the company was improving its efficiency. This meant getting the best out of stock and personnel by the cheapest effective means, but within a safe working environment. This brought another aspect of Raven's job, namely to be involved with the discipline of the running department. In such a hierarchical structure with its written and verbal codes of practice, he had to abide by the rules set down for his position.[8] His 1894–1895 log book reveals both general and individual staff concerns. For instance, he notes the inefficiency of communication between sheds and men in the Northern Division (for which he had lately been responsible) and mentions Hartlepool by name (18 November 1894). The mileage per hour of minerals is in the Northern than in the Central division He also is concerned about the repairs on northern mainline and thinks transfer of repair facilities from Berwick to Edinburgh could be a better arrangement (24 November 1894). This is a theme he returns to in his 1898 'Report on Cambrian Railways' and later in his role as commissioner on various enquiries.

Regarding personnel matters, Raven had to listen and make judgements within his jurisdiction. He had to be even-handed and impartial in dealing with staff members within known rules. Staff needed to know where they stood with him especially as he had so recently been promoted. Yielding would have only confused and weakened his position. The Unions would certainly have been quick to note bias in his attitude. The matters he records in his log book are as varied as are his responses. Some concern earlier dismissals. Here he is firm in refusing to reconsider someone dismissed by Graham, his predecessor, in April 1892 (6 August 1894). Yet of another man, a cleaner, who had ventured on to the footplate of an engine, he forbearingly acknowledges that he would raise no objection to re-employing, if his line manager agrees; another cleaner is not working hard enough according to his line manager, Raven admonished him to do better, saying he does not want to hear anything more about him in the future (2 March 1895). One man's wife came to him because her husband was in prison for debt (unspecified). Raven let her down quite gently, telling her that her husband can come and see him on discharge from prison but that at present his place had been taken (25 January 1894).

Some disciplinary interviews are to do with suspensions of engine drivers and inappropriate alcohol consumption and its relation to work. He deals with one by saying he will have to wait for the enquiry into his suspension. In other words, it was out of his hands. The other is a report of a sixty-four-year-old man, who had given up drink due to 'rheumatism', but whose work is unsatisfactory in the opinion of his line manager. In February 1894, Raven, following procedure, advises the man to let his manager know if he is ill but to keep better time, so that he (Raven) does not hear of him again. Another the same day (5 March 1895) dismissed for drink, asks for any other job; Raven refers him to Worsdell. This problem with drink and its effects on employees will arise phoenix-like in the Knox affair and with men at Woolwich Arsenal.

Some incidents were to do with health matters, other than drink-related. He was firm in his refusal for return to work of a Shildon man, who asked him to have another test (presumably a medical one), 'when he is very bad in colour' (5 January 1895). All the above items impinged directly or indirectly on Raven's responsibility for safety and its breaches by staff. For instance, he denied an appeal against a fine of a driver at Shildon for giving a shunter a lift (6 August 1894) and refused to lift a suspension of another driver who had entered a single line without staff (8 October 1894). During this period Raven was again promoted and became assistant mechanical engineer, when he began to tackle further projects.

A prestige demonstration of prowess for the East Coast mainline operators was a trial fast run from London to Aberdeen. So during August of 1895, the second Great Rail Race to the North began. The goals were to see which line enabled the fastest travel from London to Aberdeen with the locomotives and carriages available. Earlier the fastest route from London and Aberdeen had been by the West Coast Route. The successful bridging of the Tay Bridge in 1882 and then the Forth by the world famous cantilever bridge in 1890 allowed the Scottish section of East Coast route, via Edinburgh and Dunfermline to be put in contention. The whole East Coast route was shorter and therefore potentially faster than the West Coast route.

The battle was soon in full swing between the East and West Coast mainlines. On Tuesday, the day after the 'glorious' 12 August, i.e. the beginning of the grouse season, the East Coast companies met for a council of war at York. Those present were David Deuchar, superintendent of the Line; Matthew Holmes, LS for North British Railway (NBR); F.P. Cockshott from GNR; John Welburn, NER superintendent of the line; Raven, the assistant LS from NER. They agreed that from 19 to 23 August, the arrival time of 8 p.m. from King's Cross to Aberdeen should be 5.40 a.m., about twenty minutes faster than the West Coast. There were to be six (not more than seven) coaches. The GNR would have some difficulties with the accelerated time schedule.[9] There was keen interest from reporters in *The Times* and *The Yorkshire Post*. *The Post*'s correspondent on 21 August appears to have ridden on the record-breaking train.

Raven travelled all the way from York to Edinburgh on the footplate. First he rode on the footplate of class 'M' 4-4-0 '1621', built in 1893, from York to Newcastle. The engine was driven by G. Turner, who was keen on making a record trip to Edinburgh with Fireman Elijah Hodgson and it showed itself to be as sturdy a performer as a Stirling single wheeler. Despite an unspecified incident that took place during the changeover of engines at Newcastle,[10] Raven changed to the footplate of 'M' class 4-4-0 '1620' for the journey from Newcastle to Edinburgh, 124 miles in 112 minutes, with driver Bob Nicholson and fireman Tom Blades (later the driver of Raven's *Pacific*). It was a triumph for the East Coast teams. Later Raven would be remembered as the man who promoted the then fastest average time of 66mph between English and Scottish capitals.

Someone who knew Raven and appreciated his potential was Charles Sherwood Denniss, who was moving to Cambrian Railways as GM. They were both present at the opening on 21 October 1895 of the Wear Valley Extension Railway, authorised in 1892 after nearly thirty years of proposals, planning and recession in lead and ironstone industry. The company included:

Sir David Dale, Bart, director – NER and Lady Dale
Charles Sherwood Denniss administrator – NER, soon to be GM (Cambrian Railways)
Sir William Cresswell Gray, director – NER
Edward White Lyall, later chairman – NER
J. Cudworth Kendall
Henry Tennant, GM – NER
Right Honourable John Lloyd Wharton, MP (Durham), director – NER
Christopher Newman Wilkinson Secretary – NER
Wilson Worsdell, LS – NER[11]

On 27 November 1896, Raven gave a paper on his signalling apparatus. This was his first extant public address. Worsdell introduced him personally to the meeting of the Association of Railway Locomotive Engineers (ARLE), which had been inaugurated on 15 January 1890.[12] This was the first paper that he would present at the St Pancras Hotel to his peers, a group of railway locomotive engineering notables, all at various stages in their careers. They included:

Charles Sherwood Denniss,
LS of Cambrian Railways from
1896–1914.

John Audley Frederick Aspinall, LS to L&YR
William Dean, LS for GWR
James Holden, LS to GER
Samuel Waite Johnson LS to MR
Thomas Hurry Riches, LS to Taff Vale Railway
James Stirling, LS for South Eastern Railway
Matthew Stirling, LS for H&BR
Wilson Worsdell

A special meeting of the RCA was called in late March 1897 by Gladstonian Liberal, Sir Joseph Whitwell Pease, Bart, MP for Barnard Castle and chairman of NER. He typically had large coal and iron interests in the North East. Much to the consternation of other member companies, he announced that the NER Board would seek arbitration covering wages and conditions; when in dispute with its employees and George Gibb, the GM of NER supported him, refusing to back down despite pressure from them. In this case, NER ploughed a lonely furrow.[13] As will be seen later, such far-sightedness and attempts by largely Quaker Board and Executive to be even handed in labour relations would not be acknowledged by the workmen either.[14]

Unfortunately, one of the juggling acts that all concerned with the NER as a company had to keep in mind was the balancing of the books. In a period lasting from 1874 to 1913, the financial picture was as follows:

During 1874–1883, expenditure was steady about £50 million and revenue at about £6 million p.a., but dividends varied from just under 8 per cent (1874), falling (in 1877/78) to a low of 4.5 per cent (1879), but restored to nearly 8 per cent for next four years.

The next decade (1884–1893), little change in expenditure was again steady about £50 million or revenue at about £6 million pa, but dividends varied from just under 8 per cent (1884) to between 4 per cent (1891) and 5 per cent (1885/88).

Institution of Civil Engineers, Great George Street, Westminster.

During 1894–1903, expenditure had risen to about £60 million as had revenue, starting at about £7 million rising each year to about 7.5 million p.a. (1903), with dividends dropping to about 4.5 per cent each year.

During 1904–1913, expenditure had again risen to about £70 million and revenue over £8 million but dividends dropped slightly varying between 4 to 4.5 per cent each year.

There was an early falling off in investment of railway stocks, so that by the end of 1897, there was a £606,000 overdraft between capital income from share issues and capital expenditure on new works.[15]

This lack of investment became permanent and underpinned the need for economy of resources and the lack of expansion for schemes. It put an onus on Gibb, Worsdell and others to improve the whole performance of the railway, hence the move for larger locomotives, wagons and carriages. It became obvious that bulk transport with larger trains, whether goods, mineral or passenger, were more economic of resources, whether mechanical or manpower, than running many small units with lesser loads.

Having submitted a candidate's circular to the Institution of Civil Engineers (ICE), Raven was proposed by James Kitson, Lord Airedale, an NER director, seconded by Members of ICE:

John Audley Frederick Aspinall (LS – LYR)
Sir Lowthian Bell – another NER Director
Henry Alfred Ivatt (LS – GNR)
A. T. Walker, plus his former superior T. W. Worsdell, AMICE

The fine but unoccupied Oswestry Station complex in 2004, the former HQ of Cambrian Railways.

Raven was duly elected as associate member of the Institution of Civil Engineers on 10 February 1898.[16] Such a membership no doubt would have increased his professional credibility as well as contacts through the exchange of theory and practice with his peers from other companies. Darlington ordered its cylinders from Kitson & Co. of Leeds, whereas Gateshead did so from Robert Stephenson & Co. in Newcastle. There were obvious business connections between Raven and Kitson. As Lord Airedale, Kitson would be there when Raven was approved as MICE in 1910.

He was asked by Charles Sherwood Denniss (now in his third year as GM – Cambrian Railways) during the course of the year 1898 to go to Cambrian Railways HQ at Oswestry. The company had 2,442 miles of mostly single track through terrain, reminiscent, on a much grander scale, of the Wear Valley. Its mainline ran across mid-Wales from Flintshire via Oswestry to Aberystwyth; connected to this were winding links down the southern Welsh Marches and a line up the west coast to Pwllheli. Surrounded by larger companies, it had end-on contact with LNWR, GWR, Cheshire Lines Committee and MR. Internally it had a number of smaller standard-gauge branches to isolated villages and narrow-gauge subsidiary enterprises. Besides rural passenger traffic, there was lead mining on Mawddwy and Vale of Rheidol, carriage of crops on the Farmers Railway – the Welshpool and Llanfair and flannel production at Welshpool. The mainline came to provide a tourist link to the western Welsh coastal resorts, with hotels in Pwllheli, Criccieth and Harlech and later in Aberystwyth, via through carriages from GWR and LNWR. It had running powers into Chester, Crewe and Warrington.

As a commercial enterprise, it started off somewhat shakily both financially and managerially. In the 1870s it was in the red, but by 1880 had managed to break even. It provided a deal of local employment, but at a cost. Its management style was autocratic and exacting enough for an enquiry to be held into its practices. Denniss had moved into post when they were a number of new senior managers appointed. Because freight usage and hence returns were on the decline, he decided to promote very actively the railway's tourist potential.

The LS William Aston had been in post since 1879, and had produced twenty highly regarded light 4-4-0s and 12 0-6-0s, each very reminiscent of Alexander McDonnell's efforts on both sides of the Irish Sea. The company had ninety drivers on its books in 1898, while its locomotive stock was 85 1899 (mainly 4-4-0s for passenger trains, 0-6-0 for freight). It had 282 non-corridor carriages by end of 1901 and approximately 2,574 wagons.[17] These had been built to order by various manufacturers and maintained at the company's works at Oswestry (an English town!).

All was not well with the running of the department of LS. This was shown by Aston being previously held to account on 8 November 1893. He was asked to report on why three new passenger locomotives, delivered in April and May, where being repaired in Oswestry Works. His obsessively perfectionist attitude possibly stood in the way of GM Alfred Aslett's ideas. When Denniss took over as GM in about 1896, he brought Raven in to investigate and report on the state of their locomotives and their maintenance at Oswestry Works. It is rather unusual for an assistant LS to report in this way on a person of senior rank, albeit from a much larger and wealthier company then the Cambrian. Denniss must have appreciated Raven's abilities and arranged for him to be given the authority to conduct the investigation and produce the report.

Raven's meticulous report to the Board was given in autumn 1898. While not coming to any definite conclusions, it showed that productivity from maintenance staff was not high in Oswestry; 137 men were employed, compared with 578 at York. Oswestry, on his calculations, should have about seventy-five men to carry out the work a similar amount of repair work at York. He would later repeat this logistic employment exercise for the Ministry of Munitions during the First World War and also for the LNER after grouping. The Cambrian Board considered it and another report, submitted to them by Aston. The result was unanimous. They asked for L.S. Aston's resignation on 21 December 1898, which he duly tendered on 25 March 1899. Sadly, he died in 1901 from a severe haemoptosis, caused by tuberculosis.[18]

Economic considerations in the early 1900s became even more important to NER and other railway companies. This partly arose from a desire to compete with what other locomotive companies were achieving not only in Britain, but also on the Continent and the USA. Also, investment in the company had fallen off, so there was a need to balance the books by increased revenues. The financial state of NER was not helped by the crash of its bank, the J. & J.W. Pease,. It meant a loss of £125,000 as a result.

The main source of revenue was mineral transport, which dominated haulage, goods and passenger traffic playing a lesser, but important, part. There was also wisdom in seeking to work with the Unions, who could affect the prosperity of the company both positively and negatively especially in industrial action. The new century would see this conflict between workforce and management played out and continued until the First World War and afterwards.

The first round in the contest went to the employers, when in August 1900, the Taff Vale Railway Co. sued the ASRS for damages, in the Taff Vale Railway v. Osborne case, taken by the company as a result of the action of the Union men in a trade dispute. After the case, the House of Lords gave a final decision against the Union, which was required to pay £23,000 damages with expenses of the case being awarded against a further £19,000. The belief that Unions would be immune to damages, due to the actions of their members was temporarily shattered. In reply, the ASRS and GRWU and the Unions urged its reversal. The concerted effort lead to the formation of the modern Labour Party which was able after the general election of 1906, to effect the passing of the 1906 Trades Disputes Act, ensuring Unions immunity from damages.

Worsdell and his support team thus had incentives to increase the size and scope of engines. They were needed to haul either larger loads of goods and minerals or increase the speed of passenger trains. These would continue to be main considerations that urged Raven to seek out, consider and develop new methods of rail haulage power of various types, especially electromotive power, when he became CME.

Gibb and the other executives now had to examine how to produce more efficiency in train loading:

(1) Increase the number of loaded wagons per train, and haul the resulting heavy load with more powerful locomotives
(2) Increase the carrying capacity of individual wagons
(3) Improve the loading of wagons, so that fewer ran part-loaded
(4) Improve transhipping arrangements
(5) Encourage by means of favourable rates, the dispatch by traders of larger loads[19]

The steam locomotive is not an energy-conserving machine, having a mechanical efficiency of around 12 per cent. Much of the energy available from coal is lost in the water-heating process and resistance to movement, not to mention the loss of valuable chemicals as exhaust into the air. It also was prodigal in using water. Neither of these resources were in short supply normally in nineteenth- and early twentieth-century Britain. Therefore, steam locomotive building from its inception was, from an engineering point of view, a balancing act between the best use of energy from coal to generate steam, which in turn drove the machine and those factors, reducing internal and external mechanical resistances, which could retard or inhibit such movement and the rising costs of materials and maintenance. One of the main drawbacks to British development of the steam engine was the restricted loading gauge when compared with the Continent, USA and Russia. The British norm (reduced to 16ft high, when LNER introduced composite loading gauge) was a semicircular arch of 13½ft or 4,115mm maximum height at centre of arch, sloping to 10¾ft or 3,276mm at the sides x 9½ft or 2,896mm width.

This was not a problem while boilers were small, with frames supporting them and overhanging cylinders being kept well within loading-gauge limits. However, by the end of the nineteenth century, various developments and demands to improve performance and power had resulted in the top of the gauge being reached. This is demonstrated by the length of locomotive chimneys. Originally little more than a stove pipe, they had become shorter as boilers became bigger, until they were quite short and stubby. They had a dual function: not only did they provide an exhaust system, but they were important in drawing air through the heating system to assist burning of the fuel.

Once locomotive boilers were enlarged to the greatest height permissible within the gauge and cylinders or other apparatus had reached loading gauge width, there was only one way to move and that was to increase the boiler length or tuck the protruding apparatus within the locomotives' frame and running boards. The effect of this was to make access, and therefore maintenance, difficult. It will be noted how cylinder sizes (and piston valve stroke) changed little in size over this period, while the power, size and weight of locomotives did. The compression resulting from installing three cylinders, as Raven later did, made things very crowded between the running boards and frames, and maintenance increasingly difficult, even if it usually improved the aesthetic appearance of the locomotive (for details see Appendix 11 – comparative chart of Wilson Worsdell's and Raven's locomotives from 1899–1923).

External resistances to locomotive movement include the weight of its engine and its fuel (plus for steam engines water), plus the weight (and drag) of any load it is designed to pull, were important considerations in engine design and function. Internal resistances derive from its moving parts. The pistons, valves, gears, cranks, coupling rods and wheels of the locomotive (especially the drivers) have to be able to move and exert sufficient adhesion on the track to overcome inertia and resistances in starting up as well as when braking and seeking to stop. Wheel-slip is a waste of energy and possible source of danger, especially with heavy loads. The size and weight of the engine itself by 1900 had been greatly increased and efforts were made to distribute load on driving wheel axles, which helped to ensure smooth riding and consistent performance from start to stop as well as balancing out some of the mechanical stresses and reducing wear and tear.

Added to engineering considerations were commercial ones deriving from ever increasing costs of production and maintenance, plus demands for larger loads and greater speed, not to mention, safety considerations for both workers and users. Thus progress in locomotive development was determined by the demands of commerce and industry, as well as advances in technology. By the end of the nineteenth century, when Raven was becoming increasingly involved with it, the whole process had become much more sophisticated.

Nonetheless, all functional considerations were cost-driven. Improvements in particular aspects of functioning resulted from considering what had gone before and how it could be bettered and what new developments were going on in the international engineering field, where the NER particularly was influenced by innovations in both Germany and the USA. Besides improving tractive output, particularly by developing certain aspects of performance of its constituent parts, there was a need to see them all in interaction so that the working parts were in some kind of balance, for instance balancing output from cylinders. Friction and hence wear and tear were reduced, as well as discomfort in travelling both for operatives and users. This meant that a new locomotive should provide a smooth ride from stop to start coupled with an ability to move its load with ease at all speeds. The design should ensure easy access to those responsible for providing easy maintenance and renewal of its working parts. It should make as efficient use of coal in its water heating and steam generation as possible. Lessons learned from previous designs either within the company or elsewhere should mark any improvement on a predecessor. Locomotive design thus had its focus in the functional rather than the aesthetic. Yet the merits of steam locomotives when considered as expressions of contemporary design were not far removed from other artefacts derived from the aesthetic tenets of the contemporary 'Arts and Crafts' Movement. This happily allied function to beauty and simplicity of form. Such tenets were probably applied unconsciously, but are certainly increasingly evident in the locomotive design in Britain, where usually harmonious proportions and uncluttered outlines in locomotives and stock are frequently demonstrated. This process was often further enhanced by the application of a particular livery. Although primarily livery was intended to 'flag up' to its users the uniqueness of the company and its corporate pride, it served to underline the good quality of many designs not only of a company's locomotives but also for its passenger and freight rolling stock, which it displayed.

Wilson Worsdell made NER move into the larger locomotive era, a prominent characteristic of the twentieth century, by the introduction from 1899 of his classes 'S' and 'S1' 4-6-0s, built at Gateshead. They were intended to eliminate the necessary double heading needed when the previous class 'Q' 4-4-0s pull heavily loaded East Coast expresses. These new locomotives had a double claim to contemporary fame. They were the first British passenger engines with 4-6-0 wheel arrangement (Jones Highland Railway goods engines in 1894 were the very first 4-6-0s) and were the most powerful engines of their day in Britain. They combined increased power with a graciously uncluttered profile and brass trumpet case over the Ramsbottom safety valves. One of the group, 2006, went on to win the Gold Medal at the Paris Universal Exhibition of 1900.

Forty-five (forty class 'S' with 6ft 1¼in driving wheels, five class 'S1' with 6ft 8¼ ins driving wheels were constructed. The larger size was quickly shown to make little difference in practice) would be built in all. Their main drawback in running was due to the inadequate arrangement of the comparatively shallow ash pan and its consequent effect on airflow, especially when ash accumulated on a long and heavy run. Strangely enough, this problem persisted with all the class 'S' locomotives produced during the regimes of Wilson Worsdell and Raven.[21] Initially intended for express passenger work, they were displaced by *Atlantics*, once Worsdell had been to USA and became convinced of their superiority as express engines. They did sterling work on mixed traffic, secondary or relief passenger work.

The introduction of class 'T' 0-8-0s did much the same for heavier freight and mineral traffic. These classes, the bases for further development by Raven successors, would continue to fulfil the need of an expanding express freight service, the NER's 'lifeblood' from now onwards until the economic depression in 1921 at reduced cost, once the initial outlay of building the stock had been met. As Wilson Worsdell was on good terms with John George Robinson, CME -GCR and his 4-6-0 and 0-8-0 locomotives introduced in 1902 were clearly influenced by Worsdell's designs.[21]

The most immediate effect of this was for Wilson Worsdell to introduce more powerful heavy goods locomotives, the class 'T' class 0-8-0s, which came out from Gateshead in August 1901. They were the more elegantly designed precursors of Raven's sturdier-looking classes 'T2' and 'T3', produced from 1913 onwards. Ten class 'T's built at Gateshead, were released in August 1901 with Smith segmental ring piston valves and ten 'T1's built there between March and June 1902. The two methods were initially used to test the comparative of the different valves and thirty more were built between December 1902 and May 1904 with ordinary slide valves.[22] (See Appendix 1 – Comparative chart of Wilson Worsdell's and Raven's locomotives from 1899–1923).

NER was the most extensive dock owner among railway companies. This meant that not only did the dock machinery need to seen to and renewed, but the CME had responsibility for many types of shipping beside tugboats, mentioned above. There were a number of dredgers and lighters working in each port.

During 1900, after much discussion and argument, it was agreed that the Middlesbrough docks should be fitted with electric cranes rather than hydraulic ones. As the control of electrical power had passed to the LS office, it meant that Raven was involved with this scheme, his first involvement with applying electric power to industrial machinery. It is likely that he worked with 'Charlie' Baister, who had experience of dock machinery fifteen years before. The Middlesbrough scheme was delayed because of the time taken to complete work on the reconstruction of these docks and not finally completed until 1906. These were 10-ton cranes operating at 80/200ft per minute, 3-ton cranes operating at 100/200ft per minute and capstans operating at 20 cwt pull, with a travelling speed of 200ft per minute. A simpler scheme of cranes and capstans were put into operation at 'A' and 'C' jetties at Union Dock, West Hartlepool, in 1901. The electric cranes soon showed their superiority in performance.

These cranes have a business-like look. Their range is wide and they are admirably adapted to the purpose they serve – the rapid transfer of timber, ore and general cargo, direct from vessel to truck and vice versa.[23]

Raven followed this with a paper, describing the scheme in 1904 for the ICE Annual Conference, that year held in Chicago.

Having gained the required permission from the NER Board on 1 July 1901, GM Gibb, in a typical quest for new ideas and ways of working, set off to see at first hand what was happening – not, as might be expected, going to mainland Europe and in particular to view the very real developments occurring in France (witness De Glehn compounds) and Germany, but to the USA. Accompanying him as part of a five-man group were Philip Burtt, superintendent of the line, Charles Augustus Harrison, the chief engineer (Northern Division), T.M. Newall, docks superintendent, and Wilson Worsdell CME. Time spent by the Worsdell brothers in USA may have helped to influence the decision.

The tour of thirty-one days caused them to travel exhaustively over more than 4,500 miles of track in the more easterly states of the USA. The party travelled to New York, Buffalo on Lake Erie, Chicago on Lake Michigan and Pittsburgh and Altoona in Pennsylvania, cities all lying within the Pennsylvania Railroad franchise, where they investigated management and operating practices, spoke with many railway workers on the Pennsylvania Railroad, and also visited the New York Central Railway[24] and one of its rivals, the Lehigh Valley Railroad.[25] These both were the arterial railroads, carrying great loads of coal and ore to and from the mines and steel works to the ports of the Atlantic seaboard.

The long journey home by sea was a useful part of trip; thrown together day after day without the distractions of their usual responsibilities, the railwaymen discussed what they had seen and how best to make use of it.[26]

At this point in time, Raven had not been included, but was left to 'hold the fort' at Greenesfield and Darlington with Smith, Heppel and the rest of the team.

1 The house lay to the rear of the site now occupied now by B&Q. The 1855 map shows Alpine Cottage as a S&DR house, with a siding on its south side, and across that was North Road Station. By Raven's time, the north aspect was no longer open fields, but a road had been built over the short lane coming from North Road, Whessoe Street. It was lined with cottages opposite Alpine Cottage, and behind them lay a large tract of land covered by North Road Works, with Darlington NER Literary Institute on the corner of Whessoe Street and North Road

2 Reminiscences made by Mrs Smith who lived next to the Ravens in Railway Cottages. Alpine Villa (originally owned by S&DR) and all the cottages were owned by NER. This was taped in 1970s and is in Darlington library

3 It is now closed, but is a Grade II listed building and was given permission to be converted into a large private residence in 2002

4 *Northern Echo*, Friday 27 September 1895 and 20 July 1896 respectively, sole entries about Norman

5 Norman appears there in 1901 Census. Frederick appears at Mount School in the 1901 Census

6 Nock Oswald S., 1954, *Locomotives of the North Eastern Railway*, Ian Allan Ltd, p.89

7 Jackson David, 1996, *J.G. Robinson: A Lifetime's Work*, The Oakwood Press, p.64

8 Grafton in *Sir Vincent Raven and the North Eastern Railway* misreads this role in the log book and ends up portraying Raven as a martinet and unsympathetic to his staff. He then expresses surprise later when he finds Raven was indeed kindly to the people for whom he was responsible. Careful analysis of the log book indeed shows Raven to have been flexible, fair and at times compassionate within the limits imposed on him

9 Wilson C. David, 1995, *Racing Trains, the 1895 Railway Races to the North*, Alan Sutton Publishing Ltd, p.118

10 Wilson C. David, 1995, *vide supra*, p.92

11 Hoole Ken, 1967 reprint by Augustus M. Kelley, New York, 1967, of Tomlinson William Weaver, 1914, *North Eastern Railway: its rise and development, with new notes, corrections and updating by K. Hoole*, p.778

12 It would not be until 1911 that Raven finally joined the ARLE

13 Vaughan Adrian, 1997, *Railwaymen, Politics & Money*, John Murray, p.282

14 Grafton, in his *Sir Vincent Raven and the North Eastern Railway*, seems to be puzzled by their stance in favour of positive industrial relations with the workforce and their Unions. Taken from a viewpoint of Quaker belief and humanitarianism, it is entirely logical.

15 Alderman Geoffrey, 1973, *The Railway Interest*, Leicester University Press, p.165

16 Proceedings of Institution of Civil Engineers, item 276, 14 March 1898

17 Christiansen Rex and Miller R.W, 1968, Volume 2: 1889-1968, David & Charles, Newtown Abbott, p.20

18 National Archive RAIL 92/67 and 140

19 Teasdale John G., February 2002, 'Transatlantic traffic: being a consideration upon how American Railway Practices Influenced those of the North Eastern Railway', *The North Eastern Express*, vol.41, no.165, p.8

20 Romans Mike, 1987, *North Eastern Railway 4-6-0's*, Ian Allan Ltd, p.5-6

21 Jackson David, 1996, *J.G. Robinson: A Lifetime's Work*, The Oakwood Press, p.57

22 Aves William A.T., 1998, 'NER Eight-coupled Locomotives' (*Locomotives Illustrated* 123), RAS Publishing, p.7

23 *NER Magazine* vol.1, no.11 September 1911, p.213

24 New York Central Railway (1853-1968) had 10,700 miles of track in the eastern highly populated and industrialised states, including the four-track Water Level Route, providing passenger and freight services along the major rivers and the Great Lakes from New York and Boston to the midwest cities, Chicago, Detroit, St Louis, Cincinnati and Cleveland

25 Lehigh Valley Railroad (1853-1970) had only 1,362 miles of track which provided a coal hauling as well as a passenger service from western New York State around Buffalo through Pennsylvania on to the New Jersey ports

26 Teasdale John G., February 2002, 'Transatlantic traffic: being a consideration upon how American Railway Practices Influenced those of the North Eastern Railway', *The North Eastern Express*, vol.41, no.165, p.8

V

ASSISTANT CHIEF MECHANICAL ENGINEER (1902–1910)

Once he returned to Britain, Gibb was quick to implement some of the lessons he had learned from his American visit. He set about reorganising much of NER internal management arrangements. He reordered the traffic department in York. From 1 March 1902, commercial activities, run by a chief goods manager, were separated from operational activities, run by a chief passenger agent. They answered to the superintendent of the line, now called general superintendent, who was responsible for operating passenger, goods and mineral trains. They were all to report to the general traffic manager.

Similarly, the locomotive department was reorganised with the technical separated from the financial. Following the American practice of re-titling and expanding the role of locomotive superintendent as a chief mechanical engineer (CME), Worsdell was reappointed as CME to the NER. The expansion of the role included, on top of responsibility for building developing and maintaining steam locomotives, experimentation and development of other forms of locomotion on rail, land and sea, notably the application of electric, petrol and diesel engines to rail traction.

On land, there was responsibility for steam fire engines, as well as steam lorries and tractors to provide for goods haulage and petrol bus fleets, which were all beginning to provide more and more passenger services to reach areas the railway did not reach, i.e. in a 'feeder' capacity. They could alternatively bring passengers and freight to and from convenient railheads. On the water, his responsibility covered NER-owned boats, such as lighters, tugboats, hoppers and dredgers, plus cranes within the docks, as well as shipping on the North Sea to and from other East Coast ports and across to Dutch German and Danish port on the including Continent.

Raven became assistant CME in 1902 with a salary of £1,400 p.a., while Charlie Baister's was increased also to £450 p.a. and Stamer's to £400 p.a. Thus Raven now entered a fourth and vital phase in his career. He now moved back to Gateshead, to which he travelled from Darlington, having the appropriate rail pass. He became a part of the Wilson Worsdell/Smith/Heppell locomotive design team and had a variety of other duties as will be seen as the decade continued. All this marked his preparation for the role of CME, especially when Smith's death in 1906 made his position as next CME look even more likely and inevitable.

He had as his own assistant, Worsdell's first cousin, Arthur Collinson. Collinson's mother was a paternal aunt of T.W. and Wilson Worsdell. Born in Halifax, he attended Quaker schools at Ackworth (1883–1886) and then at Bootham, York (1886–1889). Apprenticed at Gateshead from 1889–1893 to both T.W. and Wilson, he became chief inspector of materials from 1894–1897, with added responsibility as chief boiler inspector from 1897–1900. Before moving into CME's office, he was manager of York locomotive works.

Raven's everyday role consisted of dealing with departmental wages, costing of new items of rolling stock as well as the development of steam locomotives and running costs, especially important in the light of a permanent overspend by NER. It allowed him to become involved with applications of electric power to different aspects of rail mechanics, not only to rail traction, but also to trackside safety measures and dockyard and electric cranes in North Road workshops. Worsdell was also investigating uses of petrol-electric engines applied to locomotion and worked via Raven with the progress of carriage design for the East Coast Joint Stock (ECJS) and GN/NE stock as well as developments in the structure and capacity of wagons, especially for coal, iron ore, steel and other mineral traffic.

When Worsdell returned to NER, he set about introducing new *Atlantics* of his own design, the NER class 'V', equipped with 5ft 6in boilers. Worsdell had been very impressed with the *Atlantics* of the Reading Co.,[2] which worked the *Atlantic City Flyers*. They had larger boilers than the engines at home. It was Baldwin, who had introduced locomotives with 4-4-2 wheel arrangement in 1896 at the Atlantic City Railroad. They were soon nicknamed the *Atlantics*.[3] This initiative was followed in 1898 by the Pennsylvania Railroad,[4] which went on to produce an even larger engine of the same wheelbase in 1901. Therefore, when Worsdell's *Atlantics* emerged in 1903 as a version of class 'R1' 4-4-0s, they came to be were known affectionately as 'Gateshead Infants'.[5]

Worsdell's teamwork approach to management is next seen in action, warts and all. The usual course of events would be for the CME to instruct his chief draughtsman to elaborate the necessary design, approve the results and commence construction. At this crucial point Walter Smith was sick and so saw virtually nothing of the design until it was completed. When he did see it, he did not like it – and said so. What is more, Smith told his chief that he could do better, and could produce a loco which would be more economical to run and capable of producing more power. In fact, the design had been produced by George Heppel, who had acted as chief draughtsman in Smith's absence. There was a lot of antagonism between the two. Worsdell decided it was too late to change and when they were introduced proved a worthwhile addition to the NER fleet of express locomotives.

In fact, this was a period when NER investigated other means of passenger and freight traction to reduce expenditure. For instance, as part of on-going modernisation from 1901–1915 it sought to provide electrically powered signalling for some of its mainline. Raven became more and more involved with the innovations of the time, especially where alternatives to traditional practice were being sought in the engineering field. He took an interest in petrol-driven means of locomotion, but only intermittently.

In considering electrical applications to railway practice, Raven would both learn and develop his ideas thanks to Charles Hesterman Merz, the very energetic electrical engineering consultant to NER. Merz was born in 1874 in Gateshead, of an emigré family, originally from Darmstadt. His grandfather had made contact with the Unitarians in Manchester, and his son, John Theodor, was born there in 1840, although the family returned to Germany when he was two years old. John Theodor, educated initially by his father, entered the University of Geissen to study mathematics, physics and especially chemistry, rapidly becoming a renowned chemist. Full of intellectual energy and hence quite restless, he read voraciously, gaining a PhD at twenty-four years of age. Banned from West Prussia in the wake of the 1870 Franco–Prussian War, he settled in Newcastle, finding Oxford and elsewhere congenial to his philosophical ideas, which sought to probe the philosophical connections between science and religion. He continued to pursue an active career as an industrialist in the chemical sector, eventually turning to the emerging electrical sphere of science. It is possible that Raven attended some of the lectures on electricity, which Theodor gave at Armstrong College in Newcastle in the 1870s.

His son Charles followed his father's interest in this area with characteristic Merz energy. With William McLelland, he set up in 1899 the now world-famous consultancy firm of Merz & McLellan (M&M) with offices at 28 Victoria Street, London. He persuaded Reyrolle, the

French entrepreneur, to relocate from London to Hebburn in 1901 so that he could supply the Newcastle-upon-Tyne Electric Supply Co. (NESCO) with equipment. During the next four years, the firm was so successful that its workforce rose from fifty-eight to 110. The stage was being set for rail electrification by NER in a series of projects.

One of the basic tenets of British rail electrification policy from the turn of the nineteenth century onwards was the idea that it was more economical to electrify suburban short-haul lines than mainlines. Financial overheads for mainline projects would outweigh any savings made in replacing steam by electric traction. Electrification is an extremely costly process in its initial stages; equipment has to be installed and electricity-generating capability built up and extended as demand increases. As a one-off capital cost, it only becomes supportable when the system offers clear assurances of future high-density movement of passengers and/or freight. Where and when such a 'market' is thought to be available, i.e. most notably in large conurbations or in fast and efficient connections between major cities, it makes sense to proceed with electrification on the basis of comparatively few electricity-generating stations of high capacity, located strategically to feed power to the electric motors of locomotives by means of overhead wires or a conducting rail system on the ground. It then allows a company to have simpler, cheaper and more easily maintained locomotives, which did not need to generate their own power. Thus, rail electrification becomes viable in economic terms, only when there is a high level of traffic.[6]

Raven, having been involved with electric cranes, now began to work with the Tyneside electrification scheme. The NER Board viewed with some anxiety the fall in railway passengers following the introduction of electric tramways in three Tyneside areas in 1901–1902, namely in Tynemouth/Whitley Bay area on 18 March, in Gateshead on 18 May and in Newcastle City boundary on 16 December 1901, and then in the Wallsend/Walker to Gosforth areas on 29 September 1902.[7] A memorandum by Gibb to the Board of Directors on 17 February 1902 noted that Raven had a pronounced interest in rail electrification and that he was working closely with M&M concerning the new NER North Tyneside Scheme.[8]

This scheme had started as a result of a meeting Gibb had had with Merz. He advised Gibb on how to deal with local tramway competition. He proposed entering into competition with them by bidding for those passengers making journeys which were longer than two miles, i.e. local suburban and inter-urban services. Trams had proved to be eminently suitable for short on-street journeys. He proposed an electrified system, with a large loop line from Newcastle Central Station eastwards along the banks of the Tyne to the coastal resorts of Tynemouth, Cullercoats, Whitley Bay and Monkseaton, returning in a westerly direction via Backworth to South Gosforth to join up with the riverside section at Manors (New Bridge Street). The key to its success in the initial stages would be a frequent service, similar to that which the tramcars provided on the streets, with extra coaches being added at peak times. Merz also at this time recommended that the short Quayside line should be electrified. He advocated making a triangular junction at South Gosforth to give more than one direction access to the proposed branch, which was to run to Ponteland. The year 1909 was envisaged as a likely date for the extension of electrification to this branch, as well as along the south bank of the Tyne to the peninsula on which South Shields stands. A latter extension was proposed to Colleywell Bay (as Seaton Sluice was named) from Monkseaton. The First World War would put paid to this proposal, when it was considered seriously in 1913.

By 3 July 1902, Wilson Worsdell was authorised by the NER Board to advertise for tenders for the project. Merz was awarded £10,000 for his professional services at the rate of £1,000 a quarter until the work was completed. British Thomson-Houston Co. Ltd won the contract to provide to supply bogies, motors and electrical equipment for fifty clerestoried motor coaches and fifty trailers with vertical match-boarding, painted in a bright scarlet and cream colour scheme, new to NER, designed by Worsdell.

Electrical equipment was delivered to NER Carriage Works at York. In addition, Newcastle-upon-Tyne Electric Supply Co. (NESCO) were to supply the power via sub-stations for third rail electrification of the track at 600v dc. Siemens Bros & Co. were contracted to provide and lay the high-tension cables and British Westinghouse & Electric Manufacturing Co. for sub-station equipment (owned and run by another associate of Merz, the American George Westinghouse). The scheduled completion date was 31 December 1903.

Following up the earlier visit to view US railway practices by NER officials, a second party, consisting of Raven, Henry Angus Watson, general superintendent, W.J. Cudworth, CE – Southern Division from 1902, was sent out to USA.

Concerning the coal traffic, the officers observed several companies' coal staiths, and concluded that they were not as good as the North Eastern itself was using. Many of the very large-capacity bogie coal wagons they saw bowed in the centre. On their return, they recommended to Gibb in their report that 20-ton wagons would suit NER best. (Unfortunately they had already taken delivery of 40-ton bogie wagons.) The three man group also looked and talked to American railroad officials concerning automatic signalling systems [see sections on electrical cab signalling]; the working of goods traffic in marshalling yards and in good sheds; the operation of locomotive sheds and repair; the arrangements made for handling passengers and their luggage.[9]

Unlike the stations, workshops and offices at home so solidly crafted in stone, concrete and wood, designed by NER's own architect William Bell, the Americans built railway buildings with cheap materials, so that they those buildings could easily be expanded, moved, or even discarded if traffic requirements changed.

The Americans only used steel in fabricating fireboxes (introduced to NER as part of McDonnell's reforms at Greenesfield in 1883), and therefore not a new measure to the NER team. All working parts of the locomotive were easily accessible. Raven may have agreed with this in principle, but in practice the NER trend continued to be placing as much as possible between the frames. While this resulted visually in smooth, uncluttered lines, it was to be a constant source of complaint from NER locomotive repair and running shops. Not too much paint was spent on American locomotives, this again a practice that ran counter to best NER practice with its detailed livery reflecting high standards of presentation.

On a different tack, they noted the efficiency of clerical staff and their support with time-saving devices such as telephones, telegraphs, typewriters and pneumatic tubes. Their recommendations were that:

1. NER experimentally install automatic signals of three different types (electric, electro-pneumatic, low pressure pneumatic). [Automatic signalling was introduced of an American electro-gas type between Alne and Green Lane Junction, Thirsk by Hall Signal Co.];
2. Wagons be fitted with cast iron wheels and ball bearings;
3. To save clerical expense, a number of staff paid monthly should be increased (but not by cheque as this required a 1d stamp);
4. Starting times of workshop staff should be changed from 6 a.m. to 7, as the Americans had shown that men starting later had had their breakfast and worked harder;
5. The use of larger capacity wagons was correct.
   Barrow-ways were laid right through the serried ranks of wagons on adjacent tracks via the wagons' central doors. Goods loaded into the wagons were put in the ends of those wagons, leaving the barrow-ways clear.

The NER observers were so impressed with this that they drew up a scheme for practice on NER with current wagons, until larger ones could be introduced. A pair of open or covered wagons would be semi-permanently coupled. The inner end wall of each wagon would be replaced by a bottom-hinged door. When a pair of wagons was to be loaded, their doors would be folded down flat to form a barrow-way between them.

However, this idea was not followed up.[10] As can be seen, the foundations for some of Raven's later ideas and reports resulted from this visit, especially when it came to looking to American practice with electric locomotives.

Progress was now made both on the third rail electrification and the building of new coaching stock. By 29 August 1903 the carriage works manager at York reported that thirteen cars were built and six were partly built, and on 17 September 1903 the first train was hauled to the Old Station at York to be inspected by Mr Worsdell, the chief mechanical engineer, Mr Raven, the assistant chief mechanical engineer, Mr Gibb, the general manager and the NER directors.[11]

M&M were able to report more fully on the success of the consultancy by presenting a retrospective paper entitled 'The Use of Electricity on the North Eastern Railway and upon Tyneside' in 1904 to a meeting of the British Association at Cambridge on the electrification system and its stock. The report showed how advanced the North East was in the public supply of electricity (Merz had advised this as a means of keeping cost down and revenues up for NER, instead of it to go to the expense of providing its own electricity supply). It described how sixty-five major companies, employing 40,000 men, used electric power as well as the 200 collieries between mid-County Durham and Morpeth, i.e. those 'feeders' of coal to the industry, north and south of the Tyne made the electricity supply so plentiful that NER did not need to supply its own. NESCO therefore supplied the new NER with electricity via third rail at 600v dc through four sub-stations, the largest sub-station being at Pandon Dene, near Manors Station, to the north-east of Newcastle Central Station.

The system was to be run initially by a fleet of ninety (not 100 as originally ordered) open clerestory vehicles, with lower panels outside having vertical match-boarding and wider windows than the 1898 ECJS third-class stock, for instance with their small paned corridor carriages. It gave the new stock a somewhat American appearance. Sixty-two of 106 new vehicles were motor coaches. (Twenty-five further units were added between 1905 and 1909.) A typical working set consisted usually of a motor coach and trailer, sometimes a three-car set. Twenty-four of the first eighty-eight cars had first-class accommodation.[12]

George F. Groves, the chief wagon and carriage draughtsman, following an instruction made to him during January 1904, sent Raven a scheme, which he had been asked to draw up for introducing one or two lavatories into the North Tyneside electric stock. Despite sending the required drawings on to Raven, changes were not carried out, possibly for economic reasons. More seriously, he next reported to Raven following complaints that construction of the bodies of the cars built in 1904 were substandard in that the frames and supports did not fit and had been filled in with wood and bits of timber, with the glass windows being too small, thus allowing rain to get in.

Nevertheless, the new system got under way: there was a special train consisting of NER officials preceding the first electric train. On 29 March 1904 the North Tyneside scheme officially came into operation, although it was quite a nominal journey to carry the public the four miles, seven chains from New Bridge Street (Newcastle) to Benton.[13] The remainder of this part of the system was completed and opened in stages, Benton to Monkseaton by 6 June, Monkseaton to Tynemouth by 21 June and Newcastle Central to Tynemouth, via the Riverside loop by 1 July 1904. Much later, on 1 January 1909, a three-quarter-mile link was made between Manors and New Bridge Street. G.S. Gibb, eager to promote the speed of the new electric transport system, remarked:

> The time allowed for each station stop is 20 seconds, and in actual working this can only be secured if passengers will do their best to enter and leave their coaches with as great rapidity as possible, and endeavour to lessen as much as possible the quantity of luggage carried.[13]

The L&YR's electrified line from Liverpool to Southport managed to beat the NER scheme to inherit the title of first electrified scheme outside London. Nevertheless, the NER scheme was a financial success and passengers returned, after a drop from 9,847 million in 1901 to 5,887 million passengers in 1904 to 7.335 million in 1908 and 10,192 million in 1913.

On a more literally prosaic note, on 31 March 1904, the annual meeting of the Gateshead NER Literary Institute was held at Gateshead, of which Raven, Norman Lockyear, Ramsay Kendall's replacement as works manager at North Road, and George Heppell, were among the vice presidents elected, nominated probably because they were NER senior officials. Raven's interest in application of electricity was shown to be wider than being about traction. Using his annotated experience with the electric cranes, Raven now prepared a paper for a meeting of IMechE held as part of the Engineering Congress in Chicago, held by the American Society of Mechanical Engineers from 31 May to 3 June 1904 on the ninth floor of the Auditorium Hotel. Raven gave his paper as the second speaker of the morning, which started at 9.30 a.m. on 2 June. Its title was 'Electrical and Hydraulic Power'. It was detailed with terse argument and many tables, which are used to compare performance, energy consumption, lubrication, effects on manpower and speeds between hydraulic and electrical cranes, used in as fair a test situation as could be devised.

Opening of 1904 Tyneside elecrification scheme. This was the new car at Manors Station, Newcastle.

Auditorium Building, Chicago.

The tenth floor of this hotel was the site for the 1904 IMechE conference at which Raven gave his paper on 'Hydro-electric cranes'.

Description	Hydraulics	Electrical	Saving efficiency by electricity
Numbers used for comparison	825	834	–
Total wt. of rails lifted (tons)	1,210.4	1,224.9	–
Total time for lifts made	7hrs 0 mins	5hrs 15 mins	1hr 45 mins
Total coal burnt at power station during test (lb)	3,584	2,912	632
Total cost of working at power station during test (pence)	167.34	151.38	15.96
Total lost working at station capital and repairs during test (pence)	436.74	351.48	85.26

Total cost of handling during test (pence)	3,528	2,646	882
Total cost of handling (pence)	3,984.74	2,947.48	967.4
Total cost per 100 tons	327.5	244.7	82.8
Total saving of effort by electric cranes	–	–	82.8
Total saving per cent by electrical cranes (per cent)	–	–	25

Summary of comparison between hydraulic and electrical lifts.

He concludes:

> ... from this it appeared that the results of special and exhaustive tests proved not only that the electric cranes were 25 per cent more economical that the hydraulic cranes on the dock, but that in handling some 1,220 tons of traffic, they effected a saving of time equal to 25 per cent of that taken by electric cranes an equally impossible advantage in dock working. [14]

Accompanying the British delegates, there were fifteen wives, so it is possible that Mrs Raven travelled to the meeting with her husband. He also worked with electric fog-signalling apparatus at the time.

From 1903 or so onwards, probably as part of his increased responsibility after being up-graded, Raven took a more active part in dealing with ECJS. There had been Joint Stock running on the East Coast mainline from the 1860s, funded from the three main constituent companies involved, GNR to fund 47.75 per cent, NER 37.75 per cent and NBR 14.5 per cent, although this changed over time to became 40 per cent, 35 per cent and 25 per cent respectively. In practice, while all three companies contributed to the cost, GNR came to dominate the overall design, to which NER usually gave approval.

Raven had to deal internally with J.D. Twinberrow, chief design officer to NER in the Gateshead design office from 1903 to 1907, and externally with GNR carriage and wagon superintendent, Herbert Nigel Gresley, who took up the post from 1905. The meetings held over many years would become the basis for a permanent friendship, surviving well beyond Gresley's eventual overtaking of Raven in competition for CME – LNER.

Many NER staff thought that NER was too dominated by GNR. For instance, on 29 May 1905, Raven wrote to Twinberrow about doors in compartment carriages, and he strongly advised Raven to eliminate side doors, apart from entry. He pointed out that they would make for reduced weight and cost, increased stiffness and greater security against collapse in accidents. The appearance would also be enhanced. Raven could not immediately reply as things were changing, various suggestions for new ECJS design were being considered. Raven and Gresley were good at working out any differences between them, usually coming to an agreement. Raven would add marginal notes to material produced and sent to him.[15] Raven wrote to Gresley on 9 January 1906, concerned about the vibration in sleeping cars and consequently the need to work on carriage frames on 25 January.

On 18 July 1905, the GN would not agree with NER, who wished to have both straight matchboard-sided vehicles and elliptical roofs for ECJS. However, by 10 November 1905 the GM of NER, in concert with his counterparts in GNR and NBR, had approved the GNR design for ECJS drawn up by Gresley. Furthermore, on 14 February 1906, they approved the replacement of eighty-four obsolete ECJS six-wheelers by the construction of seventy-eight differing corridor vehicles. Details differed depending on which carriage works built the stock, NER's at York or by GNR at Doncaster. NBR would not be involved in either ECJS carriage design or construction. The new stock was to have elliptical roofs (with which Raven agreed) and buck-eye couplings. By 1907, Gresley had begun to design and produce articulated carriages, with six-wheel bogies being introduced, following USA practice. It was agreed from 1907 to use steel under-frames, electric lighting and steam heating. The ECJS livery was to have varnished teak sides. Also, from 1904, there was collaboration between GNR and NER on GN & NE joint stock, i.e. that for use on lines used by both companies, other than East Coast mainline. For instance, new six-wheel coaches were introduced with straight-sided vertical panels without any waist, but they were comfortable inside. They were probably another effect of the American visit, looking un-British and more like North Tyneside electric stock. There was a similar eight-wheel dining car version from 1905. Authorised in 1907, four first-class sleepers for GN & NE use were added to the fleet, two built at York and two at Doncaster.[16]

In all subsequent design matters for ECJS and Joint NE & GN stock, it is difficult to separate out what contributions each man made to the final process. Gresley probably took the lead and Raven either acquiesced or suggested other ways of improving the eventual outcome, if necessary in consultation with other officers like Twinberrow, although the decisions made did not always satisfy him. He wrote to Raven in January 1907, commenting:

> I do not like the GN plan of building mainline carriages with single pillars between the large lights, I consider double pillars and a small panel a much better mechanical job, and free from a certain vulgarity of appearance.

Underneath this grumble was a firmly held view that NER should be the prime builder of ECJS. He did not agree with what he saw as incursions from GNR, when he reported to Raven in 1906:

> The Joint Committee and others appear to evince a preference for GNR recommendations; it is advisable to place NER recommendations on record, for reference when the course of time shall establish their superior soundness.

Other NER staff resented what they felt was GNR dominance, when the preferred NER practice in making vestibuled stock was being passed over in favour of Doncaster workshops and championed by Gresley, despite the fact that such stock was little used on NER.[17] Nevertheless, some elegant, wider-windowed elliptical third-class corridor stock with bow ends and similarly profiled full brake stock were produced for more secondary mainline use on NER. For stopping trains, a plainer profiled, elliptical non-corridor stock was introduced. The consultations between Gresley and Raven continued up to the beginning of the First World War and resumed more sparsely after it.

1905 first-class dining car. Note the American-influenced straight sides.

In 1904, the NER Board sent yet another group of six NER senior officials to the USA:

Cyril Francis Bengough, CE
'Charlie' Baister
Arthur C. Stamer
J.H. Smeddle
H.H. Carrick
S. Holliday

Like the earlier parties, they visited key railroads mainly in the North Eastern States, and other places too, in a more holiday mood. Their brief was 'to study American locomotive practice and conditions of transport'.

Among the places they visited were:

Philadephia	Baldwin Locomotive works, with a trip to Atlantic City on the famous 'flyer'[18]
Schenectady	General Electric & American Locomotives Cos' Works[19]
Albany	New York Central Co.'s Works
Reading	Philadelphia & Reading Co.'s Works
Washington	('a most beautiful city')
	The Capitol and White House
Altoona	Pennsylvania Co.'s Works
Chicago	Burlington, Chicago and & Quincy Co.'s Yards
	The itinerary also comprised St Louis, Pittsburgh, Buffalo, & Co.

No doubt they were able to update Worsdell and his team, including Raven, Smith and Heppell, and were thus keep the CME's team up to date about American practice. Raven, of course, still had to deal with staff problems. As he was now more senior, he could adopt a comparatively easy-going attitude to approaches made by the men, offering a pay rise to wagon greasers (to 24s) and examiners (18s), with a day's pay for the time lost at work for this discussion, held on 5 November 1904. He obviously responded to reasonable approaches from the workforce, where the solution encouraged better performance from them. Another electrification project was to do with a short freight line to Newcastle Quayside.

The section of track, leading eastwards from the Trafalgar Yard, Manors Station, in Newcastle descended a 1 in 28 gradient through a badly ventilated two-mile tunnel, of hairpin shape, i.e. having two ninety-degree bends before emerging lower down running now in a westerly direction along the Quayside. Steam traction had been used from 1870 to 1905, when it was electrified, a very early example of reducing industrial pollution, not only for the environment, but for the workers involved.

Electric goods locomotives:
Two locomotives were built in 1905 by British Thomson Houston in Rugby (a subsidiary of General Electric Company) and were numbered 1 and 2. The motors were supplied by General Electric Co. Bogies and central cab were supplied by Brush Electrical Engineering Co. of Loughborough. They were capable of starting a 150-ton train on gradient. They worked until 1964 and No.1 is preserved.

Wheel arrangement:	Bo-Bo
Driving wheel diameter:	3ft
Locomotive length:	38ft
Locomotive weight:	56 tons
No. and power of motors:	4 150hp
Current:	600v dc overhead by bow collector initially (later changed to pantograph) and 3rd rail shoe pickup
Horsepower per axle:	275hp
Tractive effort:	1100hp

The two neat Bo-Bo electric locomotives, possibly of American design, brought from one of the trips there, originally had a dual pick-up system, using either shoes on a third rail within the tunnel (or to return to the at first to Walkergate, and after the fire there in 1918 to the South Gosforth shed on the already electrified system) or using overhead wires above and below the tunnel, the current being picked up by a bow collectors at first situated at edge of one of the sloping ends of the locomotive above the buffers. The collector had to be raised and lowered by driver as necessary. After three early mishaps, because the driver forgot to lower it on entering the Quayside tunnel, it was replaced around 1907 by a pantograph on the driver's roof. This enhanced the overall appearance of the locomotive, whose design thus appeared completely symmetrical in broad profile. The interior of the centrally placed (the so called 'steeple') cab was spacious and provided better shelter for its operators, when compared with the heat draughts and exposure to weather in many steam locomotives of the time. The electric machinery was housed under the sloping ends, making the interior, compared with a steam locomotive cab, surprisingly spacious and airy. It is likely that Raven was involved as part of the production team, at least with the electro-mechanical part of the new locomotive. Two points of especial interest are his later proposals to have this dual pick-up system for his later mainline electrification and that electric locomotives provided better working space for their operators. Almost identical designs were used by Italian Railways on their line from Milan to Varese as well as the very similar except smaller and squatter locomotives built by Siemens Bros for the innovative scheme for linking the four South Shields collieries in 1909. These two schemes solved local problems for NER. The first successfully forestalled trams developed further outside city boundaries by gaining that market, thus deterring their further movement into an 'intercity' mode as done on the Continent. The second solved the difficulties of the tunnel down to the Quayside branch by adopting what had been done on the Baltimore Railroad earlier (1896).

There were other locomotive engineering initiatives, experimenting in how to apply Daimler's petrol engine and Dr Diesel's engine to railway locomotion. The NER's Alexander Docks in the Hull area saw William Dent Priestman's 12hp diesel engine with mechanical transmission in 1894 propel a dockyard shunter, with yet another 9hp diesel locomotive, constructed by Hornsby & Sons of Grantham at the Woolwich Arsenal in 1896. As early as June 1902, the NER abandoned a long-mooted scheme for a light railway to serve the coastal area of Holderness, go east of Beverley and Hull, using petrol-driven cars, but the ideas about their possible use in lightly used passenger lines particularly in rural areas lingered on until May 1903, when the idea was revived. Two petrol electric cars, numbered 3170 and 3171, were developed, looking like a very truncated versions of a single unit of North Tyneside electric stock. Their details were:

Napier engine driving dynamo at 550v
2 x 5hp electric motors
4 x cylinders: 8½ins diameter with 10ins stroke
Capacity of petrol: 30 to 70 gallons
Use of petrol: 3½ gallons slow/10 gallons express

They were introduced to work between Billingham Junction and Port Clarence.

The use of the petrol railcar lead to a request from Groves, the carriage and works department manager, to Raven about obtaining Brill and Brush trucks for them and in 1904 a four-wheel car with a 23ft wheelbase was introduced.[20] Two bogie petrol cars were introduced in 1908 and worked the Selby to Cawood route. They were not a long-term success and the cost of petrol against coal ensured that the experiment was not repeated, although Raven returned to look at diesel engines after the war. Ironically, what would be a more serious threat to railway passenger transport in the coming decades and an outstanding success was the introduction of petrol buses purchased to work the Holderness area. A bus service was started on 7 September 1904 from Beverley to Beeford, which by the end of the year was extended to Driffield, as well working the Selby Goole route. It was a sign of things to come. Raven indicated another scheme – this time a 'steam' enterprise, again designed to cut running costs – of what NER was pleased to call autocars, but which were generally known as 'push-and–pull' trains. They were intended to compete with increased pressure from local bus and tram companies.[21] They were made up of either a BTP 0-4-4-T with a single carriage in front (with circular window in front for the driver to see through to the road ahead) and for heavier traffic another behind the engine, either combination working as one unit. These autocars ran from 1 April 1905 along the short, but frequent, local service from West Hartlepool around the interior harbour at Middleton to Old Hartlepool and on the newer branch opened to all traffic on 1 June 1905 from South Gosforth to Ponteland. This was extended to Darras Hall after September 1913, prior to proposed electrification of the whole branch as part of North Tyneside system, and to many more operations as time passed by. NER, however, was unique (except for GER) among British companies in not producing a steam railcar. Effecting economies in many of the areas of running practice had to be a feature of NER working for the future. It was investment in NER that was lacking rather than its revenue, so that despite a second half-year increase in 1906 of net profit of £294,500, its dividends rose by only 3/4 per cent.

Under 1906 patent nos 10507 and 14089, Raven, working again with 'Charlie' Baister, now locomotive running superintendent of the South Division, developed their original mechanical fog-warning equipment into a more elaborate electric system. Authorised in 1907, two trial installations were set up between Bensham and Durham on the NER mainline. The original apparatus was now updated with two side ramps beside the original ones, positioned approximately 100 yards from the distant signals. In addition, where there was a whole series of single ramps in the middle of the track one at the distant, more ramps placed between distant and home signals and home stop signals right on to the advance starting signal. The locomotive unit had central steel brush contact arms with wheeled contact arms on the right- and left-hand sides. The cab indicators had a semaphore arm and two pointers, able to point to one of four numbers. When the locomotive passed over the trigger position, a warning was raised as a result of hitting the centre and two side contacts. The semaphore arm was raised to danger position and set a bell ringing. Any of the three trigger ramps could independently set off the warning, giving the driver audible signal of his approach to a distant signal. The bell was cancelled by operating a cancelling lever.[22] A further test was authorised in 1910 using the double-tracked branch line from Eryholme to Richmond and Raven carried out tests for his final design of electrically operated fog signalling, which was brought into use in August 1911.[23] It was a well-worked out if rather elaborate system. Cost then, as now, was the major consideration in implementing it, however, as it cost five times more than the mechanical striker system. It was not universally adopted as a result and unfortunately did not survive the First World War.

Around this time, Collinson's replacement as assistant CME was Arthur Cowie Stamer, who would prove over the years to be such a reliable man. Born ten years after Raven on 7 March 1869 in Shrewsbury, to Revd Sir Lovelace Stamer, Suffragan bishop of Shrewsbury, he is yet another example of clerical father producing an engineer son. Educated at Rugby School, he worked from 1886–1889 at Beyer-Peacock, came to NER as improver in 1891, and was promoted to assistant shed foreman at York in 1892, attending the 1892 Thirsk rail crash. He moved in that capacity to other sheds, gaining wide experience. He was a noted local cricketer and played for Darlington, the Durham League champions of 1893. Stamer's photograph reveals a frank, yet shrewd, expression looking straight into the camera's 'eye'. The face is clean-shaven, except for a wide RAF-style moustache. Promoted to assistant divisional locomotive superintendent at York, he moved into CME's office in 1906 becoming Raven's assistant, after Arthur Collinson moved briefly to the Metropolitan railway in 1905. He remained with Raven as they both moved up the promotional ladder. Photographs dating from this period show Raven to be a neatly dressed, slightly stocky man, sporting a short-back-and-sides haircut and a moustache, carefully parted in the middle, as current fashion dictated; his expression is always slightly frowning, with penetrating eyes, giving a no-nonsense impression.[24]

An important decision at this time was for Walter Smith to be allowed to design his own '4CC' 4-cylinder 'double' compound (two outside and two inside) 4-4-2s, which came to be numbered as 730/1. It was destined to be a sole instance of such a cylinder arrangement on NER. It is likely that Smith's son John, who was chief draughtsman with the MR and was at the Paris Exhibition and saw the De Glehn compounds there, was able to provide some information about them for his father.[25] Sadly, Walter Smith died in 1906 and the two locomotives remain his memorial. His executors wrangled over terms for his design, so no more of a projected ten were built by NER. They were indeed as superior in performance and economic in running as he predicted. Like their contemporaries, class S/07' 4-6-0s, they had splashers rising from similar continuous box frames. The tops of the frames were concave, while Raven's were convex and both internal and external components of the frame were deeper, meaning the splashers showed less. They subsequently became known as 'Raven' frames.[26]

Smith's death at sixty-four meant Raven became more than ever Worsdell's right-hand man and so the assistant leader of the locomotive building team, with George Hepple, of course, still there as chief draughtsman. Raven's future in line for the succession as CME was now reasonably certain, all being well.

Raven had continued intermittent attendance at the Darlington Lodge, being there when he was able to do so, yet had been sufficiently interested to allow himself over the years to be elected to senior positions within it. From 1904, he attended more often and so revived his participation in the activities of the Lodge. He even became one of its officers, moving from junior warden to senior warden. In December 1906 the Lodge had asked him to be Master, but he refused because of the pressure of work at the time. The death of Smith probably increased the amount of his

Arthur Cowie Stamer, Raven's
assistant from *c.*1907–1922.

responsibility as well as placing him in the running for CME, which was presumably his ultimate goal, should Worsdell retire. With regular payment of his subscription such a prominent member of the town would have been allowed to remain a member of the Lodge. Waiting six years to exclude him finally surely reflects the patience of the Lodge in this.

Raven seems to have undergone a change of his attitude to Lodge membership, which amounted to indifference. There could well have been some issue or personality within the Lodge. For instance, when Raven did not take up the offer of becoming the Worshipful Master of the Lodge in 1906, a long-standing and devoted member, Thomas Metcalfe Barron, did agree, even breaking with tradition and moving the venue for his installation banquet to Imperial Hotel.[27] This forceful behaviour may have been enough to put Raven off. Certainly, he was a man who liked clear organisation and control, set within known frameworks. He would actively resist anyone if thwarted, with expressions of anger, if need be.

Raven continued with his Masonic meetings, becoming senior warden at the Lodge. His attendance at March and April meetings of 1906 made it look that he would become Master of the Lodge for 1907.

Next summer he was busy as he was called in to advise the Scottish North British Railway (NBR) Co. It provided the Scottish link for East Coast mainline service from King's Cross to Aberdeen, its metals running from Berwick via Edinburgh to Aberdeen. Their first massive new *Atlantic* No.868, *Aberdonian* had been unveiled and run for the first time on 1 July 1906 from the locomotive workshops at Cowlairs Haymarket, Edinburgh. It had been designed by William Paton Reid, the recently (July 1904) appointed locomotive superintendent. It would be the precursor of a further fourteen at this time.[28] James Bell,

Raven's photograph, taken in
Newcastle about this time.

the NBR's civil engineer, did not like the new locomotives. He said that they were top-heavy. The result was that during autumn 1906, there were complaints about the express services, which they were meant to head up. By the end of the year, Bell was complaining bitterly that they were also damaging the track. The *Atlantics* were withdrawn with dire effects on both freight and passenger rostering. NBR was now in a dilemma. These new engines were intended to the company's new flagships, planned to be the equal of rival companies' *Atlantics*, especially those from the GNR and NER stables. There was a boardroom crisis.[29]

Despite Reid having made some modifications, Henry Alfred Ivatt from the GNR was called in to help. Also, in spite of some recommendations having been made to ease some of the running problems, the NBR Board rejected them in April.[30] On 13 May, William Fulton Jackson, NBR general manager, was talking to NER manager, Alexander Kay Butterworth. He promised NER could help and by return of post, following Jackson's letter, Raven, with the NER Board's blessing, was given permission to act as consulting engineer on a temporary basis to NBR. Raven wrote also to Reid to tell him about as a matter of professional courtesy.

Raven was supplied with drawings and gradient profiles just as Ivatt had received. He travelled up to Edinburgh at the end of May to meet Reid and Bell. In a positive response to the situation, he was convinced that the *Atlantics* were the right engines for the job and proposed alterations in the piston rings. Reid was instructed to carry out Raven's changes on *Aberdonian*'s sister locomotive, No.876 *Waverley*. Raven got authorisation to send a man to Gateshead to obtain precise particulars of the alteration proposed.

Typically thorough, Raven, in addition, planned a return to NBR for a three-day visit from Monday 10 to Wednesday 12 June. He wanted to see how the *Atlantics* performed for himself. On Monday, he proposed to ride on the footplate of the 3.50 Carlisle–Edinburgh Express. On Tuesday, he would go on runs with the other *Atlantics*. On Wednesday, he would travel from Edinburgh to Newcastle and back, using the NE dynamometer car (acquired also in 1906) on the train. On Thursday he would have for a report to bring back to a NBR Board meeting.

Waverley was to be the engine used on Monday. When Raven arrived at Carlisle, it was not heading the train. Reid had not finished the alterations in time, much to GM Jackson's annoyance. On Tuesday Raven saw what difficulties the hilly, winding route posed for the NBR locomotives. On Wednesday, No.879 *Abbotsford* headed the 10.10 Edinburgh–Newcastle run, with Raven and his assistants in the dynamometer car. The same locomotive headed the 3.36 p.m. return journey. The read-outs from the dynamometer car no longer exist, but what was revealed is partly indicated in a letter from Jackson to Raven in the stilted 'office' English of the time on 21 July, asking him to send 'sunprints' of a table Raven had made 879's speed, drawbar pull and hp when it ran on 12 July from Edinburgh and Newcastle, offering to fill in any blanks on the chart.

On 10 July, Raven was present for the 3.50 p.m. Carlisle to Edinburgh run, following which he proposed changes to the valves. He repeated this run again on 2 August, after modifications had been made. By 13 September, Reid was able to report to NBR Board in favour of the trials with the piston ring. The Board responded by ordering that the other *Atlantics* should be modified also. Raven's recommendation that the Aberdeen block trains be slowed, was also accepted by the oard. It paid him 200 guineas for his services.[31] The next year, 1908, there were locomotives exchanges between the NER and NBR.

The same year, 1907, besides continuing with Gateshead NER Institute, Raven continued to be actively involved with Darlington Institute, becoming with Ramsay Kendall a member of its house and entertainment committee and president of the NER Centre for St John's Ambulance, whose committee consisted of Raven's colleagues, Cyril Francis Bengough and Ramsay Kendall with J.E. Parkinson, H.M. Sinclair, W.C. Stephenson and J.C. Valentine.[32]

1909 was to have been the time when the electrified North Tyneside line would be extended to South Shields and to the Ponteland branch, and even to the Colleywell Bay (as Seaton Sluice) from Monkseaton. Following a memo in July 1907, Merz and McClellan produced a report on 5 December 1908 advocating further development of electrical working to Sunderland and between Sunderland and South Shields, but increasing financial stringency caused by a trade recession meant these extensions to the North Tyneside electric rail network had to be postponed.

More significantly, in light of future events, was the introduction of rail electrification in the same year by the Harton Coal Co. to connect two of their collieries on the South Shields peninsula between Tyne and North Sea, namely St Hilda's (behind the Town Square) and Westoe (close to the sea) to coaling staithes near the mouth of the Tyne in order to convey coal and coaling waste from the collieries there. The nine Bo-Bo electric locomotives, supplied by Siemens Bros, worked exclusively via overhead power at 550v dc (the German standard). They were similar to the Quayside locomotives in design and track gauge, but smaller and squatter as they had to negotiate tight curves and a smaller loading gauge. They gained their electricity supply from a line provided by the Durham Electric Co. – a subsidiary of NESCO, marking yet another incidence of influence with M&M. (By this time they were working on a variety of commissions, e.g. in 1908 around Melbourne, Victoria, on their suburban electrification scheme, then later on in New Zealand and India.)

The electric locomotives showed that they were able to pull twice the loads of coal and colliery spoil compared to steam engines and they eliminated the need for a stationary winding engine at the Bents. The lessons derived from such a singular development within

875 'Midlothian', one of 'Waverley' NBR class 4-4-2 express passenger locomotives.

NER territory must have influenced Raven and Merz, when they considered the 1913 NER freight electrification, a much larger concern.

A scheme in the East Riding (named the Scarborough and East Riding Railway) was proposed to link Scarborough and Bridlington as seaside resorts with industrialised West Riding towns through the rural towns of Market Weighton and Driffield to connect with the H&BR at Howden. This was accepted by the majority of the company, but a minority went on to promote the line as Scarborough, Bridlington & West Junction Railway, which had gained parliamentary sanction for it in 1885, the line opening for traffic in 1890. Much to its own advantage, NER always worked the line, which gave the East Yorkshire coastal towns direct access to West Riding. From 1909 to 1913, there was a movement to incorporate it into NER. Raven gave evidence on behalf of NER and it was incorporated in 1913.

From 1906 onwards there was another series of rounds in the workforce versus employers continuing contest, when the November 1906 ASRS Conference drew up a National Programme for England and Wales, which laid out:

A standard eight-hour day for all men moving of vehicles in traffic;
Ten hours for the rest, except platemen;
At least nine hours rest between duties;
Overtime at time and a quarter;
Sundays and special days at time and a half;
A guaranteed weeks' wages to full-time employees;
An advance of 2s per week to all grades not receiving the eight-hour day.

The 'Programme', reminiscent of earlier company's plans to regulate pay and conditions, was submitted to the RCA in January 1907 by Mr R. Bell, secretary of the ASRS. He asked the RCA to meet him and representatives from the workforce. The companies did not answer. A ballot showed 76,925 votes in favour and 8,773 against. A general railway strike was called to get an agreement from RCA for the 'Programme', including the principle of 'recognition' of the Unions. The Board of Trade now intervened. Despite no meeting being held between the two sides, an agreement for a scheme of conciliation and arbitration resulted. This resulted in a 'Report of the Royal Commission' to investigate and report on the working of the railway conciliation and arbitration scheme of 1907. NER continued to try to work out suitable ways of arbitration to avert the damaging strikes; a Conciliation Conference was sanctioned by NER Board on 14 August 1908[33] and a first arbitration meeting was held on 30 March 1909. It was a probable result of being a member of the Conciliation Conference of NER on 30 March 1909 that Raven now became involved with the 1909 258-page document entitled 'North Eastern Railway Hours and Report', a statement on behalf of NER, examining the duties and wages of those for whom the CME's department was responsible. Raven collated evidence for his report from his own observations and opinions and used material derived from drivers, firemen and inspectors.

He noted that drivers and firemen had a job which meant they were idle for about half a turn of duty, waiting for return journeys; this was partly solved by mixed traffic rosters taking a passenger train one way and a goods train back. In November there was an award by Sir James Woodhouse of wages and conditions of service for company railway staff.

The next steam locomotive, the penultimate design from Gateshead, proved even more significant in the light of future developments. They were a modernised version of Worsdell's original 1899 'R' class 4-4-0s bearing many hallmarks of Raven's influence. While the wheels and cylinders remained the same, the frames ('Raven' now, of course) were longer, although the boiler was a shortened version used for the 1903 *Atlantics* of class 'V'. With their large firebox, they were coal hungry, and the firemen had to work harder to 'feed' them, so they were unpopular. They were not particularly good performers, despite a handsome appearance. When displaced from mainline working, their heavy axle weight precluded from light branch running.

The last six engines of Worsdell's graciously proportioned goods class 'X' 4-8-0Ts became the swansong of the historic Gateshead works; being the very last engines to be built at Gateshead in 1909–1910, these ten locomotives were intended for short but heavy runs around and within marshalling yards; they were rebuilt between 1914–1917, when the frames were extended to provide a larger bunker, which necessitated the support of two trailing wheels. Like many other of NER locomotives, they were coal-hungry machines.

Worsdell had also ordered the class 'Y' 4-6-2-T for similar freight work. Their main fault was the cramped cab, where their bunker intruded into the cabin space. Raven merely reordered them when he succeeded to the post of CME. (See Appendix 11 – Comparative chart of Wilson Worsdell's and Raven's locomotives from 1899–1923.)

Class 'X' 4-8-0T, a goods tank in whose design Raven is very likely to have been involved.

Because of the cramped site on the south bank of the Tyne, expansion of the Greenesfield works was not possible. So, in 1909, NER ended an era at Gateshead. It would move 1,800 of their locomotive building staff (and of course their families) to the locomotive building works in Darlington, with 1,500 men remaining behind to continue to run the works for locomotive repair only. Norman Lockyear was among those who moved from the historic Gateshead site, now no longer a place to build locomotives. Despite all the arbitration mentioned above, the NER men would still have to tow the line, which the company dictated as can be seen, when for more than 3,300 men employed at Greenesfield works in Gateshead a major change was announced.

At the Darlington end, it meant that the 3,500 men employed by NER would come to constitute 17 per cent of the borough's workforce. A spin-off from the NER's point of view was a reduction of running costs, as it did not have to pay urban rates in Darlington, being classed, unlike urban Gateshead, as a country town.[34] A similar movement occurred for the men at York. As Raven had been settled in Darlington since 1894, it is likely that he was involved in the decision, as it caused all locomotive building to be in one location under his control.

A pleasant diversion each year was the annual golf match in April. In 1910, Raven played for NER *v.* MR at Ganton course, south of Scarborough. NER would provide him with membership of the prestigious Felix Ferry Golf Club, only rescinded in 1924 by Butterworth, when LNER needed to 'tighten its belt'.

1 Teasdale John G., February 2002, 'Transatlantic traffic: being a consideration upon how American Railway Practices Influenced those of the North Eastern Railway', *The North Eastern Express*, vol.41. no.165, p.8 and National Archive Rail 527/1027 GM's circular no.582: the Reorganisation of the Traffic Department

2 Reading Railroad (1896-1976) – a compact system (1,300 miles), famed as a basis for the board game, Monopoly, provided extensive passenger services and the movement of coal in Eastern Philadelphia

3 Atlantic City Railroad (from 1883 a subsidiary of Reading Co.) running in New Jersey between Camden and Atlantic City

4 Pennsylvania Railroad – see Chapter 3, note 9

5 Atkins Philip, September 2000, 'Career Moves – George Heppel', *Back Track*, p.502-03

6 Chant Christopher, 2001, *The World's Railways*, Regency House Publishing Ltd, p.327

7 Staddon S A et al, 1978, 'Horse Tram to Metro: One Hundred Years of Local Public Transport in Tyne and Wear', Tyne and Wear Transport Executive, p.8

8 Hoole Ken, 1986, 3rd edition, *The North East, vol.4 – A Regional History of the Railways of Great Britain*, David & Charles, p.234

9 Teasdale John G., February 2002, 'Transatlantic traffic: being a consideration upon how American Railway Practices Influenced those of the North Eastern Railway', *The North Eastern Express*, vol.41. no.165, p.8-10

10 Teasdale John G., February 2002, ibid p. 9/10, based on National Archive Rail 527/432

11 Hoole Ken, 1987, 'The North Eastern Electrics: the History of the Tyneside Electric Passenger Services (1904-1967)', *Locomotion Papers* 165, The Oakwood Press, p.4-6

12 Semmens Peter William Brett, 1991, *Electrifying the East Coast Route: the making of the first 140 mph railway*, Patrick Stephens p.22-28

13 Semmens Peter, 'Tyneside Electrics Then and Now', August 2000, *Railway Magazine*, p.48, quoting from same journal, May 1904

14 Hoole Ken, 1987, 'The North Eastern Electrics: the History of the Tyneside Electric Passenger Services (1904–1967)', *Locomotion Papers* 165, The Oakwood Press, p.39

15 Proceedings of the IMechE, June 1904, p.787-827

16 National Archive, 23 February 1907, correspondence between Raven and Gresley

17 Bell R., 1951, *Twenty-five Years of the North Eastern Railway, Harrison and Sons Ltd*, p.28

18 The massive works were sited at Eddystone, Pennysylvania

19 The two works amalgamated later, General Electric Co. sited at Erie, Pennsylvania, specialising in electric locomotives, American Locomotive Co. (ALCO) at Schenactady, New York State, making steam locomotives

20 see Hoole Ken, February 1969, 'The North Eastern Railway Buses, Lorries and Autocars', Nidd Valley NGR Ltd for details

21 Groundwater Ken, 1998, *Newcastle's Railways: a View from the Past*, Ian Allan Publishing, p.76

22 Kitchenside Geoffrey and Williams Alan, 1998, *Two Centuries of Railway Signalling*, Oxford Publishing Co. p.157-58

23 Hoole Ken, 1986, *The North East Volume 4 - A Regional History of the Railways of Great Britain*, David & Charles, p.107-08

24 A similar, dark-eyed intense direct gaze is to be seen in photographs of 'Connie' and her son Michael

25 Atkins Philip, August 2000, '4-cylinder Compounds of the North Eastern Railway,' *Back Track*, p.424-29

26 Fleming M.J. 2000, North Eastern Record, vol.3 'A Survey of Locomotives of the North Eastern Railway', Historical Model Railway Society, p.127

27 Hattersley Ken, January 1997, *The Marquess of Ripon Lodge Number 1379 125th Anniversary History 1872-1997*, p.51

28 Thomas John, 1972, *North British Atlantics*, David Charles, Newton Abbot, p.56

29 Thomas John, 1972, ibid, p.76-78

30 Thomas John, 1972, ibid, p.76-78

31 Thomas John, 1972, ibid, p.87-92

32 Annual report for 1907-08 of Darlington NER Institute

33 National Archive RAIL 527/30

34 Biddle Gordon, 1990, *The Railway Surveyors*, Ian Allan Ltd, p.141

VI

CME TO NER (1910–1912)

Wilson Worsdell retired from Tuesday 31 May 1910 as CME, becoming a consultant engineer to NER, much as his brother had done. The post lasted until the end of the year, giving a salary of £ 2,000 p.a. Worsdell was a guest at a reception held by salaried staff at the Old Assembly Rooms, Newcastle, on Friday 29 May 1931. Raven presided. In his speech, he drew attention to the progress made by NER during Wilson's time, going on to praise him and his wife for their charity work. The staff gave him an antique secretaire.

Raven followed on as his natural successor, having worked with Wilson for seventeen years. He started his new post on 1 June 1910, remaining in it until 31 December 1922. Raven was to be:

> … engaged on the design, construction, repair, working etc. of railway rolling stock; and the design, construction and repair of outside machinery, such as electric and hydraulic cranes, bridge machinery, hoists, lifts, conveyors etc. and also tug boats. The North Eastern Railway has 2000 locomotives, 4600 coaching vehicles and 11200 wagons; and docks at Hull, Middlesbrough, Hartlepool, Tyne Dock, Blyth etc. [2]

There were 2,250 men working in North Road Works alone.

The scope of the post was even wider in practice than the summary above would indicate. It included responsibility during his occupation of the post for purchase, maintenance and replacement of an average of forty-five sailing vessels, including eleven steamships, which provided the North Sea passenger services, dealing with both emigration and immigration traffic, through Hull in particular. One and a half million Jews travelled through the port from 1884 to 1914.[3] There were the supporting dock vessels at all the North East ports to be serviced renewed or scrapped, such as tug boats, hoppers and dredgers working in the various east-coast docks owned by NER.

He had to oversee the increasing number of road vehicles of various kinds, namely steam- or petrol-driven lorries, which undertook freight haulage from and to railway depots and stations. To supplement local passenger services, charabancs and petrol-driven buses were used for the fledgling passenger services being developed, initially around Durham city and progressively on many more local routes.

Added to these was the overall responsibility for designing, building, updating, maintenance and replacement of carriages for passengers, whether first or third class, for use within NER territory and beyond. Here, sometimes, Raven had to develop new proposals for carriages, when required. There was also the ongoing development of the prestigious ECJS and that for GN/NE joint workings, which he and Gresley worked together as required.

Similarly, he oversaw building, maintenance and replacement of the multitude (11,200) of types of wagons, which NER needed to provide for its very lucrative work in goods and mineral traffic. Hand in glove with development of carriages and locomotives were wagons. As loads became bigger, where necessary, he provided his own solutions to difficulties that might arise.

Despite Raven having shown some interest in petrol engines adapted for rail locomotion, his overriding interest was in producing larger and more powerful steam and electric locomotives. Raven showed how well he had learned his lessons from his predecessors. He kept the model of managing a team, which Wilson Worsdell had used, with the CME at the top as an obvious controller/figurehead.

Once it had been decided that a new locomotive or rolling stock was needed and approval been given by the Board, it was up to Raven as CME to decide within the known resources available in the company whether to commission work from inside the company or for it to be tendered and put to an outside contactor. He had to ensure that all the different elements within his jurisdiction ran efficiently and could be easily maintained. Spares, such as resulted from crashes or wear and tear, would need to be readily available.

Furthermore, there was a widespread personnel function, arising from being responsible for thousands of personnel of all kinds. He had to ensure disciplinary procedures were carried out and that Union agreements were honoured by management and workers as well as deal with the effects of any dispute which occurred. In a more paternal vein, he sought to support rail welfare and recreational organisations in an active way by attendance at meetings and his patronage as president.

The salary for Raven's post was £2,500 p.a.[4] In addition, there were other 'perks' that went with the job. There was a locomotive for his use on inspections – a Fletcher 2-4-0 No.11 rebuilt with a Worsdell-type boiler, which presumably had an attendant driver and fireman and a six-wheel carriage. There was a locomotive in another sense – a car driven by his own chauffeur, Arthur Caldwell, employed from 2 August 1910. When not in his horse-drawn carriage, he was driven from Alpine Cottage (or Grantly, once he moved there) to work and back in his car (as well as presumably going to urban or rural destinations, not accessible by NER rail system). In early 1911, two more inspector cars were obtained. Lastly, Raven was allowed by the Board to take up to five 'premiums' apprentices, who were charged £105 p.a., a 'perk', which he could keep for himself. His last pupil was Maurice Hall who moved after his apprenticeship to the steel industry.

Another aspect of his new position of responsibility, as the organisation within the CME's offices at Stooperdale in 1911 will make clear, was the number of different staff over which Raven would be in charge; for instance, finance services for departmental staff and total costings of projects in the department under his control, plus the effects of such events on his budget as revenue lost due to strikes or in giving out loyalty payments to non-strikers or providing for Royal visits.

To sum up, Raven now developed his spheres of influence in four different, but linked directions. Firstly, he continued to develop Worsdell's initiatives with steam and electric locomotive traction as well as efforts to improve safety devices, the design and building of wagons and coaches. They were all part of his normal working brief. Secondly, in line with this, he assumed increasingly the patronage of a number of local railway workers' associations in the expected paternalistic way by becoming their president. Thirdly, he also became increasingly involved with the development of engineering interests, both locally via Darlington Technical College and nationally in further participation in associations and institutions. Fourthly, and lastly, on becoming CME Raven appears to have gained more confidence in accepting socially important civic roles in and for Darlington.

The first matter with which he became involved[5] was, in fact, none of the above, but a local example of industrial strife known as 'the Great Unrest', so common from 1910 until the start of the First World War. Strikes were aimed to gain Union recognition as well as to provoke industrial conflict. They were often led by ordinary Union members, influenced by a small number of Marxists The nominal dispute was for improved wages, hours of work and working conditions or perceived oppression by management. In the case of NER, their cause was not always justified as will be seen.

Raven, the new CME, unfortunately could not escape the effects of this industrial unrest. Having been a member of the Conciliation Conference of NER since 30 March 1909, in the future he was to learn what the industrial strife meant. For the time being, in mid-July 1910, he would only be marginally involved. He was among the chief officials of NER met at the Central Station to deal with the stoppage about a local decision to transfer a head shunter called Goodchild from the east end to the west end of Park Lane sidings in Gateshead. He refused to work at the west end. He was, therefore, told to go home, and thereupon the shunters on duty in the yard at the time ceased work, and the others, who were due on duty later in the day, refused to start work. Subsequently, a number of men, including drivers, firemen, guards, teemers and good warehouse staff at other centres also ceased work.

At first a local dispute and on the surface a comparatively minor issue, it spread quickly and caused disruption to both passenger and freight services around the Tyne and Wear areas and their hinterland. Services were provided by local tramcar companies and did much to mitigate the pressure. They ran a quick service from the Central (to the coast) and their tramcars were packed to the doors throughout the course of the entire day. Raven appears briefly as an angel of mercy, when an excursion train from Crook, with Sunday-school scholars and teachers, was delayed for nearly an hour at Newcastle. It was bound for Whitley Bay, but the driver did not know the road, and for some time it appeared that the hopes of the little ones were to be blighted. The situation was saved by the arrival on the scene of Mr Raven, the chief mechanical engineer, who at once volunteered to assist the driver, and the train went out on its journey amidst the cheers of its youthful freight.

There were between 5,000 and 6,000 men in the Gateshead and Newcastle areas on strike. Meanwhile, the NER officials stayed on to produce an official statement, of which the town hall meeting had a copy also. The general manager expressed his willingness to meet the men's representatives after the mass meeting, giving out his official statement to the Press, giving the terms which the NER would agree to:

> All men now on strike to return to work immediately – casuals included.
>
> No legal proceedings to be taken against men who have struck, and no entries recorded against them in their histories.
>
> The General Manager undertakes that a number of grievances which the men say, exist shall be enquired into without delay, and if the men so desire, he will himself receive a deputation within a week to discuss the mode of such enquiry.
>
> The General Superintendent will meet Shunter Goodchild and, if he so desires, two of his mates to hear the objections to his removal from the east to the west end of Park Lane Yard.

Despite discussion late into Wednesday evening, the dispute was still not resolved. The next day, Thursday 21 July, things looked the same, until Williams, as general secretary of ASRS, reminded the assembled ASRS members in no uncertain terms that the general manager of NER had been very fair, especially over the first three proposals he made, and that he had made it clear that he was not prepared to budge on the fourth. Both sides met again in the afternoon at the town hall, the strikers indicating that it was their own affair, not the Union's. Whereupon, another shunter called Ned Scott (a member of NER Conciliation Board) pointed out that the Union secretary had put a lot of work into getting the NER officials to consider the case and that they had only one course – namely, to accept the NER offers. There was great uproar, but eventually Walter Hudson MP (Newcastle-on-Tyne) gained control and Scott continued to point out that all along Goodchild had disobeyed orders and had had to go home, yet the company was willing to pay his wages while the grievance was investigated. This had been the case on Monday, why should it not the same today, Thursday? His logic prevailed and they voted for a return to work. A new deputation from the strikers, Messrs Williams, Hudson, Sleigh and Scott, now went to the NER Board Room at the Central Station, where a conference began at 9.15 p.m.

Members of the NER Conciliation Board	Representing the NER Company	Representing the Men
W. Crosthwaite	Alexander Butterworth Kaye, general manager – presiding	C.A. Henderson, JP, secretary, Tyne Dock Branch ASRS
T. Dickinson	Philip Burtt, deputy general manager	J.W. Dowens, rulleyman, secretary, South Shields Branch ASRS
J. Foote	S. Halliday, District Goods Superintendent	Walter Hughill, Secretary, Newcastle City Branch ASRS
T. Harrison	George Hope, mineral manager	James Sleigh, fireman, Gateshead secretary, Gateshead Branch ASRS and NER Conciliation Board
Councillor J. Patrick	Vincent Litchfield Raven, CME	J. Brodie
W. Race	Henry Angus Watson, general superintendent	J. Drinnan
W. Ramshaw	Ralph Lewis Wedgwood, divisional goods manager	J. Moffatt
Edward (Ted) Scott	E.F. Wilkinson, district passenger agent	T. Parker
James Sleigh, fireman, Gateshead, secretary, Gateshead Branch ASRS and NER Conciliation Board	H.H. Carrick, district superintendent, Sunderland	J. Wilkinson
		T. Wilson

The parties involved in settling the July 1910 strike.

By 10.30 a.m., they finished and Philip Burtt was able to tell the Press:

> The strike may now be regarded as over, the men having accepted the Company's terms unconditionally... The men will return to work immediately.

The GM's terms remained exactly as laid out above.[6] Like many another dispute, there was no victory for either side. The management could take the higher moral ground as they had not broken the agreement and as the strike was no legal, the ASRS had to capitulate.

Raven now began to embark cautiously at first in national professional matters. He submitted a 'candidate circular' (or Curriculum Vitae) to the meeting of 7 September 1910 at the ICE in order to be transferred from Associate Membership to Full Membership. Those who ratified his election were all members themselves of ICE, namely:

Messrs Airedale, (presumably James Kitson, Lord Airedale);
Oliver Robert Hancke Bury (GM of GNR);
Henry Copperthwaite, NER;
Henry Alfred Ivatt (CME for GNR);
James Livesey, consultant engineer;
A. Henry Meysey-Thompson MP (director on NER Board);
A. and F.W. Fannet-Walker;
J.D. Wardale;
Lindsay Wood;
T.W. and Wilson Worsdell (ex-CME's of NER).

As a conclusion to the 1910 dispute, Raven next appeared on 28 September as one of the representatives of the NER company executive, when Alexander Kaye Butterworth, GM-NER, was asked to present evidence, detailing for the management's case in past disputes by the Royal Commission on Railway Conciliation Schemes of 1907. He did not present any evidence. By 1 October, a set of rules was produced about what to do in strikes. Later, both management and workers' representatives were elected to their respective bodies, with a view to industrial peace. The onset of war during 1914 and the following war years focussed attention away from disputes, although in the longer term, it merely deferred the industrial strife.

Also around this time Raven completed the round of decisions about centralising facilities at Darlington, a movement which Fletcher had started in the late 1870s and which had been followed afterwards by McDonnell, in particular. Darlington now was to become the main centre for NER CME-led operations, York being the administrative centre. Once Gateshead had ceased as a locomotive-building centre for NER from 1909, Darlington became the sole site for NER locomotive building. Despite the July and August industrial action in Gateshead, from 1 October 1910 the CME, his operations and staff were moved to Darlington. This meant, as had happened earlier, that 1,500 Gateshead men were transferred to Darlington. Those 1,500 men, who remained at Greenesfield to carry on with locomotive repair and maintenance work, felt that they might become unemployed in the future, like so many others in the Gateshead area at that time.

There were three particular areas of responsibility, to which he had to pay specific attention, all to do with keeping the railways moving greater loads at greater speeds, namely carriages, wagons and locomotives. The time available for this work, viewed with hindsight, would fall into two phases, positioned on each side of Raven's 'war duties', the first lasting from 1911 to 1915, the other from 1919 to 1922. What is noticeable is the continuity of Raven's approach in all three areas with what had gone before under Wilson Worsdell. Raven followed his predecessor's practices closely, knowing them well as he had, in fact, worked on them himself. Later developments would add features, which he estimated would fulfil new needs or improve performance.

In 1908, NER owned 3,979 carriages, 1,574 bogie stock and 2,365 four- to six-wheel stock. Raven would oversee approximately the same number on coming into office regarding their design, building, development, maintenance and replacement. The First World War marked a divide in the building of carriages and wagons. Up to 1914, there was a notable variety in the building, but during the war there was more stringency, which meant that only more particular needs were met because of the war effort, and centrally more nationally focussed administration. This attitude persisted during the post-war years to amalgamation.

Raven continued his involvement with ECJS and GN/NE, continuing his collaboration with Gresley, so sharing responsibility for 213 ECJS and seventeen GN/NE stock, the estimate for such stock in 1913. These corridor carriages were produced at Doncaster and York, their roofs were semi-elliptical, they had standard gangways and at 53ft 6in long they were, in general, similar in appearance (dining cars were 65ft long). However, detailed differences emerged from the two workshops. The York-built carriages had indisputable NER features. For instance, they had their own NER-pressed steel bogies on an 8ft wheelbase and chassis with more moulded details. Raven's specific contribution to this series was three kitchen cars.

For more particular NER use in the pre-war period, there were non-corridor 49ft compartment third-class carriages with semi-elliptical roofs, produced in 1911; non-corridor 52ft composites in 1912; and corridor at 52ft first class and third class, all mounted on 8ft bogies, in 1912–13. Raven also designed a pair of first-class 'invalid' coaches with sixteen seats from 1911.[7]

A similar remit regarding design, building, development, maintenance and replacement of a vast array of wagons saw a move towards greater size as befitted the increasing demands for more consumer goods, especially perishables, often having to move from market garden or fish quay to be at the markets within a few hours. These were produced in three phases – before, during and after the First World War – much as Raven's carriages and locomotives were. He authorised such particular items as: short base 30T ironstone wagons for working on sharp curves near blast furnaces as early as June 1910; 12-ton low-sided plate wagons, produced from 1911 onwards (eventually totalling 1,300), bogie wagons of different weights and construction, 20T, 25T and 40T, including ones converted from tenders. For mineral traffic, there were the 11,000 11T coal hopper wagons, 550 10T covered fish vans, continuing to build 10T perishable goods vans, until a total of 245 was reached (fifty of which were converted to refrigerator vans

Above: First-class invalid carriage with sixteen seats from 1911.

Opposite below: 60445, a low-sided two-plank flat wagon from October 1920.

48426, a short base 30T ironstone wagon for working on sharp curves near blast furnaces from June 1910.

481, a low-sided wagon from March 1912, with steel frames and wooden sides.

70651/35415 flat top wagons, converted from tenders from April 1911.

10846, a cross-beamed open goods wagon from 1916.

23130, an open cattle van built from February 1918.

by 1923); there was also the servicing of 2,000 8/10T cattle vans. During the war, production of new lines became more specified and included not only a new steam crane in 1918, but wagons for carrying heavy goods, glass and aeroplane parts, and still more coal wagons.

This reflects the wide range of goods and their vehicles transported by rail at that time. Sometimes Raven, as CME, would be asked to deal with unusually shaped or heavy loads.[8] He was concerned with the effect that private wagons were having on the service, especially the cost of repairing them, which fell to NER when the private wagons ran on their metals

Dates	Outside Contractor's Prices (e.g. Pease and Partners)	NER Own Prices from Shildon Works
1898	£91 15s	£85
1905	£113	£112 10s 0d
	£12,000	Total building saving on 500 wagons
1900–1910 repair to wagons per wagon	£3 16s 10d	£2 17s 1d
	£234 7s 6d	Total repair saving on 500 wagons

Chart of comparative costs of building and repair of private wagons to NER, based on notional unit of a 12T goods wagon.

Commodity	Pence per train miles
Goods	40–125
Mineral	80–160
Passenger	40–40

To show returns on commodities from 1900–1912.

Moving to Raven's main output, steam locomotives, there is a basic pattern underlying what he was concerned with doing as he incorporated a number of features. While not in themselves unique when some of the details of other contemporary British locomotive designs are considered, they are sufficiently individual to make the locomotives recognisably his, both visually and functionally. Not all aspects of this model will apply to every class of locomotive he built.

54883, a coal wagon with bottom
doors from 21 January.

All Raven's engines were large, whether tank or tender, filling the available NER loading
gauge. He had had to increase boiler size when it became necessary to make locomotives more
and more powerful and capable of higher speeds. Worsdell had already lifted boilers to near
the maximum height allowed for the NER loading gauge restrictions, when he built his class
'S/S1' 4-6-0s. So, now the only way to increase boiler size was to make them longer. Raven's
boilers were always straight sided and cylindrical (not tapered at the front, as was GWR
practice). There was a small circular handle on the single circular smoke box door. Through
boiler cladding, they appeared to be with the round-topped firebox, which in turn led into
the front of the cab, making for reduced cab space. (Belpaire fireboxes were not commonly
used on NER.) The locomotive's superstructure usually rested on 'Raven' frames, which had
internal convex ends at the front, between the running plates. (Raven raised the middle section
of the running plate above the last leading wheels and the drivers at the end of his NER
career for classes 'P3' and 'S3' and for his *Pacifics*, possibly as a response for better access for the
maintenance men than he had with his earlier designs.)

Chimneys were shortened throughout the series, being a very truncated conical shape
with rims, and often at the front a *capuchon* (the delightful Geordie term for them was 'wind-
jabbers'). These often partially wore away and in many cases were dispensed with later; under
the LNER composite loading gauge was lowered to 13ft). Domes were always situated in the
middle of the boiler. Like chimneys, as the boiler size rose they became less and less 'hay-stack'
in profile, becoming almost hemispherical in shape.

Frames were planned to form a supporting structure with the addition of leading and
trailing wheels below them as additional support where necessary. Additionally, they helped to
distribute axle loads, improve 'riding' qualities and adhesion. Similarly, he usually fitted three
cylinders, one placed at either side of the frames (sometimes internally, sometimes externally),
the third inside the frames (exceptionally, pre-war classes 'P2' and 'S2' had only two cylinders).
By this, he sought to improve stability, again enhance 'riding' and to reduce the effects of torque.
Both these measures were aimed at reducing stress on the crank-axle, lessening the need for
maintenance and replacement of locomotive parts as well reducing wear on the track.

Raven started to introduce superheating for all the major classes of NER locomotive,
including his own – a feature which he pursued enthusiastically once he was convinced about
it and had decided how it improved performance. Originally developed by Wilhelm Schmidt,
the Prussian engineer, as early as 1897, Churchward (CME for GWR) and George Hughes
(CME for L&YR) from 1906 onwards had both developed applications to their locomotives.
Therefore, it is not surprising that Raven should set out to investigate superheating
for himself, instituting comparative trials between non-superheated and superheated
locomotives. One of the arguments which persuaded Raven to use superheating was its ability
to reduce boiler pressure, yet provide increased power. This reduced the wear and tear on
the boiler – a welcome economy, although reduction of coal and water which also occurred
seems not to have been a prime consideration at this stage. Each class had Stephenson gear and

piston valves, which usually drove on to the second set of coupled wheels (again classes 'P2', 'P3' and *Pacifics* were exceptions in that they drove onto a third set of coupled wheels). Above all, driving wheels were smaller splashers than formerly on Worsdell's bigger engines, because 'Raven' frames were so deep. The culmination of this was his *Pacific*. He also had a preference for the cylinders and their pistons to drive on to the second pair of driving wheels, connected to the other 'drivers' by connecting rods. While cabs provided driver and firemen with overall roofs, the space available was cramped usually by the intrusion of the firebox into it. For many years Ramsbottoms' safety valves had been the standard, capped by brass 'trumpets', but after 1911 these were replaced by poppet safety valves without cover.

On a more aesthetic note, Raven locomotives were in tune with the Arts and Crafts movement, in which simplicity and elegance of design went hand in hand with function. The Raven (and the earlier Worsdell and Smith designs) had uncluttered profiles, enhanced by their spatial relationships. In profile, the vertical arrangement of wheels, frames and boiler is balanced by the positioning of chimney over smoke box. The smoke dome always lies about midway between it and the cab in a horizontal movement, complemented by the lower splashers at running plate level. Comparison between 4-4-4Ts designed by Raven and later 4-6-2Ts by Robinson reveal how neatly Raven fits frames and boiler and much of the important mechanical components between the side tanks, adding chimney, cab and bunker into design in graceful proportion, while Robinson's design looks slightly top-heavy. Similarly Reid's NBR *Atlantics* with their large boilers looked a bit pot-bellied beside the sleeker NER class 'Z' *Atlantic*, which Raven produced.

These class 'Y' 4-6-2T freight tanks were the first engines for whose design Raven took responsibility. They had been on the drawing board, as it were, before Raven took office and their similarity to Wilson's Worsdell's class 'X' 4-8-0T is clear. They were 3-cylinder freight tanks, but now had larger boilers with 1,648sq. ft at a pressure of 180lb per sq in and so better able to realise the power available to them from their 3-cylinders, unlike the smaller-boilered class 'X', which, despite a pressure of 1,75lb per sq in, had only a heating area of 1,310 sq ft.

Both these tanks were unusual for that date in having three cylinders, although there was the example of Robinson's 1907 3-cylinder 0-8-4Ts for Raven to evaluate and learn from. Class 'Y's were intended for heavy loaded runs of 1,000 tons at 20mph on level track, but they were used on short runs with mineral trains over the steep gradients in County Durham, leading from inland collieries to the North East coast ports. Twenty were built in Darlington works between October 1910 and June 1911. Saturated at first, they later had superheaters added.

Class 'Y' 4-6-2T, a fine design for heavy shunting.

2006, Class 'S/S1' of Worsdell, the mixed traffic precursor of Raven's class 'S2' and 'S3'.

797, Class 'S2', the Raven expansion of the previous picture, which, apart from Raven frames, higher splashers and different safety valves, was in many ways similar in profile and performance.

Next came developments of Wilson Worsdell's classes 'S' and 'S1'. Built during 1911–1912 as class 'S2', they had the same sized drivers, leading wheels, cylinders, Stephenson gear and piston valves as their predecessors. The main development was a larger boiler and later from 1913, superheaters were added (at first with a form of 'Robinson' heater and elements, but later those of the 'Schmidt' type). The first twenty engines of this new class 'S2' were to be earmarked for express passenger use. History, however, repeated itself and once Raven's new class of 'Z' *Atlantics* became available, the class 'S2' was quickly put to mixed traffic duties. This meant that class 'S2' could haul an express passenger train in one direction, but could be rostered to return with a fully fitted express goods train in the other direction. This reduced time in running 'light' back home, reduced the movement of locomotives and promoted the use of large express goods trains, particularly necessary in transporting perishables like fish. There was a real drive for transporting trains as quickly and efficiently as possible in each direction. The class proved reliable enough engines,[9] and a further ten were built in 1913, but their cabs were rather cramped for those who had to work them, the position of their narrow firebox doors making stoking difficult. Nor were things made easier by difficulties with steaming due to restricted air flow in the firebox, if the shallow ash pan was banked up too much.

More attention has been paid to No.825, the last of its class, which had originally appeared in March 1913. Raven used it experimentally by fitting the Stümpf Uniflow system for steam distribution, in an attempt to reduce heat loss and hence energy gained from burning of coal. Its aim was to stop reversal of steam flow in the cylinders and consequent condensation therein. It had been developed from a stationary engine in 1908 for use by locomotives by Johannes Stümpf of the Königliche Technische Hochschule in Berlin-Charlottenberg, where he introduced it in 1909. Raven mentions briefly a visit to Germany in his April 1913 address to engineering students in Darlington Technical College. It is possible that he had been in touch with Stümpf, even visited him.

A25, the last class 'S2', fitted with Stümph 'Uniflow' apparatus.

2212, the 'Uniflow' *Atlantic*, the apparatus heavily disguised by prolonging leading bogie, which while distorting the front end, avoids the ugliness of calls 2, No.325.

Aesthetically, the addition of the system interrupted the smooth lines of the class to a ludicrous degree, by raising the front end and cutting onto the running plates in order to mount the external cylinder on each side. It was the only Raven engine to receive Walschaert's valve gear. It is not clear whether the changes improved in any way the performance of 825 over its untreated brothers. There were problems in running. It could be difficult to start. The central part of the cylinder remained comparatively cooler, so it expanded less. The piston could seize up completely solidly in the middle of its travel. The whole class could be only deemed a moderate success and were a midway stage on the way towards class 'S3', one of Raven's long-lasting practical and elegant masterpieces. The class was scrapped in two batches, five in 1937 and the remaining fifteen between 1944 and 1947.

The next locomotives classes 'Z/ Z1' 4-4-2 *Atlantic* express passenger engines were built because Raven pointed out to the directors of NER that there was an urgent need of further large passenger engines. There were at that time only 22 Atlantics – ten class V, then class V/o9 and the two Smith compounds and ten class R1 4-4-0s.

The original proposal had been for them to be a 3-cylinder version of Worsdell's last group of class 'R/R1' 4-4-0s. His new *Atlantics* were a development of both Smith' s '4CCs' and of Worsdell's classes 'V/ Vo9', whose external design with the continuous box-like lines of external frames and the shape of convex front end to the locomotive frames had already shown Raven's influence. His new engines were intended for express passenger use, twenty of which were built by North British Locomotives in 1911, ten with saturated steam and ten with Schmidt superheaters. The last thirty of class 'Z' were built at Darlington from 1914–18, all of which were superheated from 1914.[10] They quickly became a success for a number of reasons. They rode more smoothly at speed than Wilson Worsdell's classes 'V' and 'R1' because the three cylinders provided a more even torque. They used less coal and produced greater mileage between servicing and required less repairing.[11] When Gresley tested this class later in 1925 against Ivatt *Atlantics*, he decided that there was little difference between them. Raven's could move trains slightly better, even if they used more coal to do it and did not need to run double-headed like the Ivatt's.

Later, in 1918, one of them, No.2212, was built with one massive casting to house the three *Uniflow* cylinders under an extended leading bogie. While it thus avoided the very ungainly

Above: 2013, one of Worsdell's class 'R', 4-4-0. Note the Raven frames.

Left: Worsdell class 'V' Atlantic.

Below: 731, the second of Smith's class 4CC *Atlantics*.

Bottom: 2201, one of Raven's development of both the above, class 'Z' *Atlantic* — powerful function and simplicity in design.

look of the S2 *Uniflow*, it looked a little too long in the overall wheelbase compared to its sister engines. Another, 2202, was converted to oil-burning in 1921–1922. They were scrapped between 1944 and 1948. (For details see Appendix 11 – Comparative chart of Wilson Worsdell's and Raven's locomotives from 1899–1923.)

One of the men who worked under Raven was Edward Thompson. Thompson's father, Frances Edward, had been a master at Marlborough College, teaching Greek, and Edward was born there. As a boy, he may have known Nigel Gresley, who would have been an older pupil there. Thompson graduated in Mechanical Sciences from Pembroke College, Cambridge, in 1902, going on to work with Beyer, Peacock & Co. Ltd in Manchester, a great provider of railway engines, especially to Irish railways among many others. After a time with the MR, he moved on to Woolwich Arsenal. In 1906 he became an assistant to NER district locomotive superintendent, Bill Farrow. Worsdell moved him to Gateshead to work with Raven's associate 'Charlie' Baister, the northern running superintendent in early 1909.

Raven must have quickly appreciated Thompson's potential.[12] Thomson's administrative ability in the past could well been relayed from previous employers to his benefit, following Raven's professional contacts with them. Thompson remained behind to continue his work with 'Charlie' Baister in Gateshead during the succeeding year, after the big move to Darlington had been made.

As well as being a junior professional associate of Raven, Thompson came to know the Raven family socially. He started a lifelong friendship with Raven's son Norman Vincent, most likely through his father's contacts with Gresley and his department at GNR, where Norman was apprentice. More significantly, he came to know Guen, Raven's younger daughter, became engaged to her and eventually married her in 1913. In 1910, both families were sufficiently friendly for Thompson, plus his father and mother to send presents to Connie Raven on her marriage to George Herbert Watson.

The Watson family was a typically lower middle-class professional family. The father, George Newby Watson, was born in 1847/48 in Pimlico, London. His wife Jane, born in the year 1846, being like Raven's mother-in-law Scottish. Admitted as a solicitor in 1871, Watson moved to Darlington, working from 1873 in partnership with Hugh Dunn (Hugh Dunn and Taylor). He worked hard and largely through his own efforts so that by end of the century he had become a well-known Darlington figure for his work in the legal profession, the established church and society in general.

He seemed to move house frequently, possibly a sign of his upward social mobility. He lived initially off North Road, quite close to the railway works.[13] He joined Darlington 1379 Marquis of Ripon Lodge of the Freemasons, being initiated in 1876, becoming Lodge Grand Master in 1882, living in streets close to north road. By 1890, he had moved upmarket to the leafier suburbs of Carmel Road in west Darlington, still the more fashionable and genteel part of Darlington. He moved from house to house three times in the area during the 1890s, settling finally at Grantly, the house NER was to purchase for Raven.[14]

His sons, George Herbert (born 1879) and Lawrence Cecil (born 1880), after attending Malvern College in Worcestershire, studied also to become solicitors. George Herbert qualified in 1902 and joined his father in his practice, taking up a position as clerk to the local court. George Herbert took over from his father on his retirement in January 1909, when the practice seems to have been just Watson senior. The other Watson brother, Lawrence Cecil, was articled to his father and qualified as a solicitor in 1905. The two brothers now joined together after their father's retirement to form Watson and Watson, with their practice in Lloyd's Bank Chambers on High Row. The Watsons were involved with service in the Church of England in one way or another, sons having positions in local churches and one of his daughters marrying Revd Leonard B. Ashby, vicar of St Mary's, Barnard Castle. George Newby was also president of Darlington Choral Society, while George Herbert was organist at St Mary's, Cockerton, from 1902.

Raven and Watson senior are likely to have met at the Lodge meetings and had sufficient contact socially for Connie Raven and George Herbert to meet. Perhaps their schooling

St Cuthbert's C/E church, Darlington, where Connie and George Watson were married.

in the Malverns gave them a common theme for conversation. They became engaged and eventually get married. Their wedding on 3 November 1910 was one of the events of the year in Darlington polite society.

It was held in the historic St Cuthbert's church, Darlington, being celebrated by the bridegroom's brother-in-law, Leonard B. Ashby, assisted by three other clergymen, Revd J.T. Hammond, then newly appointed vicar of St Mary's, Woodkirk, Dewsbury, Revd D. Walker, vicar of St Cuthbert's, and Revd F. Peacock, vicar of Holy Trinity, Darlington. The choir of St Mary's, Cockerton, a daughter parish of St Cuthbert's, where George Herbert had been organist for the previous eight years, provided a personal touch, in attending and singing appropriate hymns, accompanied on the organ by Dr Hutchinson, who played the usual wedding marches as the bridal party entered and left the church.

For her wedding, Connie wore:

> … a Princess dress of soft ivory duchesse satin, with fichu of Mechlin lace, which was knotted at the left side with a bunch of orange blossom, and continued down the side and caught up on to the train with a bunch of orange blossom. Her veil was of old Honiton lace, and she wore an old pearl necklace, the gift of her mother, and carried a lovely bouquet of lilies of the valley.

Furthermore:

> Mrs Raven, the mother of the bride, wore a dress of electric blue velvet, with old gold embroidery on bodice veiled with blue ninon. Her large black hat was trimmed with blue ostrich feathers, and she carried a bouquet of Parma violets and lilies of the valley.

The men of the party wore top hats and tails. Her father gave the bride away and the bridegroom's brother Lawrence was best man, and they both signed the marriage register as witnesses. There were three bridesmaids, Guen Raven, the bride's sister, Olive Crichton (her cousin from Bath), and a Miss W. Collin.

They were attired in dresses of soft white satin, with overdress of white crepe ninon, cut up the sides and caught back with knot of same. They wore large black picture hats. Their ornaments were pearl and amethyst pendants and these and the bouquets of yellow roses which they carried were the gift of the bridegroom.

The bride gave the bridegroom a set of silver hair and clothes brushes. He gave her a diamond and sapphire ring. There were an abundance of gifts from friends, colleagues and well-wishers. The list of gifts and givers serves two useful purposes. Firstly, it provides an account of what kind of wedding gifts it was fashionable to give in 1910. There were many silver items, for use in the household, as ornaments and for personal use and adornment. There were items of furniture, tea sets and china, household linen, and paintings, while Raven gave them a cheque. Secondly, it provides a profile of the people who were living and in contact with a family sufficient to be giving gifts. First of all, gifts were received from members of the Raven family; notably they included Raven's sons Norman and Frederick, his brother Charlton and his wife (married in 1903 in Brentford), one of his sisters, Gertrude Jane and her husband, Mrs Raven, who is probably Raven's mother, aged seventy-five, yet nothing from his other brothers, two of whom were in the USA or from his other sisters.

There were gifts from Constance's maternal grandparents, her uncle George Crichton and his wife, a sister-in-law, Mrs Edward Crichton and a cousin. Similarly, the bridegroom's family received gifts from his father, mother, his brother Lawrence, his sister Mrs Ashby, her husband (the 'lead' clergyman at the wedding) and their daughter, plus his father's associates from the Bench of Justices.

Then there were gifts from her father's associates and their families in NER – Mr and Mrs 'Charlie' Baister, Mr and Mrs Philip Burtt, Mr and Mrs Harold Copperthwaite, Mr and Mrs Norman Lockyer and daughter, Mr and Mrs Arthur C. Stamer and the foremen of North Road Engine Works and, lastly, from Raven's former superior, Mr Wilson Worsdell and his wife. Edward Thompson and his father and mother also gave presents. Among the many other givers of gifts from the wider circle of friends and acquaintances, many from professional backgrounds in industry, commerce, medicine and trade, were a group of Freemason colleagues and their wives, especially Alfred Faulkner Ball, who had introduced him originally to the Masons in Newcastle and Dr Thomas Hutchinson who possibly gave his services free as a wedding tribute.

Following the reception at Alpine Cottage, the couple went to honeymoon to London and the South.

The bride's going away dress was a tailor-made blue coat with oyster grey crepe de chine, and she wore a set of sables.[15]

After moving from Grantly, probably on retirement (another solicitor Mr S. Clarke lived there from 1909 to 1911 before Raven was moved there by NER in 1912), George Newby went to live at 20 Western Parade, off Coniscliffe Road, where he lived for another five years. Connie and George Herbert, on their return from honeymoon, went to live at 20 Victoria Road,[16] but the couple moved frequently around the town.

Lawrence Cecil lived at Jasmine House, Haughton-le-Skerne, and was a loyal churchwarden at St Andrew's there. Lawrence was also a footballer in his younger days and kept up his interest in sport. He died on 14 June 1948 and after the funeral was cremated in Darlington. He left a son (Capt. A.G. Watson RASC) and a daughter (G.H.)[17]

During 1911, there were further strikes. From 6 to 11 March, there was a strike of carriage cleaners at the Central Station in Newcastle and lastly, on 11 August, a National Strike was called by ASRS; although NER workers were not involved, they came out on strike without notice. The strike finished on 25 August.

On a more genial note, Raven, in his new position as CME, moved progressively into public speaking, taking up the presidency of various NER employee institutions. He attended the tenth annual dinner at the King's Head Hotel in Darlington on 10 February 1911, where he presided as chairman, with Mr Pigg as vice-chairman. He presented a purse of gold to Anthony T. Atkinson, who had retired after thirty-seven years of service in the Mileage Department, Gateshead, on 10 December 1910.[18]

On 10 May, he attended the AGM of Gateshead NER Literary Institute where the annual report and accounts were universally adopted, dealt largely with the educational facilities and the description of members and students attending in larger numbers. Wilson Worsdell had resigned the posts of president and treasurer, and several speakers gave cordial expressions to their indebtedness to him.

Thompson followed his desire to further his career by deciding at this juncture to move south to the GNR at Doncaster as carriage and wagon superintendent. So, in late 1911, NER department gave Thompson a travelling clock and a silver-mounted pipe as farewell gifts.[19] He may have felt that he needed now to map out his own career and not be too dependent on his future father-in-law. The photographs of Thompson show that, like Raven, he was always neatly dressed, but clean shaven, showing a similar no-nonsense expression to his future father-in-law. They were destined to become closer, not only by meeting up at work for NER in the future, but by Thompson becoming engaged to Guen during 1912 and marrying her the next year.

Raven was duly elected to both positions that Wilson Worsdell had previously held. Lastly, he was proposed by H.L. Wainwright, seconded by Bowen-Cooke CME for LN&WR and accepted as a member of ARLE at their meeting of 28 November 1911 at St Pancras.

Raven, to improve performance on older stock, did what many CME had done before and after, and updated his predecessors' locomotives with what he felt to be improvements despite the fact that superheaters were not effective on short runs. They were fitted to:

T.W. Worsdell's classes	'B1' 0-6-2Ts
'C1' 0-6-0s (from 1914)	
'F' 4-4-0s	
'G' 2-4-0s	
Wilson Worsdell's classes	'M', 'Q', 'R' and 'R1' 4-4-0s
'S' 4-6-0s (between 1914 and 1924)	
'S1' 4-6-0s (between 1913 and 1917)	
'V' 4-4-2s (between 1915 and 1919)	
'V/09' 4-4-2s (between 1914 and 1920)	
20 'P' 0-6-0s (between 1914 and 1920)	
28 'P1' 0-6-0s (between 1915 and 1918	
iii) Smith's class	'4CC' 4-4-2s (in 1914).[20]

He also fitted twelve class 'R' 4-4-0s with 'Raven' frames, recognisable in that they raised the height of the frame and had a convex curve of the front end;[21] it is generally agreed that the changes improved the balance of their outlines.

Raven started to consider petrol-driven vehicles once again for his tours of inspection as CME and as a result two such inspection vehicles were built. However, more importantly, Butterworth, NER GM, now decided that future operational policy should include more electrification in NER. This resulted in Raven in latter part of 1911, traveling to the USA with Charles Merz on a fact-finding mission.[22]

Merz was now a very well-known figure in industrial application of electricity, first becoming a member of the IEE, then gaining the Faraday Prize and eventually becoming a vice-president. The pair travelled to gain first-hand experience of transatlantic methods as applied to various electrification schemes being developed there. Their interest was partly technical, partly economic. There was a need to devise economies in reducing the running costs of moving vast amounts of minerals, an operation, that some USA railroads had been notably successful in doing.

A key report from Raven and Merz was issued, dated 12 January 1912, resulting from their American study tour detailing a cost of 1.5 million for the development of a short experimental goods line between Shildon and Newport (Middlesbrough), which Butterworth proceeded to back,[23] although he was not ready to consider wholesale electrification of the system at this stage, the mainline electrification between New York and Newcastle being part of this report also. The same day, 12 January, Butterworth GM, in a typically and distinctly more cautious way, put it before the Board. This enabled Raven to begin planning the introduction of his own schemes both for electrification and the design of electric locomotives.[24] Later in the year, in a memo on 8 August, comments were made at the Board meeting that the estimated figures for the scheme were on the low side and information should be sought from existing systems.[25] Coal production throughout the United Kingdom was at its peak of 245 million tons in 1913, so Raven's advocacy of the economies arising from electrification was apt. From 1900, the mileage of trains run by the company was reduced by 15 per cent, while at the same time the volume of each separate division of its business notably increased: by 18 per cent in minerals, by 35 per cent in goods, and by 29 per cent in passengers.[26]

Raven would have to acquiesce in whatever decision was finally made. That it went ahead at all is amazing when the current (1913) NER deficit reached £4.5 million.

Another activity Raven pursued on his return home concerned his presidency of Gateshead NER Literary Institute. He chaired its half-yearly meeting on 8 December, where, unusually, his wife, not him, presented prizes to successful students. Also among those present were George Heppell, J. Pigg, Norman Copperthwaite and the principal of Rutherford Technical College (the precursor of University of Northumbria), Mr Eclair Heath. Raven was to become increasingly involved in the further education of engineers. He here only commented briefly that it gave him great pleasure to be present. He had long taken a deep interest in the education of young men in the north of England. As a member of the committee many years ago, it was his pleasure to push forward the educational side of the Institute.[27]

These comments would be later amplified in 1913 in a speech at Darlington Technical College. At the same meeting, he was re-elected for the period 1912–1914 as president and treasurer.

Also at the end of the year, he designed an unusual pair of carriages, first-class bogie saloons for invalids, numbered 2023 and 2026. They were 50ft 6in over ends long, 7ft 9¾in high and 9ft wide, with semi-elliptical roofs, an interior finish in a Sheraton style of mahogany inlaid with boxwood, Axminster carpet on the floor and mohair curtains. They also provided luggage space, a central sitting area with comfortable sofas, a private room and two lavatories. The entrance had double doors, very useful to allow invalid carriages and stretchers in easily.[28]

A large site close to the older North Road site was acquired at Stooperdale. At its east end the first building, a new boilershop, was divided into three sections: a tender repair bay, the length of the west side, on the eastern side; the remaining space was divided into two, the northern section being given over to boiler construction, repair and testing, while the southern section to cabs, splashers and tanks.[29]

It was 513ft long and 219ft wide and included a paint shop with space for twenty-four tender locomotives, with an adjacent stores department. The complex was separated by a railing from the Darlington–Barnard Castle railway line, which passed nearby.[30] Raven was based at the North Road works until April 1912, when he moved to:

> … a magnificent new building on the Stooperdale estate was ready. Known locally as 'Buckingham Palace', and standing well back from Brinkburn Road, this remarkable edifice might well pass as one of the 'stately homes of England'.[31]

These fine new offices, built during 1911, were designed by William Bell of York, the chief architect to NER. Like Raven, Bell spent his working life with the NER. Born in 1843 or 1844 in York,

Stooperdale, fine offices for the CME, designed by NER architect William Bell (they earned the nickname locally of 'Buckingham Palace'); here Raven had his office suite in the left wing.

he started in 1857 as an assistant to Thomas Prosser and Benjamin Burleigh and became chief architect at the beginning of 1877, responsible to the NER chief civil engineer. The succeeding thirty-seven years saw him providing NER with a wonderful series of stations of all sizes, fitted to rural, suburban and city environments, plus hotels, offices, workshops and warehouses.

Stooperdale, a site of 2,500 square yards, was built of Normanton brick with a south-facing frontage of 300ft in Palladian style. The central main entrance has an Italian terracotta portico with sturdy columns rising to the first floor, topped by a central pediment. Two wings with seven bays project to each side only two storeys high, each side having seven mansards let into the sloping roof. Internally, the entrance hall, which is fitted with revolving draught-proof doors, gives immediate access to the corridor, which runs the whole length of the building, the various offices running off from the corridor. The main staircase runs from the entrance hall to the top of the building and gives access to similar corridors on each floor. Terrazzo marble in Venetian mosaic is used for the floors of the entrance hall and corridors and in the steps of the staircase. The woodwork on the ground floor is fumed oak.

The private office of Mr. Vincent L. Raven, the Chief Mechanical Engineer, is situated at one end to the left of the main entrance. Next to this apartment is a room devoted to Mr. Raven's Chief Clerk, and next to this again, a large room in which 30 and 40 clerks are located. Close by, but on the opposite side of the corridor, are rooms occupied by Mr. A. C. Stamer, Assistant Mechanical Engineer and his Chief Clerk; whilst to the right of the entrance is a spacious conference hall. Further along to the right is the Accountant's Office where, under the supervision of Mr. Whitton and Mr. Miller, accounts relating to the department are dealt with. This particular room occupies the full width of the east wing of the ground floor.

The treatment of the first floor is very similar to that of the ground floor. The officers and staffs of the Outside Machinery Superintendent, the Electrical Superintendent, the Chief Boiler Inspector, the Chief Carriage and Wagon Draughtsman, and the Chief Locomotive Draughtsman [George Heppell and his deputy R. Robson].

Outside Machinery Superintendent and his staff] are all situated on this floor, where they had drawing offices. On the second floor are the chemical laboratory, the rooms of the Chief Testing Inspector, Dynamometer Car Inspector and the official photographer, a photographic room, and a dining room for such members of staff as are not able to go home to their meals, with spacious kitchen accommodation adjoining. The caretaker's quarters are on this floor. In the basement excellent provision is made for the storage of documents, etc. Boilers for heating the premises are also located here, as are the motors which work the power being obtained from the Company's own power house. An adequate system of telephone communication is also provided.

In the rear of the building is a railway siding, from which fuel (coal and supplies) may be dropped from the tracks into the cellars of the new building. A motor garage (probably to house his personal limousine) and a cycle shed are also provided. The open space in front of the offices has been neatly laid out with flowers and shrubs. [32] [33]

This detailed description provides a clear picture of the extensive management set-up around a CME, how it is functioned, and the care NER took to ensure working conditions were of a high contemporary standard for its administrative and support staff. It, however, omits to mention that Raven's own office – the only one to be so privileged – was one of the first offices to be double-glazed and had its own toilet and wash place, built on to the west side of his part of the ground floor, obvious perks of being CME.

The new HQ also meant that Raven was in relatively easy distance of Shildon Wagon Works. Locomotives had also been made by Timothy Hackworth at the famous 'Soho' works, finally closed in 1883 as part of Fletcher's early rationalisation. Shildon was another typical north-eastern one-industry town, developed like Consett, Seaham Harbour and Darlington itself to serve a particular industrial enterprise (in this instance, to make wagons). The wagon works (in 1923 covering 40 acres and employing 2,750 people) had been inherited by the NER after amalgamation with the Stockton & Darlington Railway in 1861. Raven designed new 20-ton steel wagons for transportation of Cleveland ironstone to blast furnaces, which were built at Shildon wagon works.[34] They weighed 7 tons 118 cwt each and were provided with end brakes.

The NER bought Grantly, a large house, for their CME, reminiscent of one of G.T. Andrews brick 'villa'-style stations. They were no doubt influenced in their choice by Raven, who was familiar with it as it had previously belonged to Connie's father-in-law. Being set in a 'good' area, it would consolidate both NER's and Raven's social status, being located in a more socially suitable part of town, yet still close to Stooperdale, Raven moved into it about 1912.[35]

It was Raven who was present once again at the fifty-fifth AGM of Gateshead NER Literary Institute. He sounded an educational note, as he mentioned:

... the value of evening classes and especially emphasised the value at the present time of magnetism and electricity by mechanical students.[36]

He also remembered the death of J.H. Simpson, locomotive inspector, who had died on 8 May. Perhaps he remembered the early days of his own career as inspector.

Shortly after this, Raven attended a banquet, held by the Iron and Steel Institute on 9 August 1912 at the Connaught Rooms in Great Queen Street, London. It provided him with what would be useful connections for future reports and projects, especially his time at Woolwich Arsenal and the Admiralty. (There was a hidden but obvious old boy's network, seen again and again in the meetings he attended, which would provide Raven with an important career decision before his retirement.) The guests included:

John Audley Frederick Aspinall (CME for L&YR)
Lawrence Billinton (CME for LBSCR)
Charles John Bowen-Cooke (CME for LNWR)
Lord Cavendish Duke of Devonshire (chairman of Furness Railways)
Lt-Col. Stanley Brenton von Donop (inspecting officer of railways, Board of Trade)
E.B. Elrington (president of IMechE)
Robert Abbott Hadfield (president of Iron & Steel Institute, chairman of Hadfield Co.)
F.C. Herbert
W.H. Kitson
A.L.C. Pell (manager of LCC Tramways)
W.F. Pettigrew (CME of Furness Railways)
J.M. Robertson (parliamentary secretary, Board of Trade)
Dr Frank T.C. Tudsberry (lawyer)

Things did not always run smoothly for Raven as a manager. There was a lot of disgruntlement about declining levels of pay for many workers in 1912 which came to a head in December 1912 in the so-called Knox dispute. Knox had come off duty on the afternoon of 26 October and was not to be on duty for another thirty hours. He had some tea, bread and butter and, later, he admitted to having a couple of rums with hot water between 9 p.m. and 9.40 p.m. at the Bigg Market on his way across the town centre to reach the horse-drawn bus, which ran from near the Anglican Cathedral in Newcastle over the High Level Bridge to outside the Greenesfield works. He had tried to mount the vehicle, but the conductor would not let him onto it. Two policemen tried to hustle him off the tram and he struck out at one and was promptly arrested. His case was brought before the Newcastle Magistrates Bench on 5 November. They found the evidence inconclusive from either side, but fined Knox 5s nevertheless, for being drunk, with an order to pay costs. Some witnesses within the tram related that he was unfairly handled. The whole evidence reads now as if there were faults on both sides in the incident.

Representatives of the ASRS went to talk with Raven on 22 November and he expressed his willingness to see Knox. On 29 November, Knox and John Sleigh, the Gateshead branch secretary of ASRS, had an interview with Raven at Darlington. He was not in favour of strike action. Because Knox had been found guilty, as CME, Raven felt he had to reduce Knox's position as a mainline goods engine driver of twenty-nine years experience (thirty-seven years altogether with NER) to doing duties on a pilot engine with the loss of pay of 9s per week, rather than suspending or dismissing him.

This judgement, despite Raven's blunt expression of his position, was printed in the local press on 3 December. It precipitated the strike and on 7 December 5,500 NER men left work without notice, which must have reminded Raven of the situation two years before. He was now the person with responsibility for handling it. Butterworth initially backed Raven's decision. The ASRS, joined by the GWRU officials, whipped up a process of demonisation of Raven, calling for his resignation as was reported in the local newspapers. The issue was now seen to be the right to do what one wanted when off duty rather than a safety issue. The men again shouted for the dismissal of Raven at angry meetings on 10 and 11 December. Questions were asked in the house of the Home Secretary, Reginald McKenna. He instituted a Commissioner, a London magistrate Chester Jones, to retry the case for and against Knox at a hearing on 18 December. He quashed the conviction and Knox was granted the King's Pardon.[37]

It was an expedient decision, enabling peace to be re-established immediately in the short term, so as to get the men back to work after six days' strike and reduce financial loss all round. Thus, following a Union meeting, the strike was declared over from midnight on 14 December, following Knox's reinstatement.[38] Knox comes over as having been

Horse buses waiting at the Newcastle end of High Level Bridge to travel to Gateshead, the scene of the Nichol Knox incident.

remarkably detached from the effects of the original incident in allowing the strike to happen.[39]

Nevertheless, the Union, the ASRS, had to agree that strikers should be penalised for leaving work and that the company should deal with offenders firmly.[40] It is easy to blame Raven for excessive severity, but NER was quite morally orientated and always conscious of its good name.[41] Raven's name does not appear again in industrial disputes and it is possible that Butterworth and the NER Board preferred that he did not. There is no further record of his being so personally involved in industrial relation's concerns again.

1 Geoffrey, February 1991, *The Worsdells: a Quaker Engineering Dynasty*, The Transport Publishing Co., p.159

2 Candidates circular of the Institution of Civil Engineers, 7 September 1910, p.36

3 Newman Aubrey, April 2000, 'Trains and Shelters and Ships', Paper presented at a seminar under the auspices of the Jewish Genealogical Society of Great Britain

4 Hoole Ken, 1967, *North Road Locomotive Works 1863-1966*, Roundhouse Books, p.68

5 Grafton, in *Sir Vincent Raven and the North Eastern Railway*, almost demonises Raven and fails to see that the Unions here were intent on both national and local militancy, which the workforce seemed only too willing to follow. Even if it was not always altruistic and made wrong judgements, the NER alone among 119 railway companies ploughed a lonely furrow of arbitration. Again and again, it was rewarded with industrial action for its pains. This is particularly so in the July 1910 strike over Shunter Goodchild, which Grafton (following Bagwell) does even not mention (see article in *North Eastern Express*, vol.4J, no.182, p.57-60, May 2006, by author, for further coverage of this strike). NER also continued to go through financial difficulties from 1896, so it is natural that Raven seeks to review and justify costs as the company was often in the red and he had to justify costs

6 *Daily Chronicle*, 22 July 1910

7 Taken from Harris Michael, 1973 (1994), *Gresley's Coaches: coaches built for the GNR, ECJS and LNER 1905-53*, David St John Thomas, Newton Abbott, p.125-149 (numbers given in 1973 edition do not

always correspond to later 1994 revision by this author. Presumably the latter items are the more accurate) and from Dawson John B., Forster, Colin, Mallon John F., Prattley Ron, Williamson Claire and David, 1994, *North Eastern Record* vol.2 ,North Eastern Railway Association, Chapter 2–8, p.3–65. These two books provide much information about NER carriages. However, while the carriage information from Harris is useful, the NERA book is even better and comprehensive, even if the final picture is not clear. A definitive book, linking York works and other sources of carriages, details of the carriages themselves, including their development over a half century and particularly their patterns of usage by NER and its users over the time of its existence, would be a fascinating historico-social document

8   Dawson John B.; Forster Colin; Mallon John F.; Prattley Ron, Williamson Claire; and Williamson David, 1994, *North Eastern Record* vol.2 North Eastern Railway Association. Its review of wagons is exhaustive and is the book to explore for more information but it is confusing at times, for instance total numbers of different types at any one time are difficult to deduce. Therefore even more than for carriages, a definitive book about wagons, the source of those on the NER system including private ones, their pattern of use across the whole system and beyond and their development over the years would make yet another essential and useful book

9   Nock Oswald S., 1983, *British Locomotives of the 20th Century*; vol.1, 1900–1930, Patrick Stephens, p.131 pronounced them 'successful'

10 Romans Mike, 1994, 'North Eastern Atlantics and Pacifics' (*Trains Illustrated* 93), Ian Allen, p.6,

11 Hill Geoffrey, February 1991, *The Worsdells: a Quaker Engineering Dynasty*, The Transport Publishing, p.152

12 Grafton Peter, March 1971, *Edward Thompson of the LNER*, Kestrel Books, p.17

13 Kelly's Directory for Northumberland and Durham 1876–1977

14 The name Grantly, often spelt erroneously as Grantley, shows that the Watson's were likely to be familiar with Trollope's six-volume set of novels, *Chronicles of Barsetshire*. Archdeacon Grantly and his family at times appear throughout the six novels and their name also erroneously at times gets an extra 'e' from commentators. See comment in Postscript

15 *Northern Echo*, 4 November 1910

16 This is the bridegroom's address on the marriage certificate

17 Obituary and funeral notices for L.C. and G.H. Watson, *Darlington and Stockton Times*, June 1948 and 11 August and 20 August 1949 respectively

18 *NER Magazine* vol.1, no.3, General news

19 *NER Magazine* vol.2, no.1 March 1911, general news

20 The Stephenson Locomotive Society, Jubilee (1959) Volume 1909–1959 LNER section – 'The North Eastern Railway'

21 Aves William A.T., 2000, North Eastern 4-4-0s (*Locomotives Illustrated* 132), RAS Publishing, p.7

22 Grafton Peter, March 2005, *Sir Vincent Raven and the North Eastern Railway*, Oakwood Press, p.41. He has Thompson and Stamer accompanying Raven and Merz to the US. It is unlikely that Thompson went to the USA with them, as he had moved in late 1911 to GNR at Doncaster

23   Memorandum to NER Board, from GM's Office, 8 August 1912

24 *NER Magazine*, vol.1 no.5, p.145, General news speech at Darlington Technical College in the next year (1913)

25   Hoole Ken, *The Electric Locomotives of the North Eastern Railway*, Locomotive Papers 167, Oakwood Press, p.11–15

26 Simmons Jack, 1978, *The Railway in England and Wales: Volume 1 The System and its Working*, Leicester University Press, p.258, using Irving R.J., 1976, *The North Eastern Railway Co. 1870-1914: an economic history*, Leicester University Press, p.293–99

27 *NER Magazine*, vol.1, no.12, general news

28 *NER Magazine*, vol.2, no.1, general news

29 Hoole Ken, 1967, *North Road Locomotive Works 1863–1966*, Roundhouse Books, p.33–34

30 *Dodd's Darlington Annual*, 'North Eastern Railway's New Offices in Darlington', p.19

31 Nock Oswald. S., 1954, *The Locomotives of the North Eastern Railway*, Ian Allan London, p.125

32 Based mainly on *Dodd's Darlington Annual*, 'North Eastern Railway's New Offices in Darlington', p.17/19 (additions to original text in italics inside brackets)

33 Hoole Ken, 1967, *North Road Locomotive Works 1863-1966*, Roundhouse Books, p.33

34 Bell R., 1951, *Twenty-five years of the North Eastern Railway*, Harrison and Sons Ltd, p.47-48

35 The property passed into LNER ownership becoming the LNER All-Line Operating School from 13 January 1944, then into British Rail ownership as British Railways School of Transport. This closed and training was transferred to Faverdale Hall (Stamer's former residence) in 1968. The property was then put up for sale. (*Northern Echo*, 26 July 1968)

36 *NER Magazine*, vol.2, no.6, general news

37 Knox's great nephew, John Mallon told the author at Darlington Study Centre, North Road Darlington, on 1 September 2001, that he thought that Raven had been excessively strict. He said that Knox had a highly individual rolling way of walking, which had been as a result mistaken for a drunken gait

38 Bagwell Philip S., 1963, *The Railwaymen: the History of the National Union of Railwaymen*, George Allen and Unwin. p.337-38

39 *Newcastle Daily Chronicle*, 11 December 1912

40 Irving R.J., 1976, *The North Eastern Railway Company 1870-1914: an economic history*, Leicester University Press

41 Raven was unlucky in being so involved with this case. He behaved in a characteristically open forthright way. The ensuing hub-bub was settled not because he was wrong, but because a politically neutral way out was sought. His action seems to be entirely in accord with the handling of the earlier illegal 1910 strike. The author's great-grandfather Joseph Bowes was station master at Marishes Road, near Pickering. According to his daughter – my grandmother – he was proud of having reported another employee (a guard, I think) to York for using obscene language, while on duty. It indicates the standards of behaviour expected from NER employees and how senior staff should deal with lapses

VII

DEVELOPING A CIVIC PERSONA
(1913–1914)

Raven now started to move his design-and-build team towards producing larger steam passenger mixed goods and mineral locomotives. Like Wilson Worsdell, Raven had assembled the team with whom he worked. Arthur C. Stamer was now assistant CME and George Heppell was still chief design officer and many others were involved with the design, for instance of the new class 'T2's. Much of Raven's reasoning was highlighted when he took part in a discussion on 13 January 1913 of ICE, following a paper 'Superheating Steam in Locomotives', which Henry Alfred Fowler (CME-MR) had written jointly with his chief locomotive draughtsman, now works manager, James E. Anderson, and his assistant Sanford John Symes. Fowler presented it, covering those aspects of a locomotive likely to be affected by superheating, including the effects on metal, lubrication, cylinder and valve design and maintenance. Many notables from the contemporary British railway world attended:

John Audley Frederick Aspinall (CME for L&YR)
Charles John Bowen-Cooke (CME for LNWR)
George Jackson Churchward (CME for GWR)
T. Clarkson
R.E.B. Compton
Druitt Halpin
Alfred John Hill (CME for GER)
G. Jebb
A.J. Jones
W.A. Lelean (Messrs Rendal, Palmer and Tritton, consulting engineer, especially to Indian Railways)
Loughran Pendred (later president and editor of Newcomen Society magazine)
J.J. Rosenthal
H.R. Sankey
A. Siemens
Charles Liddell Simpson, James Simpson & Co.
John William Smith, Chief Design Engineer for MR
H.A. Stenning and F.H. Trevithick (CME for Egyptian Railways)

It is interesting for future reference to note that among those who attended was one with Indian railway connections. The discussion continued on 20 and 27 January. Later, in his inaugural presidential address to the IME, Raven stated that he chose three cylinders for larger express and

2116, the first of Worsdell's class 'T' goods 0-8-0s in August 1901.

heavy freight, because of the impression made on him by the 3-cylinder 4-4-0s, designed by Walter M. Smith, NER chief draughtsmen of the time:

> It was on account of the even starting effort, given by the 120 degree cranks with a 3-cylinder engine that I was led to use it.

He found that using three high-pressure cylinders produced a more powerful torque for transmitting power to the driving wheels and hence more traction for a given adhesion weight, allowing heavier trains to be hauled and giving a better ride on the footplate. However, having three sets of cylinders with their valve gear inserted behind the running frames made for less accessibility for servicing and this remained a continuing difficulty with his locomotives.

Raven now continued with next group of locomotives, eventually 120 in number. They were again a development of a Wilson's Worsdell precursor, this time his class being 'T' 0-8-0s, Raven's becoming class 'T2'. They had the same boilers as were given to superheated class 'Z' 4-4-2s, and they steamed well under a variety of conditions, having been designed to need the minimum maintenance. Raven's class 'Y' 4-6-2T had been given three cylinders as early as October 1910. Despite it not being consistent with what he said above, these new locomotives were only given two cylinders, which may account for them not giving the smoothest rides. The drive from the gear was to the third set of driving wheels. Basically, like their earlier brothers, they were big, plain locomotives, intended to be driven hard as mineral heavy duty 'work-horses' carrying coal and ore across the steep gradients, which ran from hillside industrial sites to the seaboard in so many NER locations. Production of them started in February 1913, continuing until 1919, with thirty being built in 1913, nineteen in 1917, eight in 1918 and thirteen in 1919, all at Darlington. In addition, fifty more were built by Armstrong Whitworth at Newcastle and delivered between November 1919 and April 1921. The class was withdrawn between 1963–1968.

The next group of locomotives were class 'D' 4-4-4Ts, a wheel arrangement called 'Reading' in the USA. They were intended for lighter short-distance passenger trains. They were a rare wheel arrangement in Great Britain. Raven may read about others or even seen them when in Germany,[1] been intrigued by it and hence decided to try out for his new tanks, although his design only had two cylinders, with steam reverse and poppet safety valves instead if Ramsbottom's. The engines themselves were intended for short-distance passenger work, so replacing aging Fletcher 2-4-0s and McDonnell 4-4-0s. Despite their elegant profile and competent running over easily graded lines, their tendency to slip despite a 20-ton axle load when the line was wet did not endear them to drivers, nor did the small opening to get into the cab. They thus gained a reputation for rough riding and rolling at speed, resulting

1247, the first Raven Class 'T'2 0-8-0 in February 1913, the ubiquitous and robust mineral traffic maid of all work, seen all over the North East until the end of steam.

Class 'D' 4-4-4T, a graceful short-haul passenger tank with a noticeably narrow entrance to the cab.

in their being nicknamed 'Teddy Bears'. Forty-five in all were built: twenty authorised in 1913, built in 1913–1914, when scarcity of materials halted production during the First World War, but a further twenty-five built in 1920–1922 in Darlington. (For details see Appendix 11 – Comparative chart of Wilson Worsdell's and Raven's locomotives from 1899–1923.)

Reminiscent of earlier days in Gateshead was Raven's presence at the opening of the long-awaited new NER Railway Literary Institute in Shildon in February 1913. Designed in a suitably plain but robust restrained Queen Anne style in brown-mauve brick with stone dressings, the main building had a pediment over its main entrance, flanked by a projecting bay at each end, a design typical of NER architect William Bell. Inside there was a lecture hall for 460, and an initial library of 2,000 volumes.[2] Raven became its first president. He was on the platform for the opening ceremony with his wife, Sir Arthur F. Pease, Miss C.F. Pearce, Stamer and Mr and Mrs Ronald Worsdell, the Shildon works manager and his wife. Sir Arthur F. Pease,

Above: Shildon NER Literary Institute, designed by William Bell, opened in 1913.

Opposite: Darlington Technical College (original building).

as one of the current NER directors, performed the opening ceremony. Ronald Worsdell opened the Hall with a silver key. He also introduced a very stylish four-wheeled horsebox with an elliptical roof and upper swing doors.

Raven was now established as a man of importance in railway matters in Darlington, becoming more actively involved in the civic life of the town. This lasted beyond his official retirement in 1922. For instance, he took an active interest in Further Education. His name appears on the 1911 list of education sub-committee members for Darlington Technical College. This was also situated on North Road, further into the town at Gladstone Street and is still a striking Arts and Crafts-style building, erected in 1896. Raven became vice-chairman of its Board of Governors. He showed particular interest in being a member of the mechanical laboratory sub-committee. This had supervised the completion of a five-year project to develop a new experimental steam mechanical laboratory within the college. No doubt this, combined with his status as CME, resulted in an invitation from Alderman Edward Wooler[3] to the Annual Distribution of Prizes at the college on Wednesday 9 April 1913. He was not only to distribute the prizes, but also to declare the new laboratory officially open. The principal, Mr Scoles Hague, in presenting his report for the 1911–1912 session, remarked on the support that Raven had given to the college. Then in his address to the audience, which included Mrs Raven and Guen,[4] Hague spoke of Raven's:

> ... keen interest in the development of practical engineering education and of his great experience, he has given valuable advice in the selection and specifications of the suitable experimental machines which he had kindly inaugurated.[5]

Raven's speech in reply at this ceremony was quite lengthy. He used rather stilted and repetitious phrases as reported, but this was a keynote of his speech. The speech provides useful insights on how he viewed contemporary technical education and the place of the railway engineer in the advancement of practical science.

Mr Vincent Raven was warmly received and said they all knew he had the subject of education deeply at heart and for that reason he was extremely pleased to accept the invitation of the committee to distribute prizes that night. As a mechanical engineer, he felt he could talk to them on that branch of education with the greater confidence than others, and he had no hesitation in saying that those people who had decided to make it their study in life had before them a field so wide and far reaching, with infinite possibilities that they would never regret having entered upon it, nor complain of the monotony of the course. No science had advanced more rapidly than that of the mechanical engineer, and the difficulty was in that particular branch they should specialise, and how qualify themselves to be able to deal with it and rise to the highest position in the particular line they might elect to take up.

Becoming more fluent in his expression, he addressed the pupils' duty to be motivated and to contribute to their own learning and career development, no doubt harkening back to own formative experience at home, at Aldenham School and his apprenticeship under Fletcher and his subsequent rise through in his chosen profession.

None of them should be satisfied unless they were able to attain a position of responsibility in the path of life that had chosen to pursue, but it was indeed impossible for them to rise to easy eminence unless in early youth they considered certain qualifications which were indispensable to progress, and foremost among them were perseverance, moderation, and thoroughness. The mechanical engineer to learn his profession in the most thorough manner must have theoretical and practical training, and how they should be combined had been a matter of serious consideration for some time for many eminent and qualified engineers, and he did not know that any definite conclusion had been arrived at. But the opportunity for education of the engineer in this country had in recent years been so greatly improved that the problem did not seem so difficult to solve today as it once was. They had now a number of high-class technical schools, such as that in Darlington, in which they were enabled to learn theory in such a way as to have illustrated in the mechanical laboratory where the student might be encouraged to take a real interest in the subject being taught. He went on in an admonishing way to draw attention to a wider view of learning both from the pupil's and teacher's points of view. He struck a mildly jingoistic note, seeing a need to keep England and its students of engineering in the forefront of scientific progress:

England was for many years far behind other countries in its teaching of mechanical engineering. America and Germany were a long way ahead. Raven had had the opportunity of seeing their engineering colleges, which were so laid out and designed as to make the studies really pleasurable and interesting and over there it was the fashion to work. They all knew how insinuating it was to be in the fashion, he went on − if it was in the fashion to work they did it, and if it was in the fashion to play, they did that also, and the best of them did either or the other well. He had nothing to say against play, but it was the easiest fashion to follow, and he thought all youth would follow it more or less. But it is a good thing to work, and to do it well. They must have it put to them in such a way as to interest them thoroughly − and they had no excuse in Darlington in that direction. In these days of international rivalry, when all nations were anxious to be superior to each other, it behoved them to be among the first in the great race for mechanical knowledge.

This last sentence seems to presage the European conflict to come in 1914 − and to which Raven would contribute in his own way. He now unfolded local achievements, with some pride, and sought to place what he himself had done in context:

The introduction of steam and railway locomotives was the first real beginning of mechanical engineering less than one hundred ago, and did not that begin in Darlington? Therefore, the young men of that college with their engineering traditions with their schools and works around, having every opportunity of learning thoroughly the profession of mechanical engineering with its theory and practice combined, had no excuse that they should not become, as he had no doubt many of them would become known men in the engineering world of the future.

He then moved on to one of his pet topics − compounding and superheating − discussing their benefits. How much the audience understood of the technicalities he related is open to conjecture, but the conclusions he drew from the arguments which he put forward were clearly stated. In a sense it was a summary of what he set out to achieve with steam. The lessons in practical economics learnt from Gibbs and Geddes had not been lost on him.

As a railway engineer, he might perhaps have been expected to say a few words about a locomotive, that most interesting machine which had done its full share in assisting the great advancement going on throughout the world in the past century. There were many ways in which the locomotive had been improved, such as increased pressure being used, compounding, and the like. Compounding in a locomotive had always had drawbacks as condensors could not be used owing to the limitations of space, and to his mind compounding had never been a true success. He felt compounding in the locomotive should never be indulged in unless there is a clear and distinct advantage. An increased number of high-pressed cylinders were then used in locomotives − either three or four − with great success. They gave increased steadiness, and a better timing movement. In those days of high speeds and heavy engines, he explained, this was most important, both as regards the machine itself and the track on which it runs. The greatest improvement of that era, no doubt, he said, was the superheating of the steam locomotive. In 1911, they designed and built on the North Eastern Railway twenty express engines for working the mainline expresses between York and Edinburgh, having three high-pressed cylinders. Ten were ordinary engines with 180lb pressure and cylinders of 15²in, and ten were superheated with cylinders 16²in and 160lb pressure. In every other way, they were similar. The average coal consumption for 1912 for the non-superheated was 47.8lb per mile and for superheated 38lb per mile, which showed a saving of 9.8lb or 20 per cent. This, in those days of increasing coal bills, was of utmost importance, and then they found the cost of boiler repairs would be much less due to decreased pressure in the boiler. He had good reason to be satisfied with the superheated engines, and they were extending the practice with regard to both new engines and those re-boilered where possible.

Raven concluded with a personal view about the improvement of steam locomotives and a short, but far-sighted section praising the use of the electric locomotive as a means of traction:

> They could not prophesy the future of steam locomotive, but it was certain that it had a keen competitor in the electric, which would run it a hard race in the future. It was more a question of cost at which they could generate and transport electricity as to how soon the electric locomotive came into general use than the difficulties with regard to the locomotive itself. In itself it had everything to recommend it. Its driving motion was rotary, and it could in less space have a much more powerful machine than with the steam locomotive. It is interesting to know that hereon the North Eastern Railway and practically in the very part of it where the steam locomotive first ran, the electric locomotive would be the first in England to work heavy mineral traffic and that in Darlington shops, these locomotives would be built, and therefore they would see the locomotive on the North Eastern Railway was no means standing still.[6]

Its day in the British Isles was not to be in his lifetime, but fifty years later, he said; he probably did not realise how prophetic his vision of the future use of electricity would be as a propulsive force of the modern railway. He was merely informing his audience, and the Press who reported it, of the innovatory nature of his immediate plans.

More explicitly, now that the Board, via Butterworth, had given approval, Raven's next project was the electrification of the fifteen-mile line from Newport (the 'Erimus')[7] yard on the Tees at Middlesbrough) to Shildon, a line that ran over the main Darlington to Newcastle line without a direct connection. He justified his arguments over the expense incurred by indicating the economies to be effected by running electric locomotives. The 1,500v dc would be supplied using double copper wires to ensure good contact, supported by overhead gantries, and placed at intervals of 300ft (later intermediate supports had to be put in, because of the prevailing winds from the Pennines across the fairly exposed terrain). There were sub-stations at Preston near Aycliffe and at 'Erimus', supplied by the Cleveland and Durham Electric Power Co. (again another company closely associated with M&M and NESCO and bought out by them in 1917). The current was picked up by pantographs, placed on the roof of the locomotive. 6 June 1913 marked the date for the inauguration of the line, (the first system in the United Kingdom to use electric locomotives and the world, boasted erroneously the NER).[8][9] In fact, a development started in 1907 on goods control to bring a large area of goods traffic in the Teeside area under telephonic control at Newport; this completed in November 1910. Part of this plan covered the project as far as Bowesfield Junction, ready for the improved haulage times and loads, due to electrification, from the South Durham coalfield. It would put some of the new facilities to good use.[10]

Delayed by the outbreak of war, once the overhead wiring had been transferred from Siemens-Schukert to British Insulation and Helsby Cable Co. Ltd, the line was opened in stages. The first of the batch of locomotives, No.3, opened the section from Shildon to Bowesfield Junction (Stockton) opened on 1 July 1915, Shildon to Middridge Sidings on 30 October and from Bowesfield to Erimus on 12 November, the whole length to Newport East being finally opened on 1 January 1916. Raven's role in seeing it transformed into a working railway was cut short by his call to Woolwich Arsenal. The capable Stamer supplied the necessary supervision of the project, during 1915-1919 while Raven was away.

The ten electric goods locomotives were built in 1914 at Darlington, with electrical equipment supplied by Siemens, and were numbered 3 to 12. They were capable of hauling a 1,400-ton train at 25mph. While there was coal to haul, they fulfilled their purpose. However, the 1921 coal strike was the beginning of the end. The industrial strife of the 1920s made things worse and the markets receded. Without hope of further electrification to which the ten locomotives could be decanted should the line close, and with the system needing renewal

No.3, one of the neatly symmetrical axle-driven electric Bo-Bos for the Shildon–Newport line. Note the spacious cab, when compared to contemporary steam locomotive.

by the 1930s, the locomotives were mothballed in 1935, after being considered for conversion to diesel-electric propulsion. They were totally scrapped in 1950.

Wheel arrangement:	Bo-Bo
Wheelbase:	27ft
Driving wheel diameter:	4ft
Locomotive length:	39ft 4in
Locomotive weight:	74 tons 8 cwt
Maximum axle load:	19 tons
Current:	1.5 kv dc overhead
No. and power of engines:	275hp per axle (4)
Maximum speed:	40mph
Tractive effort:	1100hp (28800lb)

Both his sons followed their father into the emerging field of railway technology. Norman, the elder son like his father, joined the railway on leaving Darlington Grammar School. His interest, like his father, was in electrical engineering.) His father had come to know GNR engineers as working colleagues from meetings at IMechE sessions and over consultations about East Coast Joint Stock especially from 1904 onwards.

Norman became a life-long friend of Edward Thompson. They could have encountered one another as a result of Thompson's meeting the Ravens socially and visiting their home. Norman then went into the steel industry. He became an AMIEE in 1913, giving a *poste restante* address at Royal Golf Club, Sandringham, Victoria, Australia.[11] He later worked for Merz and McLellan as an electrical engineer, working on his father's new electric express passenger locomotive. His AMIEE lapsed in the 1921–1913 period. He continued to remain very friendly with Thompson and provided him with much support after his sister died.

Raven's younger son, Frederick Gifford, after a period at The Mount Boarding School in Northallerton,[12] followed his father more directly into railway work. Probably apprenticed in

Britain, he went to Brazil, probably with one of the British-owned companies, such as the metre-gauge Leopoldina Co. He did not attend Guen's marriage in 1913. He had moved on to India, working for North Western Railway in 1914 as area locomotive superintendent, based between Lahore and Karachi at the Muslim pilgrimage town of Multan in the middle of the rather arid Punjabi plain.[13]

Another part of the NER's perceived, if rather paternalistic, relationship with their workforce was to give patronage to out-of-work-hours recreational services, including providing sports facilities and buying instruments for the NER Brass Band at Darlington. A good example was the start, on 7 March, of the Darlington Railway Athletic Club with Raven as its president, Arthur C. Stamer its chairman and J.G. Crosby its secretary. Its rules were passed and three sections were set up, for cricket, for tennis and for bowls.[14]

In April 1913, Raven was asked to provide a plate wagon for NER, because of the need to transport boiler parts of 13ft 2in diameter, which exceeded the loading gauge, if transported whole. By putting sections on their sides on a wagon up to 19ft long, he was able to overcome the difficulty with a minimum of outlay. Raven was re-elected as Gateshead NER Literary Institute's president and treasurer on 16 May at its fifty-sixth AGM and the next month became involved with a new staff enterprise.

The Railway Athletic Ground for use by the NER Athletic Club was officially opened on 7 June 1913 at Hopetown, close to North Road Station. Stamer sported cricket clothes and Thompson wore a blazer; Stamer also wore a striped cap and Guen wore a straw hat and white dress. Other wives and sisters, including Mrs Raven, were among the ladies present:

> The place was decidedly 'en fête'. A lively wind thrashed the lordly flags, making a brave show of coloured devices against the new green of the trees. Someone pointed out the new pavilion, which seemed to have been placed by some gentleman out of the 'Arabian Nights'. It was an amazing apparition in brown and red, and the perfectly mown field stretching up to it only heightened the effect.

Built in the form of a triangle, the pavilion serves the joint purpose of providing accommodation for cricketers and tennis and bowls players, one side facing the cricket pitch and the other facing the tennis courts. It is a one-storey building surrounded on the two 'front' sides with a veranda.

The grounds for the two latter were not ready for play, the tennis courts being scheduled for use by the end of the year, the bowling green for the next season. There were a number of guests and officials. Besides Raven, Mrs Raven, Guen, Thompson and Stamer, there were one of the NER directors, A.F. Pease, R.G. Suggett, R.W. Worsdell, Herbert Nigel Gresley, now GNR-CME, and Henry Angus Watson. Raven presided, while Sir Arthur Francis Pease performed the opening ceremony. Raven, in his address, introduced Pease, after he praised 'the excellence of the ground. He felt sure they were all proud of the new ground.

He concluded on a slightly churlish note, saying the railway company had given them all the advantages of the ground, free of cost and, therefore, it would be their own fault if the club did not make it a thorough success and to the benefit of the railway men at Darlington.

After declaring the ground open, Pease said that they must all be indebted to Mr Raven and Mr Stamer, and they also had to thank the chairman of NER for giving them so much ground. They had for many years been working with the Great Northern Railway in running the grand service of the East Coast Route, and they would be glad to know that they had with them that day Mr Greasley (sic), representing the Great Northern Co., and a Great Northern team from Doncaster. He hoped they would spend many happy hours on the new ground.

Gresley proposed a vote of thanks, saying that next year he hoped that Doncaster would be able to entertain a team from Darlington on a new ground they were hoping to have at Doncaster.

This was seconded by Mr Whitton. There was a cricket match to close the proceedings between the NER team and the GNR team from Doncaster. The home team (Railway Athletic XI) won by 115 runs (Stamer, a well-known local cricketer scoring 8 not out) to 95 (Edward Thompson being bowled out for 2) from Doncaster XI, a gratifying result for the NER eleven. During the whole match, the NER Brass Band, under the conductorship of Mr G.A. Williams, played selections.[15][16] Raven did not the meeting of ARLE on 12 June, but sent a letter about shop staff wearing protective glasses. Our shop men would object, but if suitable glasses were available would be of great benefit, he writes. Unfortunately, no record is made of whether any were purchased of used. He is obviously concerned about their health and safety.[17]

Later in the month, on 25 June, Thomson returned to Darlington to marry Guen. Thompson was already living in what was to be the marital home, Litchfield (Raven's middle name as well as his paternal grandmother's surname), Thorne Road, Doncaster. She married him at the Holy Trinity C/E church, Woodland Road, Darlington, about 500 yards from Grantly. It was built in 1838 by Anthony Salvin, in a plain, if spacious, Early English style with a square tower, with a spirelet at its eastern corner.

For her wedding, Guen wore a gown of ivory charmeuse, one side of the corsage being draped with charmeuse, the other side and the long sleeve of Limerick lace finished with tiny seed pearls. The waist band had long sash cords beaded with white beaded trimming. The skirt was beautifully draped with lace on a train of charmeuse. The bride also wore a veil of Limerick lace with a chaplet of orange blossom leaves, finished at the side with a cluster of blossom. Her ornaments were a diamond heart and diamond and pearl rings, the gift of the bridegroom.

Furthermore:

> ... the bridal gown, veil, trousseau frocks, opera cloak, fur coat, and gown worn by the bride's mother were designed and made by Fenwicks of Newcastle.

The men of the party wore top hats and tails. Her father gave the bride away and her brother Norman was best man. Father and son signed the marriage register as witnesses. (Frederick did not seem to be there; it is possible he was still in India.) Master John Parker was the page and there were four bridesmaids, Misses Jean and Betty Johnson(e) (probably daughters of Thompson's sister Catherine), Isabel Jeffrey and nine-year-old Violet Gresley (daughter of Gresley, later married to the son of the musical family of Godfrey). This was quite to be expected as Gresley was Thompson's superior. (He was present, too.) Norman was the best man and her older sister, Mrs Constance Watson, was there. Frederick was probably still in India.[18]

The wedding service was celebrated by Revd Thomas Peacock, assisted by Revd H. Mackenzie, as for Constance's wedding, three years before. The hymns chosen were the old favourite for weddings, 'O perfect love' and 'May the grace of Christ' (the last hymn in *Hymns Ancient and Modern*). The 'Bridal March' from Wagner's *Lohengrin* provided the recessional rather than the processional.

Here, the similarities and changes with Constance's marriage in 1910 make for some interesting comparisons. There was an equally long list of presents, similar to that of Constance and her husband; this included a lot of silverware, crockery, linen and older furniture. It is interesting to note the same members of the Raven family were in sufficient contact to send gifts, but which now included Miss A. Raven, possibly his older sister, born in 1854. The gifts from the Crichtons were much the same as were the associates of Raven's and the NER, but the Thompson's circle now included associates from GNR and gifts from his immediate superior Gresley and his children, but not Gresley's wife. Raven continued to have a congenial relationship with Nigel Gresley, developed over the last decade through contact initially with ECJS and later working as CME's for their respective companies as well as more socially

Edward Thompson, Raven's son-in-law, later CME for LNER.

Raven's daughter, Guen.

Holy Trinity C/E church, Woodlands Road, Darlington, where Guen and Edward Thompson were married.

through their professional relationship with Edward Thompson. Joint professional interests no doubt developed the relationships on a more personal level. The correspondence and later contacts at meetings between Raven and Gresley reveal a mutual respect for the other's opinions. Such events as the opening of the Athletic club and Guen's wedding reinforced their friendship. Following the reception at Grantly, the couple went to honeymoon in Switzerland, returning to take up residence at Litchfield, Thorne Road, Doncaster, on the same road as the Gresleys. Thompson at this stage would seem to be on amicable terms with Gresley.

Figures reveal the importance of mineral traffic and increasingly goods (hence the need for mixed traffic locomotives), over passenger, which despite local electric transport and the threat of petrol engine were maintained as shown in returns of pence per train mile from 1900 to 1912.

Goods	40–125
Mineral	80–160
Passenger	40–40

Raven occupied the chair on 6 February 1914 at the thirteenth annual staff dinner of the CME Department, which had ninety guests. There were toasts to NER and the chairman by acting vice-chairmen S.W. Bullen, after which George Heppel proposed one for the acting vice-chairman. Musical entertainment was provided by seven staff members.[19] However, Raven was not present when Stamer presided at the AGM of Athletic Club on 2 March[20] nor on 28 November at the first annual dinner of the Athletic Club (which doubled as the fifty-second annual dinner of the North Road NER Institute) at the Alma Hotel, Cockerton, where he and the vice-president were toasted.

Since becoming CME, Raven had become more actively involved with the development of rolling stock, showing what a stickler for detail he was. For instance, when he and Gresley both made proposals for ECJS or joint NE/GN stock, he made a detailed analysis of Gresley's proposals compared with his own, justifying the reasons for his choice, e.g. that toilet space in ECJS corridor stock should become more spacious. About this time, two dynamometer cars, one from NER and one from GWR, were borrowed by Gresley to carry out rolling stock tests. Gresley found differences between the cars and asked Raven to check them. He found that the GWR produced more erratic records, because the distance recorder was 2¾ yards per mile in error and the main spring and integrator produced defective results.[21] The contact with Gresley was again made.

On a more domestic note, Raven's first grandchild was born to Constance and George on 15 October 1914 at Oakdene Terrace, the next address after 20 Victoria Road, with Connie's *Alma Mater*, Polam School, across the road. In the Thompson's visitors' book, Thompson's father and mother came to stay, for instance, from 5 to 7 August and the Ravens from 23 October to 3 November 1914.[22] It is likely that Raven's visit to Doncaster may have been to consult about matters of joint concern with Gresley, such as the refurbishment of the joint East Coast stock, the design that Raven made in 1914 for all steel kitchen cars for the *Flying Scotsman* set as a measure to fireproof the carriages, as they used gas for cooking as it was difficult to procure an adequate supply of current for electrical cookers.[23] The GNR influence is lessened by the rounded end of the coaches, full-length eaves panel and glass ventilators which are of NER provenance.[24][25] He probably took the opportunity of combining visits to his daughter and son-in-law with business.

1 E.G. Barker introduced his 4-4-4 tank as early as 1896 for Wirral Railway, but Raven's interest in the wheel arrangement may have resulted from Kuhn bringing out his 3-cylinder compound 4-4-4 in 1902-1903 for Preussiche Staatsbahn. It had two cabs, a front facing one and a second cab over the buffer beam, which gave it a look of a hybrid steam/diesel

2 *NER Magazine*, March 1913, vol.3, no.3

3 Invitation in Darlington Library File on Alderman Wooler, April 1913, p.27

4 Darlington Library File on Alderman Wooler says 'one of his daughters'

5 Darlington Library File on Alderman Wooler, April 1913, p.27

6 Darlington Library file on Alderman Wooller, April 1913, p.27

7 Erimus – 'we will be' is the motto of Middlesbrough

8 Drew Paul, 1975, 'The North Eastern Railway' (*Trains Illustrated* 15), Ian Allan, p.10

9 *NER Magazine*, 16 February 1913, vol.3, no.2, p.127-29

10 Burt Philip, 1926, *Control on the Railways, a study in method*, Unwin Brothers Ltd, p.95-96l3, Thacker's Directory of India, 1915

11 This golf club has no record of his staying there, although the IEE give that address when he became AMIEE, was he 'down under' for work (Melbourne electrification) or for pleasure or both?

12 He was a pupil there in the 1901 Census

13 Thacker's Directory for India, 1915

14 *NER Magazine*, March 1913, vol.3, no.3

15 *NER Magazine*, June, vol.3, no.6

16 *Northern Echo*, 9 June 1913, p.8

17 Minutes of ARLE, 13 June 1913

18 This is most likely to be Raven's brother and his wife, as there is no mention of his son Frederick Gifford having a wife on the war grave notice as there was later with that of Raven's grandson, Michael Watson

19 *NER Magazine*, vol.4, no.37, p.61

20 *NER Magazine*, vol.5, no.39, p.74

21 Gresley Herbert Nigel, Letter to George Jackson Churchward, 7 April 1914, Boxtest/test 4, NRM, York

22 All these dates derive from the Thompson's guest book entries. The one for the Ravens may indicate either one day visits or a period of stay as Raven made the first entry and his wife the

second later one. On 5 December 1914 and 6 February 1915, E. Bradley Kitson was there and on 6 February. Hubert R. Kitson called

23 Harris Michael, 1994, *LNER Carriages*, David St John Thomas, p.13
24 Jenkinson David, 1988, *British Railway Carriages of the 20th Century Volume 1: the end of an era 1901–22*, Patrick Stephens, p.120
25 Ibid

VIII

WAR EFFORT AND KNIGHTHOOD (1914–1918)

The Government declared war on Germany on 4 August 1914:

> ... one of the world's most fateful dates. The decision taken on that day in the name and on behalf of the British Empire altered the destiny of Europe. It is not too much to say that it gave a different turn or direction to the advance of the human race. The trumpets of war had already sounded in the East and in the West, and colossal armies were hurrying to the slaughter. Millions of men were either on the march or strapping on their armour for the conflict, and roads and railway tracks trembled with the weight of guns and munitions and all the sinister devices and mechanisms of human destruction.

The war would indeed alter Raven's life. Almost without realising it, he was being drawn into the war effort.[2] He would over the next year move to a different sphere of work. Furthermore, both his son and son-in-law would be affected in different ways. The day after the declaration of war, the railways were nationalised in all but name. They were now organised and managed through the Railway Executive Committee which had been formed for the purpose in April 1914 in its attempt to standardise the running of the rail network as national whole.

The committee had a nominal chairman, Herbert Ascombe Walker from LSWR, with War Office representatives comprising:

John Audley Frederick Aspinall CME	LYR
Sir Alexander Kaye Butterworth GM	NER
C.H. Dent	GNR
Sir Francis H. Dent, director	South East & Chatham Joint Committee
Sir Sam Fay GM	GCR
Sir Guy Granet	MR
Donald A. Matheson	Caledonian Railway
F. Potter,	Divisional Superintendent GWR
Sir Robert Turnbull, director	LNWR

They recommended that individual company's revenue, wagons and their coverings were to be put into a 'pool', while rivalries for custom between companies were to be suspended.[3] Raven sat on the War Maufacturers' sub-committee, which had GM and War Office representatives (he was replaced by Stamer, once he went to Woolwich).

This call to co-operation was to be made even clearer in October by Walter Runciman, president of the Board of Trade, to Guy Calthorp (GM–LNWR). He contacted his colleague,

CME – LNWR C.J. Bowen-Cooke (who knew Sir Frederick Donaldson, the head of Woolwich Arsenal, who had immediately preceded Raven in his post there). Drawings were produced at a meeting held at the Railway Clearing House, of equipment that was most urgently needed. The outcome was an urgent call for arms, a call which was answered by some of the railways. The CMEs of the various railway companies, including Raven, met to discuss the matter in order to produce a report about what jobs could be tackled by the railways. It was held at the Drawing Office for the Railway Clearing House on 20 October 1914. Those present included:

> Raven
> Charles John Bowen-Cooke (CME to LNWR)
> George Jackson Churchward (CME to GWR)
> Henry Fowler (CME to MR)
> Herbert Nigel Gresley (CME to GNR)
> Hughes (CME to LYR)

It was noted what was required and they agreed to assess what could be done in their own shops. Much effort was diverted from locomotive building as the major output of North Road Works into producing armaments, once a new machine shop was built for the Darlington National Projectile Factory, which was set up in 1915 at a cost of £40,610 15s 9d.

This was built at government expense but managed by the NER on the understanding that at the end of the war it would be taken over by the NER together with such of the fixed plant and machinery as would be useful for railway engineering purposes. Staffed by more than 1,000 women and girls, this factory produced more than 12 million shells and repaired more than 2 million cartridge cases.[4]

Similarly, Thomas Putnam's Darlington Forge was turned over to gun manufacture, also employing 1,000 people.

Meanwhile, back home in Darlington, Raven had become a grandfather. Mary Gifford Watson was born on 15 October at Oakdene Avenue, Darlington. Connie's father-in-law, George Newby Watson, became ill in July 1914, while staying at Southsea, Portsmouth, no doubt staying with his daughter and her husband, now vicar of St Simon's there. He died on 21 November without seeing his newly born granddaughter. He was brought back to Darlington for burial. The funeral service took place at Holy Trinity, Woodland Road, on 25 November. Revd Leonard B. Ashby, Watson's son-in-law, and the incumbent of Holy Trinity, Revd F. Peacock, conducted the service. The family mourners included his son and daughter-in-law, but no other member of the Raven family. It was noted there were a number of wreaths,[5] no doubt including theirs.

From now onwards, the *NER Magazine* begins to reflect the effects of the war in its pages from November 1914 onwards and always gives the first pages, prior to the more usual 'civilian' matters. NER had even raised its own battalion, as part of the Northumberland Fusiliers. By 1 June 1915, it had raised 7,153 men. The monthly figures were issued with details from which NER department they came. More sadly, there are accounts of the wounded and dead recorded, too. By running 'coal specials', it also contributed in another way to the war effort.

At the meeting of the IMechE on 18 December, a series of papers were read on audible and other cab signals on British railways:

> 'Audible Signalling on Railway Trains in Motion' by W.C. Acfield, Signalling Superintendent, MR;
> 'Automatic Signalling in Trains' by Leon P. Lewis, of Signalling Office, CR;
> 'Electrical System of Cab Signalling' by Raven, which was read by J. Pigg in Raven's absence;
> 'Signalling on Railway Trains in London' by W. Willcox, Engineer, Metropolitan Railway and finally,

'Combined Automatic Train Control System in use on the Great Western Railway of England' by W.A. Stanier, GWR.

Raven's paper covered much of the earlier ground described in Chapter III on electrical signalling. Mr Pigg joined the discussion afterwards, and in the correspondence afterwards, Raven added pertinent comments of his own. Possibly this paper was meant to support Raven's nomination to the committee of IMechE on 22 January 1915 at IMechE HQ. He was elected to it at the February meeting, then re-elected to the post each year until 1920.

In the next year, Raven decided to enter local politics as a local councillor, standing for West Ward where he lived, when Councillor John Widdowfield retired after nearly thirty years of service and became an Alderman of the Borough. Raven was a good choice for nominee for the vacancy, representing the borough's largest employer and contributor to the local rates, NER with all its various undertakings. At this time, candidates were chosen on their merits as citizens and the potential in running a self-governing borough, not on party political lines. As he pointed out in his short manifesto, he had lived years in Darlington and had worked only for NER, but was also on various committees to improve the borough and its facilities. He addressed a meeting at the Mechanics Institute in early March, saying he had lived in Darlington for twenty-two years.[6] After polling on 12 March at the Mechanics Institute, he was returned as councillor by 458 votes over the other contestant, which has greeted with relief in one letter to the editor. (The result was Raven – 668, Rennison – 210.) In his post-polling address, he said he hoped he would merit a continuance of the support and confidence of the burgesses in the future.[7]

Raven addressed a meeting of his election supporters on 20 March in much warmer terms than his acceptance speech. As there was to be another election on 2 April, Raven, wishing to continue to stand as councillor, said he could not claim the experience of the other two candidates. During the short period he had been a member of the council he had attended one meeting and two committees. He had not changed much since a fortnight ago, when had expressed confidence in him and he had not had time to misbehave. This was greeted with laughter. He felt that an election like that could not be carried through successfully without enthusiastic workers. He thanked them for the support they had given them and he hoped that they would repeat that support and so use their votes.[8] The election result on 2 April was:

Major B.G.D. Briggs	– 976
V.L. Raven	– 972
C.H. Leach	– 781
S. Willotts (not elected)	– 123

The three higher scoring candidates were duly elected. As a result of his election, he became a member of the Town Council's Committee for Tramways, which had been purchased by the council as a municipal service in January 1902 from privately owned Imperial Tramways Co. Ltd on the move from horse to electric traction. He also served on Committee for Electricity and Gas Undertakings provided by the council; electricity had been generated from 1900, while gas supplied two thirds of household in the borough.

In April 1915, the Railway Operating Department (ROD) of the Royal Engineers (RE) was created at the request of the War Office. Men were sent first to Longmoor for equipment and a short military training, before being dispatched with as little delay as possible. The Department was under Col. Leopold Cecil Paget. It was extremely likely that Raven's son, Frederick, was recruited in this way during 1915–1916.

Probably aware he had to appear at local functions now that he was a local councillor, he appeared at NER Assembly Rooms meeting on 21 April. On 8 May, he declared the Rifle Range of the Shooting Club Section of Darlington Railway Athletic Club officially

David Lloyd-George, Minister of
Munitions.

open. Although Raven enjoyed shooting, he did not participate in any of the clubs shooting matches. Perhaps it was too *infra dig* for a CME to do so.[9] Then, on 5 June, the 11th Yorkshire Regiment (The Green Howards) visited Darlington Railway Athletic Ground, where there was cricket, quoits and shooting. Raven, his wife, Stamer and his wife were all there. Lt-Col. Aspinall headed the military party.

> The tennis courts were kept going in full swing and on the croquet lawn one saw soldiers seeking in this decidedly quiet pastime relaxation from their strenuous physical efforts. Music was provided by the NER Prize Brass Band under the baton of G.A. Williams and the Fife and Bugle Band of the 11th Yorkshire under Drum Major Lawley. THe Athletic Club was successful in all games, with the exception of quoiting, where the soldiers showed their superior strength and staying abilities.[10]

Raven's last design-and-build effort before leaving Darlington was the six-wheeled self-trimming tender, which was capable of holding 52 tons of coal and 4,125 gallons of water and which was self-trimming, that is:

> By inclining the sides and back plate of the coal space the vibration of a tender when running induced the coal to move down the slopes and thus continually drift to wards the shovelling plate.

Sir Eric Geddes, Civilian
First Lord of Admiralty, first
Minister of Transport.

This was introduced on 17 September 1915. After the war, it would be attached to Raven's new class 'T3', 'S3' and *Pacific* locomotives. At York in 1915 two 45ft bogie Carriage Carrying Trucks (CUT) were built with elliptical roofs and matchboard sides, followed by three more in 1923. In 1917, there followed a four-wheeled version, 21ft 5in long, when four were built, six more in 192, five more in 1922 and one more in 1923. Both the designs were followed by the LNER, who built forty more of the former and four more of the latter.

The Ministry of Munitions had been set up in April 1915 with Lloyd George as its Minister, working under Lord Kitchener as Secretary of State for War with King George V's active backing. Sir Frederic Donaldson, the previous post holder, was also a railway man and a member of IMechE had resigned to become Chief Technical Advisor to the Ministry. Raven may well have been proposed as his successor in this wartime post at the Ministry of Munitions because of and as a result of efforts with munitions being made in Darlington North Road Works, the positive outcomes of the meeting held the previous year at the Board of Trade and his being known to Eric Geddes and recommended by him to Lloyd George.

The NER Board allowed Raven to be seconded to the Ministry of Munitions on full pay, but he still remained in overall control of CME's office, as various details reveal in correspondence. He even continued some civic duties, becoming a Justice of the Peace in Darlington in 1917.

From 15 September 1915, Raven was chief superintendent to the Royal Ordnance Works at Woolwich, now under the aegis of the War Office. Dating from Henry VIII's time, The Royal Arsenal had become a vast series of brass foundries and workshops, surrounded since the French Revolution by a stone wall 20ft high and twenty-two miles long. During the First World War, it employed 88,000 people, covered 1,350 acres and even had 150 miles of its own railway system. Raven wrote to Alderman Wooller saying he regretted being called away on war work, but he was helping the war effort by managing the supply of munitions. He indicated that he would stay a member of West Word, nonetheless.

Raven's responsibilities were for the more efficient production of munitions, the supply of which was lagging behind the Army's needs. He must have had accommodation in or near the Arsenal, but also travelled back north frequently enough when the need arose. He set about reorganising things so well that Lloyd George wrote in his War Memoirs:

> I appointed in his place Mr Vincent Raven, of the London and North Eastern Railway (*sic*), and his quickening influence was soon felt throughout Arsenal and resulted in an increased production of completed shell.[11]

Furthermore, he paid him a national tribute in the House of Commons on 20 December 1915 when he reported to the House of Commons in his capacity as Minister of Munitions that:

> Sir Frederick Donaldson, the distinguished engineer who is at the head of Woolwich, has gone to America and Canada, and helped us to organise new sources of supply there and has rendered very great service to us. The engineer of the North Eastern Railway Company (Mr Vincent Raven) was placed at our disposal, and he is in temporary control, and the services which he had rendered them have been conspicuous. I will give an illustration. The manufacture and filling output of various articles has increased since he took it in hand, in some cases by 60 per cent, in others by as much as 80 per cent, whereas the staff has only increased by 23 per cent. One of the things he initiated was a statistical record of output. That is having, and will continue to have, a potent effect nor only upon the output, but upon the cost of output. As an illustration of the use to which figures can be put I will mention that when the output of a certain shop or section of a shop is noted the following morning it is possible for the superintendent, or the works manager immediately to put his finger upon the fact that perhaps the flow of raw material fails, or that owing to congestion of the Arsenal railway, the output cannot be got rid of, and the cause of the inefficiency of the machinery can be checked... Such hitches in the daily work of a factory can be avoided and minimised by a most complete system of statistical control and that has been instituted at Woolwich.

It is likely that he was also responsible for the loan of four of NER's 0-4-0Ts to help with the increased traffic at the Arsenal. The munitions manufactured had to stored and were taken a few miles south to the 8,000-year-old extensive cave network at Chislehurst, which had its own narrow-gauge railway and electric light supply installed. A remarkable effort was made by women workers at Arsenal, where at cost to their health, they proved more reliable than men, who could be unpunctual often due to drink. This remarkable use of women as a workforce is reflected in the poster, setting out women's condition for work with NER, issued in his name on 16 March 1916, where he sets out regulations for women in the Shell Shop at Darlington.

The British involvement in the Balkan 'arena' in the First World War is not well known. The defeat of the Allies at Gallipoli from March 1915 onwards until the final retreat in January 1916 meant the south-eastern portions remained in Axis hands for most of the rest of the war. Here Raven's remit was peripheral. He was responsible for the provision of smoke cones, presumably important in the strategic retreat from Anzac, Suvla Bay and Helles from 8 December to 9 January. If the Allies had been successful in Gallipoli, Serbia and Macedonia would have not been so quickly lost to the Axis Powers in October 1915 and Allied support of Serbian efforts to keep Danube and its hinterland out of Axis control would have been more successful. Raven's distant contribution to this campaign was to provide boot repairing machinery for troops in Thessalonika during the severe winter snowstorms of 1915–1916 and to provide hay baling machines presumably for horse feed; in Serbia much of the supplies of armament were drawn by horses to the battle lines, not by rail as on the European Front.

On a more professional note, Raven was re-elected in February 1916 to IMechE, where he was noted as being at Woolwich. During 1916, Edward Thompson joined him before going off as director of transportation to the troops in France. Back at the NER, Lord Knaresborough, chairman of NER Board, after paying tribute to the late chairman, Lord Ridley, noted that the company's workshops were producing a large quantity of ammunition for the Government, largely exceeding the original estimate.

In Darlington, meanwhile, Raven was re-elected president of the First AGM of the NER Athletic Club on 9 March and at the NER Assembly Rooms Annual Meeting. (He was noted as being at the Ministry of Munitions.) Similarly, the AGM of the Gateshead NER Literary Institute on 31 March 1916 summed it up in a tribute to members who were serving the king in either a civil or military capacity.

During Raven's absences from NER, the ever reliable Stamer carried on as acting CME at Darlington (as well as acting president of the Athletic Club), but Raven remained its president until 1923, when Stamer took this over. Stamer was well-liked by the workmen, having the ability to see their point of view as well as promoting interest in sport and other activities as we have seen already.[12] Stamer had been responsible for the continued war effort in Darlington, having support from Lockyer, the works manager from 1909 to 1922, and from George Heppell, chief draughtsman from 1906 to 1919, who was then succeeded by his deputy R.J. Robson. He undoubtedly acted as a 'buffer' between the rather punctilious Raven and the other people in the CME's department. This meant that, despite Raven's absence until 1919, there was no halt, just a definite slow-down in production; for instance, only two locomotives were built at Darlington in 1916 due to munitions work. The new workshop built for this munitions project was bought by the NER for £22,444 4s 7d and proved a useful addition to the total workshop complex.[13] Thompson also returned once again to the GNR, but remained friendly with Stamer at Darlington.[14] The production of carriages also stopped, starting up again briefly in 1920–1921 prior to amalgamation.

On 11 April, Woolwich was privileged by another visit by King George V. He had visited it the year before, but obviously came this time to see the improvements Raven had made. Raven looks uncomfortable, posing with the military 'brass' around him. He is the only one who has uncovered his head in the presence of the king.

In June 1916, after the death at sea of Lord Kitchener (and Sir Frederick Donaldson) when HMS *Hampshire* hit a mine, Lloyd George became Secretary of State for War. He was succeeded by Christopher Addison.

By December 1916, Lloyd George had became Prime Minister of the Coalition government and so was responsible for drawing up the New Year's Honour's list. For his war efforts, Raven was awarded a knighthood on 13 February 1917 – a tribute indeed to his management skills in efficiently improving the output of the works at the highest national level.

> From personal observation of Sir Vincent Litchfield Raven's labours for his country in her time of stress, no one deserved the honour more than which Sir Vincent had been the recipient of.[15]

On 31 March, the Gateshead chairman and committee of the NER Literary Institute, of which he was still honorary president and treasurer, sent from their meeting congratulations to Raven on his knighthood.

At the outbreak of war, Raven's son Frederick had returned home to join the British Army in 1916, probably spending time in military railway training at Applepie Camp at Longmoor. He went to work in the ROD of the RE (the 'Sappers'), a largely unarmed section of the forces, started in April 1915. He rose to rank of Lieutenant in the Railway Transport Sector, ROD.

The repeat visit of King George V to Woolwich Arsenal, with Raven the only civilian.

Frederick was somewhere in Northern France, no doubt where convoys of ships were used for carrying coal from Britain to France, guarding themselves as best as they could against the very successful German submarine campaign being waged against British shipping. The port of Le Havre, besides receiving military supplies, was No.1 base for the British Expeditionary Force. The ROD was involved in getting supplies inland from British ships to the Front despite the retreat of the Germans in February to the so-called Hindenburg line. His father also travelled over to France, probably in connection with the war effort, where he may have taken an opportunity to see Frederick and discuss the needs of the ROD. Raven would have known and authorised, with the NER Board's approval, the transfer of the entire batch of 50 Wilson Worsdell's class 'T1' slide valve 0-8-0s to the ROD. Here they brought honour to themselves by working from the Channel Ports into Normandy and Belgium, proving better than their LNWR and GCR counterparts, because of their efficient reverse gear. Their large cabs were appreciated also. Furthermore, twenty of class 'P' 0-6-0s were also prepared for a similar service to ROD and sent to Hull (Borough Gardens) for shipment, but the order was cancelled so they were not sent. Frederick:

> ... was wounded by a high explosive shell receiving serious injuries. For several days, his condition was not unfavourable under the circumstances, but it was then understood that his wounds were poisoned and hopes for his recovery were sorrowfully abandoned.[16]

Sadly, twenty-seven-year-old Frederick, now a captain in RE, died from his wounds on 24 March in Le Havre. He is buried in Sainte Marie Cemetery, Le Havre. From the same NER Literary Institute meeting noted above, the committee sent condolences to Raven and his wife. Raven had crossed over to France in March probably to see his son or his grave, as well as touring the dreadful conditions in front-line trenches at first hand.

> Sir Vincent had our sympathy with him in the loss he had sustained by the death of his son.[17]

Sainte Marie Cemetery, Le Havre, the resting place of Frederick Gifford, Raven's younger son.

Raven may have been instrumental in obtaining on loan a NER 0-4-0T for use at the Kyle of Lochalsh and two 0-6-0 crane tanks and another 0-6-0 for another unspecified destination.[18] He was not of course alone in being 'borrowed' from railway company employment. For instance, Henry Fowler from MR was also at Munitions and Sir Sam Fay GM of GCR from 1917 to 1918 was Director of Movements and Railways and, from 1918 to 1919, Director General at the War Office.

In May 1917, Raven became Deputy Controller of Armament Production for the Admiralty (and controller from autumn 1917), being responsible to Eric Geddes, who became controller of the Navy at the same time. He eventually ousted Lord Jellicoe, the first Sea Lord. Born in India, the son a Scottish civil engineer, Geddes had had experience in the USA on the Baltimore & Ohio Railroad,[19] then in India as traffic manager to the Rohilkhund and Kumoan Railway in northern India. Appointed as a claims agent with supervision of all claims made on NER in October 1904, he had early impressed Gibb with his ability flexibility and application to the job. After December 1905, he acted as commercial agent with the duties of watching trade movements, searching for new courses of traffic and locating new factories in NE territory. He took charge of the goods department as chief goods manager in 1907 after acting as deputy for a few months in 1906, replacing William Robinson, who had been basically unenterprising and content to let things run along. By 1911, Geddes had become deputy general manager. Ralph Lewis Wedgwood had become chief goods manager in 1912, when Geddes became traffic superintendent. His quick rise through this variety of posts would lead him to become NER GM in 1914. His career, like Raven's, would take a new direction as a result of the country entering the First World War.

The NER Board gave him permission to leave the company in order to work for Lloyd George, the Minister of Munitions, as Deputy Director General of Munitions Supply. The department had been formed in May 1915, because there was not enough of any type of armament, especially shells to support the battle lines, as had become clear from the Spring Offensive of 1915. By August 1916, Geddes was in France as Director General of Transportation to reorganise transport and the proper use of standard-gauge railways for the war effort. In October he became, despite being a civilian, the Director General of Military Railways under the auspices of the War Office (as well as Haig's Inspector General of Transport). Raven's son-in-law Edward Thompson had gone back to the Arsenal in 1916, but left to join Geddes' transportation staff in France, where he was twice mentioned in dispatches and finally gained the rank of Lieutenant-Colonel. The result of Geddes' activity was a programme of railway construction in France by the end of the war, laying 2,500 miles of standard-gauge track and metre-gauge track from specified railheads to the Front. The Admiralty at this time was regulated by members of a council of ten – three MPs, six naval officers and a permanent secretary. Raven's responsibility was important as part of the strategy to increase British shipping against German submarines and concerned 'all matters pertaining to the manufacture and purchase of ordinance etc, torpedoes and mines etc.'[20]

Meanwhile, Lloyd George had become Prime Minister and Winston Churchill became Minister for Munitions. Raven, in the first list published on 25 August 1917, was further honoured, becoming a Knight Commander of the British Empire in recognition of his war effort at the Royal Arsenal and Admiralty.[21]

The Most Excellent Order of the British Empire was instituted by King George V as recently as 4 June 1917, including women for the first time in any Order, it had been instituted to honour large numbers of people in the British Isles and other parts of the Empire, who were helping with war effort, either as combatants or civilians on the home front in any realm of activity. The reigning monarch is the Grand Master, and the order has five divisions to be conferred on men and women equally, namely:
Knight and dame grand cross (KCBE);
Knight and dame commander (KBE or DBE);
Commander (CBE);
Officer (OBE);
Member (MBE).

The two highest divisions entail admission to knighthood. It means that the person entitled to do so can surround their coat of arms with the circle and motto of the order (For God and Empire) and can suspend a representation of their ribbon and badge from their coat of arms. The investiture in the chapel of the Order in the crypt of St Paul's Cathedral took place. Geddes got the highest honour, GBE, and Raven received a KBE, as did Sir Henry Fowler on 20 February 1918 for his work at the Ministry of Munitions and with aircraft at Farnborough. After the war Edward Thompson was awarded an MBE, Military Division, and his friend Raven's other son Norman Vincent, who was by then a lieutenant, also received an MBE in 1919.

Despite his war work, Raven had remained active in the town and it was noted in the council statistics that as member since 1913 election of the Town Council's Committee for Tramways and Electricity and Gas undertakings, he had not missed any council meetings at all – a truly remarkable performance and typical of his dedication to task in hand and his meticulous time management, no doubt helped out by use of passes on the express trains between Darlington and King's Cross, for which he was responsible in part during peacetime. The Gateshead NER Literary Institute contacted him about pass for an excursion. His reply indicated that he 'thought the time was not opportune for it and did not know on any other which has being held'.[22] He was making it quite clear that he could still have the final say.

Raven was sworn in as a JP in Darlington Borough in July 1917. This meant attendance at the Quarter Sessions four times a year, Easter, Whitsuntide, Michaelmas and Epiphany.[23] It meant a careful ordering of his time for him, to enable him to attend the court on a regular basis, but his rail 'Gold Pass' undoubtedly proved invaluable. He would remain as Borough JP until 1925, the year after he had left the town.[24]

Raven could also rejoice in having a grandson, Michael Litchfield, born to Constance and George Newby on 17 March 1918. It is likely that while Raven was away in London, Lady Raven, as she now was, would be with her older daughter in Darlington at this time. Mary and Michael Watson would carry forward the Raven line, with their great-grandchildren, alive today. Two of Raven's brothers who had emigrated to USA died in 1918, Ernest Woodhouse in August, aged fifty-one, and on 23 November, Hubert, aged forty-nine, a civil engineer in Princetown.[25]

1 Lloyd-George, David, *War Memoirs of David Lloyd-George*, vol.1, 1938, Odhams Press Ltd, p.42

2 Pratt, Edwin A., 1921, *British Railways and the Great War*, Blount Odhams, p.589-90, 629-32

3 Vaughan Adrian, 1997, *Railwaymen, Politics & Money*, John Murray, p.299

4 Hoole Ken, 1967, *North Road Locomotive works 1863-1966*, Roundhouse Books, p.38

5 Obituary and funeral notices from *Northern Echo*, 23 and 25/11/1914

6 *Stockton and Darlington Times*, March 1915

7 *Stockton and Darlington Times*, 13 March 1915

8 *Stockton and Darlington Times*, 20 March 1915

9 *NER Magazine*, vol.5, no.55, p.196

10 *NER Magazine*, vol.5, no.55, p.172

11 Lloyd-George, David, *War Memoirs of David Lloyd-George*, vol.1, Odhams Press Ltd, p.353

12 Nock Oswald. S., 1954, *The Locomotives of the North Eastern Railway*, Ian Allan London, p.173

13 Hoole Ken, 1967, *North Road Locomotive Works 1863-1966*, Roundhouse Books, p.69

14 Grafton Peter, March 1971, *Edward Thompson of the LNER*, Kestrel Books, Knaresborough, p.19-20

15 Gateshead NER Literary Institute AGM minutes, 16 May 1917

16 *Darlington and Stockton Times*, 31 March 1917, p.7

17 Gateshead NER Literary Institute AGM minutes, 16 May 1917

18 Stephenson Locomotive Society Journal, November 1975, p.345

19 Baltimore & Ohio Railroad (1827–1987), 10,000 miles of track, linking the East Coast with the Mid-West, worked as a carrier of both goods and passenger traffic from its inception

20 Darlington Library newspaper cuttings, 1914-18, *Teesdale Mercury* dated 2 June 1917

21 There is a letter from Raven to Wooller thanking him for his congratulations on receiving his knighthood, dated 14 February, in Alderman Wooller's file

22 Gateshead NER Literary Institute minutes, 24 May 1917. They replied to him that they appreciated the position, but asked for a special case that no single journey pass be made. Raven's reply is not recorded

23 Lloyd-George, David, *War Memoirs of David Lloyd-George*, vol.1, 1938, Odhams Press Ltd, p.42

24 *Stockton and Darlington Times*, 13 March 1915

25 *Stockton and Darlington Times*, March 1915

IX

RETURN FROM WAR
(1919–1921)

Peace was declared on 11 November 1918 and by early 1919, Raven was fully back at work with NER. Alderman Wooller of Darlington had written to congratulate him on his knighthood and he gratefully replied to him. Even better from a financial point of view, the NER Board of directors welcomed him home with a bonus in addition to the £3,000 p.a. he had been receiving during his secondment away from NER:

> In view of the fact that Sir Vincent Raven has received no bonus or advance of salary during the war and been put to considerable expenses during his residence in London since 1915 during the time he was working at the Ministry of Munitions and at the Admiralty - resolved that a special grant of £2000 be made.
> Signed
> Knaresborough – Chairman.[1]

During the war, there were moves to produce a standard locomotive. The ARLE had, for instance, selected and adapted Robinson's design of a mixed traffic 2-8-0 from a GCR prototype as its standard. However, once they were back at work, he and Gresley resisted any thought of standardisation between their respective companies' locomotives, and in some ways each of their new *Pacifics* becoming symbols of this. Raven's time away from the NER disadvantaged him, as his energy had had to be redirected to armaments for four years. Gresley had not left his post during the war years. Unlike Fowler and Raven, he remained CME to GNR throughout the war. This allowed him to devote time to uninterrupted experimental thinking and to test and modify any developments he wanted to make concerning his new *Pacifics* and other new locomotives at GNR.

Raven's attitude on his return to his post as CME after the war can only be surmised. Like others seconded out of their post, he had to pick up many of the threads of departmental running again. As it turned out, the actions he hoped to carry out to realise his own ideas about future development would fall into three phases. The first showed him displaying a consistent eagerness to develop new and more powerful steam locomotives and really promote the launching of the NER mainline electrification scheme. The second phase was one in which Raven faced reality and came to terms with all the political, economic and industrial factors affecting the nation, the North East and the NER as a result of the war. This meant increasing uncertainty for him in terms of his fulfilling plans for the immediate future. Lastly, in a sense cornered by events, he had to appraise and make decisions about what his role was going to be within the new dispensation, which grouping would inaugurate on 1 January 1923.

Although there was a brief resumption of ECJS work in collaboration with Gresley in 1920–1922, this was ended by the 1923 grouping. On the positive side, Edward Thompson came back to NER in 1920, to York, gaining further experience as carriage works manager, which also meant that Guen was nearer to her parents and her sister Constance, and it was easier for them to visit each other.

Raven now set to work with a will, making mainline electrification an important issue not only for discussion and planning within NER, but also making sure his intentions were known on at national and European level. The scheme focussed now on complementing in a major way the Newport–Shildon freight – workings with a mainline electrified from York to Newcastle to the same voltage. At the time, the mainline carried about three quarters of NER's total freight and passenger traffic. However, the contemporary received view of rail electrification was that the high cost of introducing the system was justified if it was for intensive suburban usage, but there were doubts and reservations about it the costs if it were introduced for mainline passenger and freight work. Therefore, for Raven and Merz to propose such a scheme was a daring move in the face of the fear and prejudice of British rail companies about mainline electrification.[2]

The Newport–Shildon line had seemed to be a pre-war, one-off experiment. The after effects of a global war, marked financial stringency and unrest at home completely hindered any repeat attempt by NER (or LNER, for that matter) to back that kind of experiment. The only companies considering mainline electrification at the time were the MR, whose 1908 Lancaster–Morecombe–Heysham line was a trial run for Derby to Manchester electrification, and the London, Brighton & South Coast Railway for their mainline from London to Brighton. In the event, the latter was not carried out until 1925. Aspinall at L&YR was also giving thought to West Coast mainline electrification between Crewe and Carlisle and Captain H.E. O'Brien was appointed electric engineer to the new joint L&YR and LN&WR, giving the idea much commitment.[3]

As an early inkling of what it was going to mean to him, Raven gave a paper on the York to Newcastle electrification in February 1919 to IEE. He was convinced that it was an important element in the future development of railways and in particular it was one of the ways of dealing with some of the congestion between York and Newcastle: quadrupling the track was another. He was involved in particular with Francis Lydall (formerly with Siemens, but now the representative of M&M in this particular project, later to become a partner in the firm) and his own son Norman Vincent, also working with M&M as an electrical engineer of some ability in his own right. Both the Ravens provided much input towards the final choice of locomotive, its planning and construction.

The upshot was a memo from him to the NER Board requesting that a sample electric locomotive be built. This was approved on 19 March 1919. Following a simulation exercise done on 27 March 1919, it was demonstrated that there would also be a reduction in the amount of locomotives needed for the same amount of work.

Following frequent consultation with the Ravens, Merz submitted a full feasibility study for the NER Board about the scheme before he left for South Africa, fairly assured that from now on the electrification scheme would go ahead. The NER Board minutes for 25 July 1919 note:

> The General Manager submitted a report on a proposal to electrify the line from York to Newcastle. It was agreed that a committee should be appointed as under:
> Mr Pease; Sir Hugh Bell; Captain Kitson; Mr Lupton,
> signed Knaresborough, chairman.[4]

The Board heard from this committee on 19 September:

The committee have examined the proposals and have satisfied themselves in view of the fact that there are considerable arrears of engine maintenance to be made good and that electric working would enable the traffic to be worked by a much smaller number of locomotives, the substitution of electric for steam power could be carried out at a figure which would justify the initial outlay provided agreement could be made for a supply of current. Resolved that the scheme be approved and submitted to the Ministry of Transport,
signed Knaresborough, chairman.[5]

Thus, the Board's approval at this stage vindicated Raven's scheme and the prospects for the future of NER mainline electrification were now at their highest point of expectation, especially as NER were even more in the red at £4.8 million than before the war. This positive feeling must have been reinforced by the installation of two further traffic control schemes like the Newport one earlier, but more ambitious. The earlier one was opened in Newcastle in September 1917 to cover Tyneside and, more significantly still, the other opened in York in autumn 1922, covering Newcastle to Doncaster.[6]

However, the first negative omen, prefiguring the eventual abandonment of the whole scheme, appeared on 27 September when the National Rail Strike took place. Despite this, Raven himself prepared a second memorandum to the NER Board about the extension of electrification on the network, providing alternative designs for locomotives, which Merz and he had considered, whether the mechanism would be either rod, gearless or quill drive. He later produced a report in conjunction with Henry Angus Watson, the Superintendent of the Line, dated October 1919, which was submitted to the NER Board. It used the knowledge and experience gained on the earlier passenger and freight schemes. Eighteen pages long with two coloured diagrams, it proposed the electrification of eighty miles of mainline from York, beginning at Dringhouses signal box, between Holgate Bridge and Challoner's Whin junctions to finish in Newcastle Central Station. There would be a parallel line diverging from Northallerton through to Ferryhill, via Stockton, where it could link up with the Shildon to Newport scheme and continue on into Middlesbrough. This connection meant that all the freight traffic from the Erimus yard at Middlesbrough could have access to the mainline and be electrically hauled without need of further change of locomotive while within the NER system.

Curiously, there was no proposal to integrate the Tyneside scheme of 1904, fed at 660v dc even at some future date. On the advice of Merz, Raven proposed that the system used a dual power supply system, primarily third rail (as for North Tyneside system), with catenary in stations and goods yards (as for Shildon to Newport line), all at 1.5kV.[7] Out of the 395 miles proposed to be electrified, 282 were to use third rail and 115 the overhead supply. Raven stated that third rail was cheaper to install at £2,850 per track mile than overhead at £4,340 per track mile. Moreover, although third rail was more expensive to maintain, it depreciated less readily, it could be maintained by permanent way gangers and seemingly posed no foreseeable problems on bridges and tunnels. However, Merz advocated boxing 'the third rail' in with wood, based on experience with the Central Argentine Railway. There could be some danger to platelayers, who would be close to it. There could also be problems with current leakage, as high voltage current tends to seek earth readily, but it could be laid easily for extensions. Raven privately (and, in the event of what happened, over optimistically) envisaged the system extending to Carlisle and Berwick in his dream for the future.

Overhead catenaries were not seen as conducive to high speed trains; Raven, however, quite quickly changed his commitment to third rail, preferring overhead by 1921 to be the main method of pick-up. Where there were marshalling yards alongside the electrified line, the first 100 yards would have electric power, after which battery locomotives would take over. Enterprisingly, quarry and mine branches would be electrified, if their output source lay at less than two miles from the mainline.

Overhead catenaries needed to be installed in more urban situations to avoid gaps in provision in supply, where junctions and level crossings occurred. York, Thirsk, Northallerton,

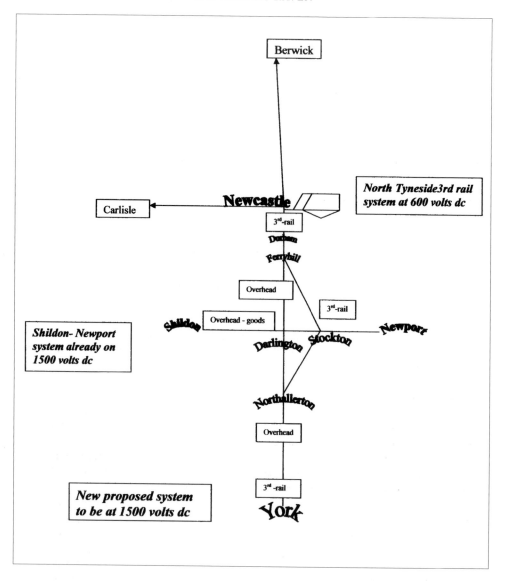

Diagram of proposed electrification.

Darlington, Durham, Low Fell and Newcastle Central, plus on the eastern loop, Ferryhill and Stockton were all be provided with overhead wiring. Power would be supplied at 1,500v dc at 2d per unit by NESCO once negotiations with NER were complete. Sub-stations would be provided at York, Pilmoor, Darlington, Ferryhill, Durham and Newcastle. Merz had remarked in his report that should the electrification spread to GNR territory at Doncaster, South Yorkshire Power Co.'s supply could be approached in use. Financial arguments included the more economical performance of the electric locomotive over comparable mileage with steam locomotives and the effect electrification would have on reducing manning rosters.

Type of traffic	No. of steam locomotives	No. of electric locomotives	Saving %
Passenger	54	29	25
Freight	155	80	75
Total	209	109	100

Comparison of projected steam *v.* electric locomotives requirements.

Raven argued that the locomotive figures included those due for replacement anyhow, due to depreciation of stock during the recent war. The total cost, minus notional savings, would be revised as £956,400.

Summary of costs for electrification

Track equipment	£1,302 000
Updating signalling	£93,800
29 electric passenger locomotives (notionally replacing 54 steam locomotives)	£12,800 each
80 electric locomotives (notionally replacing 155 steam engines)	£11,500 each

less saving in costs from ceasing to run steam locomotives

Total	£186,468 p.a.
Wages	£53,197
Coal	£110,122
Stores	£109,395
Repairs	£107,391
less new maintenance for new locomotives	£65,443
Total net savings	£121,025 p.a..

Running costs

Steam locomotives	£658,865
add their depreciation (5 per cent p.a.)	£19,167
Electric locomotives	£472,397
add their depreciation (5 per cent p.a.)	£14,294

Comparative estimates of total costs of electrification.

On 9 January 1920:

The General Manager reported he had received a letter from the Minister of Transport that the Minister approved in principle the proposal to electrify the mainline and the immediate construction of electric locomotives. The minister was of the opinion that the time had come when an attempt should be made to obtain more uniformity of type, signed Knaresborough, Chairman.[8]

Thus, the Board was able to give provisional approval for Raven now to proceed with a prototype locomotive, for which he was accountable to a special sub-committee. Next, Raven had to decide what prototype locomotive he was going to build. He had a number of alternatives for freight and passenger use for consideration:

(i) Freight and mineral Bo-Bo
Merz had suggested a version of those used on Shildon line.

(ii) 0-C-0 (0-6-0) – one engine
This single engine was converted from a standard tender frame to have a vertical worm-drive on middle axle, the motor being supported by the frame, to reduce the deadweight on the axle. Built in 1921, it was intended to test bevel as part of preparations for main line electrification with pick-up shoes, rather than overhead source; it was tried out on the line from Jesmond and Gosforth.[9]

Length:	24ft 4¾in
Frame:	standard tender
Super-structure:	box-shaped
Wheels:	6 x 3ft 9¾in
Weight:	31 tons 8 cwt

iii) Gearless 2-Co-Co-2
This type of locomotive derived from a massive General Electric Co. of America design at Schenectady, which both Raven senior and Lydall had seen. A similar design was used on the Milwaukee Railroad.[10] It was to be designed and built to the same specifications and included maximum speed of 90mph, which No.13 would have (details below), but had a wheelbase of 62ft 8in (No.13 was 53ft 6in long) and weighed about 105 tons (as against No.13's 102 ton).
   Raven was refused permission to build it by the special sub-committee for the Board.

iv) Ordinary passenger locomotive
Merz produced a gearless design because he thought a lighter locomotive was suitable for ordinary passenger work.

v) Heavy duty passenger locomotive
A second design by Merz was for a geared quill, derived from iii) above, e.g. with slotted quills for easier axle inspection, being close to the design actually used by Raven for No.13.

vi) Freight Co-Co
This was an articulated 108-ton freight quill drive box-cab locomotive, which was capable of a pull of 15 tons which would haul a train of 1,000 tons up a gradient of 1 in 100 at 30mph. He compares it with a notional 134-ton 0-8-2 steam engine of comparable strength.[11]

vi) Raven's choice – No.13 – Passenger electric
This quill drive locomotive became the actual NER prototype. Design work went on until the end of 1920. Much of the drafting of details was worked out by a senior draughtsman, Hinchcliffe, who had previously worked on the Shildon electric locomotives. The official order was placed on 21 January 1921. The mechanical equipment cost £5,000. It was built at Darlington at an overall cost estimated at £20,000. (Stamer later thought it was more like £27,767 in actual practice.) The electrical equipment, costing £15,000, was manufactured by Metropolitan-Vickers at their own works at Trafford Park, Manchester.

They had their own representative in Darlington, R.T. Brookes as liaison officer.[12] Norman Vincent Raven acted as the M&M representative and was present to oversee things. The reason for the large 'steam' type driving wheels was that their six half spokes and six trifurcated spokes could resist the heavy pressures exerted on the wheels by the quill drive. When its large helical springs were compressed, it meant that it could move quietly away as it rapidly accelerated, a marked change from the 'puffing' of the steam locomotive on acceleration.

Weight:	102 tons – 18 tons, 10 cwt per driving axle
Weight per driving axle:	18 tons ,10 cwt
Weight per bogie axle:	11 tons, 12 cwt
Wheel arrangement:	2 – Co. - 2 (rigid wheelbase = 16ft)
Driving wheels:	6ft 8in
Total Wheelbase:	43ft 8in
Driving wheel diameter:	6ft 8in
Bogie wheels:	3ft 7¾in
Overall length:	53ft 6in
Width:	8ft 10in
Height:	13ft c in (when pantograph locked down)
Current:	1500v dc overhead
Tractive effort:	5,900lb (1hr @ 43mph),
	9,480 (continuous @ 50.5mph)
Horsepower:	300 each motor = 1,800 total
Top speed:	90mph
Centre of Gravity:	4ft 10in above rail level [13][14]

The 4-6-4 'Baltic' wheel arrangement of the locomotive was unusual, but had been used for steam engines by Robert H. Whitelegg for his elegant mixed traffic tanks for London Tilbury and Southend Railway (1912) and later for his Glasgow and South Western Railway (*c.*1919). This, coupled with the 'steam'-size driving wheels, arose from Raven's desire for balance under the frames in order to promote smooth riding and reducing wear and tear on the track. He had been in correspondence with Lawson B. Billinton, who had produced his own graciously proportioned 'Baltic' Tanks for LBSCR for just the same reason. (Raven used the same 'Baltic' wheel arrangement in his drawing of a diesel engine and, of course, Gresley later adopted it for his 'Hush-Hush' streamlined locomotive of 1929.)

So, the prototype was completed and added to stock as No.13 in May 1922. The proportions of the whole design were typically late NER in that they were harmoniously symmetrical yet gave an impression of great power. The only asymmetrical elements were the forwarding placing of the driver's access door and the fact that it ran with only one of its two pantographs up. While not streamlined, there were rounded edges over power units and cab and 'steam' main frames had been adapted to run over the entire length, but raised over the large driving wheels and even the sandboxes were geometrical in shape. All of these features made for a gracious profile. It was fitted for dual operation, electrical pick-up being either by pantograph for overhead or by shoe for third rail. Overall, it was an English refinement of the contemporary Continental and American designs.

While new, it was painted in grey livery, but it was eventually painted in Saxony green with a lemon lining in the autumn of 1922. Trials were held on the Shildon–Newport line, the only available length of track, during the summer and autumn of 1922, often with a dynamometer car to gather technical data. They were keen to promote the new venture:

Main line electric locomotive; actual test results. This locomotive which is intended for hauling East Coast Main Line trains over the electrified portion of the NER was recently subjected to a severe test of on the heavy mineral line between Shildon and Newport

(Erimus yard). The train comprised of 17 vehicles weighing 460 tons maintained an average speed of 42 m.p.h. on a ruling gradient of 1 in 103 – equivalent to a drawbar pull of 6.5 tons. On a gradient of 1 in 200 it attained 58 m.p.h. – a drawbar pull of 5 tons and an overall average of 5.5 tons. Such results have not been produced on the same section of railway with a steam locomotive.

Furthermore, at Shildon shed the new locomotive had a series of human 'acolytes' who had experience of working with Raven as well as running the Shildon line and its locomotives; they were the shed master J.W. Thackeray, the charge fitter R. Brownlees, who seemed to know both engine and Raven senior well, and William Hopper, who became No.13's chief driver.

On one trial trip, Brownlees found the locomotive's electrical contactors were too small. Using twenty-two carriages of the East Coast Stock, No.13 moved from Shildon to Bowesfiled Junction and stopped. It had burnt out the contactors. Raven followed on in his special locomotive and carriage. He was, of course, furious at the stoppage and let those assembled around the halted engine know it. Brownlees stopped him as he came down to the engine, explaining what had happened, but Raven went on in front of the experts assembled to view the performance of his new engine. He turned on his heel and told his driver to go off to Darlington. Brownlees now spoke to the Metrovick representative, R.T. Brookes, saying that it might be better if he could get to Darlington, before Raven arrived at the North Road Works and exploded there. Brookes got a taxi and arrived at North Road to find a message that he should telephone Raven at Grantly. He was told that he, Brookes, should render No.13 operational within the week.[15] Metrovick actually did this, sending the replacements from Trafford by car within seven days.[16]

This ground-breaking locomotive was stored first in Darlington. In July 1925 it was towed to the Fighting Cocks and exhibited at the Stockton and Darlington Centenary celebrations. After that, it was shown again over the next four years or so at various 'Open Days' at Faverdale, Middlesbrough, Shildon and Darlington works, basically as a curiosity. Eventually placed in Gosforth sheds, it stayed there until its official withdrawal from stock on 21 August 1950, travelling to Catcliffe, near Rotherham, on 15 December to be cut up. A sad end for an enterprise of such promise and missed opportunity for the North East primarily and for the rest of the British rail network.

NER Board on 11 June 1920 noted that the government would not be providing any funding for the electrification.[17] This marked the beginning of the end for the scheme, as well as the beginning of a second more disillusioning phase of Raven's post-war career. To avoid backing 'a possible dead horse', the Ministry of Transport had asked the NER to postpone the scheme, while it allowed an advisory committee to sit for a whole year on it from July 1920 to June 1921.

Nothing daunted, and probably hoping to put some pressure on NER directors, Raven and Francis Lydall, the M&M representative, wrote a further report produced in October 1920 after their visit to the USA. It is a veritable reporting *tour de force* in its detailed analysis of the American railways visited, full of background information gained during the visit to USA. NER Board minutes for 10 December 1920 said that:

> Chief Mechanical Engineer reported on his visit to the United States. Suggestions in the report are that:
> an electric locomotive of the gearless design should be constructed.
> the main line from Darlington to Newcastle is electrified.
> Resolved the matter be referred to the committee appointed on 25th July 1919.
> signed Knaresborough, Chairman.[18]

This reads like a last-ditch attempt by Raven and the Board, who were attempting to salvage the scheme by authorising a 'gearless' machine, although the prototype was a 'quill' engine.

The reduced length of track to be electrified was a mere thirty-four miles to Newcastle, which would start at Darlington rather than York, and there was no mention of a link with Newport–Shildon line, which would pass over it.

In a paper, 'The Advantages of Electric Traction on Railways', and to the York Railway and Lecture Debating Society on 25 January 1921 with Ralph Wedgwood, deputy GM-NER in the chair, Raven now indicated that he would like to build a gearless locomotive to compare with the geared and quilled drive of the one he had obtained permission to build. So it would seem that he saw the reduced scheme as a temporary set-back which would lead on to the larger scheme eventually.

Whilst in America, he and Lydall had had talks with the General Electric Co.'s engineers and a 4-6-6-4 (or 2-Co-Co-2) articulated engine was suggested. He put forward before his audience a number of points:

increased acceleration, higher scheduled speeds and hence more frequent service;
more even tractive effort and the ease it can be adjusted to size of a train;
higher mechanical efficiency and more constant efficiency throughout a locomotive's working life;
slower depreciation and hence maintenance cost;
increase capacity of existing tracks and fewer numbers of rolling stock needed;
double heading with a single crew and the cleanliness for crew and surroundings.

They were clear indications of how he had worked out reasons for his proposals and would continue well beyond the period of his official retirement. Sadly, they ran counter to the prevailing philosophy of development, which favoured coal as its power source.

Despite his efforts outside work, there were two committees to surmount – an NER sub-committee and a government inquiry. Merz castigated it for its lateness. The scheme's fate was further sealed, partly due to the 1921 trade recession, the miners' strike of April 1921, added to the 1921 Railways Act with its consequent 1923 grouping. The NER mainline electrification project would be permanently abandoned. It would not be done until seventy years later, minus the original proposed Northallerton to Ferryhill section, via Stockton loop and with current being derived completely from overhead supply.

There were many versions of traffic figures over the two years before the Raven-Lydall Report from the USA was officially published from CME's office in Darlington on 9 June 1921. While initially favouring the use of more third rail pick-up than overhead as a source of power supply, e.g. in drawings dated 11 November and 4 December, Raven came to change his mind, although it is not clear why, in favour of overhead cables (2,850 miles as against 4,340).[19] Possibly, he wanted to standardise the pickup from overhead catenary to be in line with the Newport–Shildon scheme, or it could have been because there were difficulties about the pick-up from the exposed rail from icing in severe weather, or possibly just the matter of maintaining safety of the exposed rail.

Seeing 'steam' and 'electric' power as complementary, Raven introduced three types of new steam locomotives, his swansong to locomotive engineering as it turned out. They would be counted among his most enduring achievements. The two classes, prior to his *Pacific* were intended to have some interchangeability. The anticipation of increased loads in both passenger and goods traffic led him to develop his earlier classes 'P2' and 'S3'.

Class 'T3', a larger version of class 'T2', was built for a post-war increase in heavy duty mineral traffic, possibly hastened by a delay in the return of class 'T' from ROD. In the event, these powerful 3-cylinder engines coped admirably with heavy mineral trains across the long gradients from west to east of County Durham in particular. They were visually a much more handsome design than class 'T2'. He provided them with new style running plates, not totally quadrilateral in horizontal profile as formerly, but raised above rear leading wheel level to a point where the last driver ended near the cab to reveal more of the driving wheel and subsequently to reduce the size of the 'splashers'. This was the new post-war standard for

901, the first of class 'T3', the powerful culmination of the Worsdell/Raven 0-8-0 classes 'T', 'T1' and 'T2'.

S3, the dignified long-lasting final version of the Worsdell/Raven mixed traffic 4-6-0.

running plates that Raven adopted also for his class 'T3' and *Pacifics*. This may have been to make access to the cylinders and internal working parts easier. It increases the visual interest of the profile and moves away from the box-like look of the earlier locomotives, enhancing the look of all three classes. They provided a sterling service, and even on trials with loads of 800 tons on gruelling gradients in Perthshire, they ran easily. They came to be used for many years afterwards, particularly on local coal traffic in the North East, right up to the demise of steam. The adding of the superheater, lengthening the smoke box, improved the locomotive's profile, when compared with class 'T2'. Fortunately, one of this once familiar group of locomotives has been preserved. It is generally agreed that Stamer headed up the enterprise. Approval was given on 9 May 1918, signed by Raven as CME and M. Gray (deputising for Butterworth) as GM; they were all built in Darlington, five in 1919 and ten in 1924.[20]

The next steam locomotives were class 'S3' 4-6-0s. All were built in Darlington, the commissioning being done by Raven as CME and A. Pease as GM of NER. They were approved in three batches, one on 14 November 1918, twenty-one on 8 May 1919 and the last thirteen on 30 March 1922, the same day as his new *Pacifics*. Raven seems to have come to recognised some of the deficiencies of his earlier class 'S2'. The result was an update of this with three cylinders (now a NER standard). This resulted in 40 per cent more power than their precursors and better starting and moving off of heavy trains. Their boilers had a larger heating surface and Schmidt superheaters, with smaller coupled wheels than the earlier S2s. (Gresley later rebuilt some of the class, further revealing gears (now Walschaerts), driving wheels and eliminating the splashers). The original version is better visually and has a more masculine air. That so many survived in their original state shows that the conversions were not necessarily major improvements or all would have been subjected to them. It may well have been a matter of putting to use what was available when time came for maintenance and renewal of parts. The LNER continued to build twenty-eight more of the class in 1923 with two more in 1924. From a design point of view, they were among his most satisfying locomotives both visually and in performance, being comparable to the Raven's *Atlantics* but larger, with the usual recognisably NER uncluttered and handsome profile. They were among Raven's most imposing and permanent contributions to NER and LNER locomotive stock.[21] Being very reliable engines, they were popular with their handlers. Their main drawback was the congestion of machinery between the frames, which made for some difficulties of maintenance, especially when adjustments had to be made.[22] One of the mainstays for rapid movement of mixed traffic, they were scrapped as late as 1962–1964. Sadly, none were preserved.

The NER Board acquired 60 acres of land at Faverdale, next to the Stooperdale property, to build a wagon works there. It cost £750,000 to build. The Cleveland Bridge & Engineering Co. began in October 1920, and the new paint shop opened in August 1923. Despite it meaning more centralisation at Darlington, the new shop was needed to provide more new wagons for NER, which had in 1914 owned 118,000 wagons (24,893 open wagons, 8,445 covered wagons and 59,815 mineral wagons, mainly for coal),[23] normally renewing 5,000 of them annually. Faverdale produced its own timberwork detail, but Shildon provided ironwork details. The war had slowed up the programme of renewing wagons, hence the need for increasing production up to 10,000 timber wagons annually.[24] Apart from that, in 1914 the future of railways on mainland Britain had been determined by the Railways Act 1921, but the details of who would be in the chief positions in the new LNER was a matter for the wheeling and dealing of railway politics. The NER was the most powerful constituent of the LNER and Geddes, the author of the act, would have been the most obvious and suitable candidate for GM as he had been deputy GM to NER and Minister of Ways and Communication from 10 January 1919.

He became prime mover after the war in securing the passage of the Railways Act 1921, which completed the idea of a national network, run via four groups, begun as a war time measure. He became the first Minister of Transport on 17 August, his Ministry being established from 23 September. He had jurisdiction over railways, but not roads, docks or harbours – a missed opportunity for an integrated system, a concept which eludes politicians to this day. In moving to the Ministry of Transport, he had left the NER Board, who granted him £50,000 severance pay in lieu of completing his contract. He was, as a result, not the person the Board would ideally choose as a new GM for LNER, preferring to support Geddes erstwhile deputy Ralph Wedgwood.

On a more personal note for Raven, on 10 January there was a gathering at Collingwood Café, Newcastle, to celebrate the retirement of 'Charlie' Baister on 31 January 1921. Promoted on 1 February 1902 to district locomotive running superintendent with his HQ at Gateshead, 'Charlie' became Northern Divisional locomotive superintendent in July 1906. Raven and his team obviously valued such a key colleague. It was Raven who very appropriately occupied the chair, supported by the faithful, 'Arthur C. Stamer, Mr H.J. Stephenson and superintendents, shop masters and member of the clerical staffs from Berwick and Carlisle to the Hartlepools'.[25]

1897, one of Worsdell's original class 'P' 0-6-0s.

2338, Raven's update of 72, as class 'P3' with superheater, larger heating surface and firebox.

Raven, in his address, which had a valedictory feeling soon to be just as appropriate to his own situation at the end of the year, said that many men in the shops would have turned up their noses at Mr Baister's first job, but from it his own pluck brought him to the important position from which he had just retired. He paid tribute to Mr Baister's energy, ability and fearlessness. Pointing the moral, he said that no man devoted to his work could ever regret joining the railway service, which presented so many avenues of advancement. NER, he added – speaking from experience – was full of good men; men on whom their chiefs could implicitly rely for help and assistance. Mr Baister had been one of them.

Baister was presented with a roll-top desk and a wallet of notes as a testimonial from the staff. Raven kept up his contract with Darlington Railway Athletic Club, being present when the Bowls Club, started in 1914, had success in winning the Darlington and District League title in 1920. He was photographed with the winning teams of 1918, 1919 and 1920. Raven had already agreed to present a cup to competition winners and further agreed to let it be named the 'Sir Vincent Raven Cup'. On it were inscribed the plinth winners' names for 1915, 1916, 1917 and 1918.

Then there was an event which must have been even more poignant for Raven, the unveiling of a War Memorial Brass, produced at North Road works to the design of C. Fenwick, an employee in the CME's office, also in January. This took place in the Mileage Department at North Road works. Before the unveiling Raven made a speech, at once both sensitive to those who had died and to those who remained, underlying the contemporary clichés. The very act of making the speech must have reminded him not only of his own role at the Ministry of Munitions and the positive attitudes of the workforce during the war, then beginning then to dissolve, but even more of the loss of his younger son Frederick. Although he did not mention his death specifically, it reads as if he took the opportunity to see his son in France, once before his death and again after it. This restraint makes the tribute more moving:

Ladies and gentlemen, fellow employees on the railway,

You have arranged to have put on your wall a tablet to commemorate the memory of those who went to fight for us and made the supreme sacrifice, and also of those spared to come back.

I do not think it is possible for you to do too much in the way of keeping in memory the names of those that went over to fight our battles on the other side, and of course, we are all agreed that those who have been unfortunate enough to remain cannot be too forcibly perpetuated in our memory.

All that we can do to show our practical remembrance is to consider the widows and orphans who are left over here to mourn.

The country, of course, is to a certain extent looking after them, but I think it is the duty of the people who know them and know their circumstances to endeavour to assist them in every way possible.

Those men over in France who fought for us, and also, indeed, everybody who worked for them over here, for, of course, it is impossible to do fighting unless there be a proper supply of munitions

Group photograph of the 1918, 1919 and 1920 winners of the Bowls League at Darlington Athletics Club, 1920, with Raven, its president, in the centre. Back row: W. Lazenby, J. Tight, J. Williamson, J. Anderson, E. Roberts; third row: J. Corrie, J. Lumley, P. Westray, F. Smith, J. Blackburn, G. Wilde, G. Charlton, R. Turner, A. Hutchinsn; second row: E. Urry, J. Hawdon, J. Clarke, M. Elliott, F. Forrest, J. Cowing, W. Keech, G. Hunter, J. Clarke, T. Chaytor; front row: K. Bertram, J. Johnson, F. Wilkinson, T. Bullock, J. Elliott, Sir Vincent Raven, J. Litton, J. Morley, A. Lumley, J. Taylor.

and the necessary transport participated in the making of history – and most important history – for it was one of the greatest wars known in the existence of this world, and that it has ended successfully... I do not think we ought to leave any stone unturned to perpetuate, as I have said, the memory of those who underwent the deprivations and hardships overseas.

I had the opportunity of going over to France on one or two occasions. The last time I was over was in March 1917, just after the retreat of the Germans following the Battle of the Somme, and when we were preparing for the Battle of Arras. It was the worst of weather, deep snow and mud in which one sank up to the knees, and the difficulties and discomforts, apart from the question of 'going over the top' were conditions that could only be released by those who had actually seen them; therefore we must never forget what those who went overseas did for us.

I am sure that everybody who works in this office in future, when they look at the tablet and see the names, the names of those who made the supreme sacrifice and the names of those who came back, will be encouraged to do their work better; it will enable them to realise when they are working on these desks, even when they are doing their everyday work, that they are working to keep up the welfare and prosperity which the previous generations fought for.

Now that the war is over, let us try to make this world better than it has ever been, and let us have greater unity among us. There is no reason why any body and everybody should not assist in attaining this end.

I will now unveil this memorial and think it reflects very great credit on the North Eastern Railway Company. We take the credit for being the first railway company in the country, and I suppose in these works, locomotives are built as well as anywhere in England; it appears that not only have we men who are able to build locomotives satisfactorily, but there are among us those with artistic talents, and it is a great satisfaction that we have been able to produce this tablet in our own works.

After the unveiling,[26] a vote of thanks was made by Councillor Maw, seconded by Mr Forrest. Ex-Lance Corporal F.W. Anderson, representing ex-servicemen, spoke about the generosity of his colleagues, rather than NER. It ended with the singing of the National Anthem.

At the sixty-fourth annual general meeting of Gateshead NER Literary Institute on 18 May, Raven was again elected president and treasurer *in absentia*. He was present at a discussion during the IME session in June 1921, concerning 'Trials in connection with the application of the vacuum-brake for long freight-trains'. Other notable engineers present included:

John Audley Frederick Aspinall (CME – LYR)
J.W. Cross
Professor W.E. Dalby (City and Guilds College – a scientific advisor to Gresley)
Sir Henry Fowler (CME – Midland Railway)
Henry Nigel Gresley (CME – GNR)
W.E. Hardy
Alfred John Hill (CME – GER)
Felix John Hookham, B Sc AMICE (British Engine Co. LTD – Shanghai)
Richard Edward Lloyd Maunsell (CME – SECR)
Robert White Reid (carriage and works superintendent – NBR)
Rendell, Westinghouse
H.W.H. Richards, EE – LBSCR and Seymour Tritton (Rendell & Robertson, consulting engineers to the India Office)

Raven also was elected vice-president of the IMechE from 1921–1923. Another important arena for his ideas was the 1921 ICE Engineering Conference, where he joined discussions with a number of contemporary engineers as the roster of names shows. The first recorded discussion was with:

Cyril Francis Bengough (chief engineer – NER)
Charles John Brown (CE – GNR)
Sir Charles Douglas Fox (consultant engineer)
William Wylie Grierson (CE – GWR), T.R. Johnson, Alexander Ross (CE – GNR) and William Booth Worthington (consulting engineer) on 29 June concerning 'The Structural Outlines of our Home Railways'

On 1 July, Raven joined in other discussions. He chaired a discussion with a heavy maritime engine-building basis concerning 'Internal Combustion Engines with Large Cylinders', presented by Sir James McKechnie, after which H.A.D. Acland, Martineau, W.F. Rabbidge and J.D.K. Restler discussed the paper. Raven's remarks were confined to the merely introductory and later intervened when things moved to the speculative, saying that he had hoped that they would have had there some representative of firms dealing with this matter (the relation of conductivity and strength of metals used in engine building) and who had built some of the large cylinder internal combustion engines, and that they would have given them the benefit of their experience. It was not much use theorising about matters of this kind. It is better to hear from people their personal experience as to the difficulties which always arose prominently in any new developments.

He seemed to be here speaking from experience of testing his new express locomotive as well as the trials of his new *Pacific*.

Also the same day, as part of a joint meeting with the Electricity Works and Power Commission, chaired by Captain H. Riall Sankey, CB, CBE, RE (retired), Raven read a paper of his, 'Mechanical Advantages of Electric Locomotives compared with Steam', which persuasively puts forward the arguments for electrification of the railways in a public statement of intent. He did not depart from the underlying basic tenets about the how and why of his beliefs, about which he enthusiastically spoke and argued in this and many other public speeches on the matter. He was obliquely pressurising his Board (and the new Ministry of Transport) to back his position.

This was the first exposition of his ideas about rail electrification, following the visit to America with Charles Merz. The paper was followed by a discussion, in which he took part with those present, namely:

Sir John Audley Aspinall (CME – LYR)
George Broughall, Assistant EE LN&WR
F.W. Carter
Lt-Col. F.A. Cortez-Leigh, (Divisional EE – LNWR)
J. Dalziel, (assistant EE –MR)
Sir Philip Dawson, MP, (consulting engineer LBSCR)
Sir Henry Fowler (CME – MR),
Henry Nigel Gresley (CME – GNR)
Charles Hesterman Merz
Sir Philip Arthur Manley Nash (mechanical engineer, chairman of Met-Vick from 1922)
Roger T. Smith (EE – GWR)

In a clear confident style, he started by outlining the pros and cons of steam against electricity as a force for railway traction. The mechanical disadvantages of the steam locomotive may be summarises as follows:

The locomotive being a completely independent unit, its power cannot be greater than the capacity of its boiler.
To increase the boiler capacity obviously implies increased dimensions and weight, both of which offer grave difficulties in regard to clearances and strengthening of bridge structures.
It is known that on many railways in Britain the limit of weight has been reached, and further development of power is only possible at enormous expense.
The boiler, cylinders, valve-gear, crankshafts and all reciprocating parts are costly to maintain.
Turntables, fuelling plant and water supply appliances must be provided.
The cab is small and open to the weather, involving discomfort to the locomotive crew.
The locomotive radiates heat and uses coal all the time steam is up, that is during many hours when it doing work, and either standing by or coasting.
The wear and tear of the locomotive on the track is considerably increased by the impossibility of accurately balancing the reciprocating parts.

The electric locomotive he pointed out was not hampered by any of the objections above, but possessed other important qualifications as follows:

Simplicity of mechanical construction and operation.
Increased power of acceleration.
Higher scheduled speed due to the possibility of heavy short period overloads resulting in more frequent service and increased use of existing tracks.
Uniform turning effort resulting in better factor of adhesion at starting and on gradients.
Absence of all reciprocating movement and accurate balance of all rotating parts.
Facilities for driving from either end of a locomotive.
Accessibility of mechanical and electrical parts.
Better accommodation for locomotive crew by reason of increased cab area and by closing in and heating the cab.
Possibility of coupling two or more locomotives together under the control of a single driver.

Now warming to his topic, he compared the economies. Regarding fuel economy, steam locomotives cannot use less than 22lb of best-quality coal per British hp/hour, in fact passenger engines on average use 32lb and goods engines 5lb per British hp/hour. The electric locomotive, using the most up-to-date contemporary electrical power could reduce consumption to 1:lbs, one half or one third, the fuel being employed being unsuitable for steam locomotives. Regarding economy in maintenance, he is able to quote the six-year experience of NER on the Newport–Shildon line. He goes to point out that in America the difference was greater than his own:

Mr Armstrong, Chairman of the *Electrification Committee* of the *General Electric Company*, give figures showing the cost of repairs per mile of three American railways varying form 6.3 cents to 14.6 cents, as compared with the cost of 60 cents per mile for a 2-8-8-2 Mallet steam engine, which is the class of engine that would have to be used to haul a similar train to that taken by the electric locomotive, the cost of repairs of which is 14.6 cents or one fourth of the steam engine.

The General Electric Co. both made parts for electrical motors of different types and complete locomotives themselves. He now moved on to describing the two main types of power transmission from motor to axle:

1. In which the motors are built direct on the driving axles, or are connected to them by reduction gearing.
2. In which the power of the motors is transmitted to the driving axles through connecting or coupling rods.

He went on to describe each in detail:

(a) Motor with reduction gear. This is most widely used method of transmitting the torque to the driving wheels. The motors are totally enclosed, each driving an axle through single reduction gearing, a pinion being mounted on the end or on each end of the armature shaft into a corresponding gear wheel, mounted on the running wheel axle. The motors are suspended by a cross suspension bar with bearings and reaction springs. These, with the motor suspension bearings on the axle, provide the motors with four points of suspension.
(b) This was what he had used in the NER locomotives, as had others in the USA and Europe.
(b) Quill Drive. The motors are mounted rigidly between the frames. Each motor is geared to a quill centred in bearings in the motor frame and surrounding the driving axle. The axle and quill are concentric. The quill is connected to the driving wheels by long helical springs which are clamped rigidly to the ends in castings which are bolted, one to the quill flange, and the other to the driving wheel. All springs with clamps are interchangeable, and any spring may be removed without disturbing any part of the running gear.
   The arrangement is such that axle, quill, pair of wheels and motor can be removed from the locomotive without disturbing the running gear. The drive secures all the advantages of a flexible gear in cushioning the transmission of torque, and lessens the vibration more. Effectively than the usual flexible gear construction and mounting. This drive was employed on the geared locomotives of the New York, New Haven and Hertford Railway[27], also the Chicago, Milwaukee and St. Paul.
Advantages of Quill drive:
(1) The driving wheels are large.
(2) The centre of gravity of the locomotive is high.
(3) The dead weight on the track is reduced to a minimum, consisting only of the wheels and axles, without the addition of any portion of the motors.
(c) Gearless. The motors are of the bi-polar type, the armature being built directly upon the driving axles, and the other parts of the motor being built into the framework of the locomotive structure. This arrangement is such that any armature with its axle and pair of wheels can be removed from the locomotive without disturbing the rest of the motor. This design is in use on the Chicago, Milwaukee and St. Paul and New York Central Railways, and is giving satisfaction.
The advantages claimed for this design are:-
simplicity of electric motor owing to the absence of motor bearings.
facility for examination of motor and removal of armature for repairs if required.
The mechanical arrangement of the complete locomotive is said to possess the required flexibility and balance to enable it to run at any speed equally well in either direction without tendency to oscillate or spread the track.

He now addressed the other classes of electric locomotive:

> The rotary motion of the motor armature is transmitted to the axles by cranks on the motor
> shafts, or on the jackshafts driven by the motors and by connecting rods coupling these cranks
> with crankpins on the driving wheels.
>
> The principal advantage of this method of drive is that the exact position of the motor in
> relation to the driving wheels is at the disposal of the designer, and he is therefore free from the
> restrictions imposed on him by the necessity for getting the motors into the space between the
> flanges of a pair of wheels as in all locomotives of class 1, and is therefore enabled to use large
> motors and place them in the most convenient position in the locomotive. This method has not
> been employed at all in this country, except for experimental purposes. In the United States there
> are a few examples, namely the locomotive on the New York section of the Pennsylvania Railroad,
> another of a different design on the Norfolk and Western Railroad[28] and on an experimental
> locomotive designed by the *Pennsylvania Railroad* for the electrification of the Altoona grade.

Generally, in the US, designs favoured class 1. On the Continent, notably in France,
Switzerland, Italy, Germany, Austria and Sweden, the connecting rod in one form or another
is almost universal. Up to the present, electrification in these countries has been carried out
mainly on the single phase or three-phase system, and Continental engineers consider that
the additional complications caused by the introduction of cranks and coupling rods are more
than compensated for by the advantage of having a free hand with the motor design.

Generally satisfactory, some problems had arisen but had been eliminated by strengthening
special parts such as crankpins, Scotch yokes, and so on, and by introducing a certain amount
of flexibility into the connections between the motors and the crankshafts.

The discussion now started with contributions from Aspinall. He generally agreed with
what Raven had said he liked the idea of motor being in the cab for easier maintenance.
He hoped that the system would be standardised; the proposal from the Electrical Advisory
Committee to the Ministry of Transport not surprisingly was 1,500v dc. Sir Philip A. Nash
was impressed with the economies, and adduced experimental figures, which expanded the
point of the wastefulness of steam locomotives. Of course, his firm had provided the electric
components for No.13! As it happened, these figures backed what Raven had written ten years
before in his 1909 report, 'North Eastern Railway Hours and Report'.

Times	In minutes	%
Standing time	190	43
Moving time	245	57
With regulator open	121	28
Total time	435	-
Remaining time standing without using power, but under steam	314	72

The chart of wastefulness of steam locomotives produced by Sir Philip Arthur Manley Nash from
Met-Vick, given at the ICE Conference on 1 July 1921.

An electric shunting locomotive would certainly be more efficient, because of its greater acceleration and movement as well as less consumption of power.

Merz pointed out that delays in electrification were due to the need for heavy capital expenditure, although Raven's figures showed it was compensated by economies in use. Another cause for delay was deciding which system to use. Sir Philip Dawson expanded this by pointing out the number of types of electric motor. He would prefer not to have those with reciprocating parts, which was merely transferring the problems of the steam locomotive to that of the electric. He asked Raven for details of the NER system and its benefits.

Smith wondered about putting electric motors in the limited space available and voiced concerns about the overseas market in the purchase and maintenance of locomotives, while J. Dalziel remarked that the improved ability of the electric engine to move loads with a minimum speed reduction was because it had reserves of power. This was important for the hilly territory that the MR covered. He also remarked on the indecision about which system to use. He favoured the quill type to solve the problem of high-speed electric locomotive. He did not favour the New York Central gearless armature type of engine; it had too many axles and its centre of gravity was too low, but it did have the motor 'upstairs'. Furthermore, the rods tended to lock each other and impose heavy stresses, affecting both maintenance and consumption of power.

Gresley, usually receptive to new ideas, argued for the continued use of steam power, understandable now that his new class of *Pacifics* was in the offing. It was about equally effective in terms of actual work on the draw-bar, in comparative studies here and in the US. A good standard that had been given for electric locomotive was 100 per 1,000 ton-miles, compared with a *Mallet* steam engine of Santa Fe Railway of 82; New York Central gave figures of 2.6lb per draw-bar hp steam and 2.5 electric. In England, 100 to 110lb was quoted for express passenger trains and 110lb during the coal strike on a train of 600 tons. He could not argue about a reduction of one third in maintenance costs, but the cost of supporting power supply systems needed to be considered. Sir Henry Fowler favoured the electrical system, as he felt that the steam was developed more or less as far it could go, but remarked that in the case of accident a part of the electrical system could be disabled more than for steam.

F.W. Carter mentioned putting engines back to back, while F.A. Cortez-Leigh commented on steam engines standing idle a third of their time. Could the new steam engine fitted with turbine and condenser be the answer? George Broughall echoed a lot of what had gone before about the economic running and maintenance of the electric locomotive, agreeing with Aspinall about the type of electrical motor to choose.

Raven summarised by reminding them of the economies that could be affected, especially in shunting. Nine electric locomotives worked the NER line, which had previously needed fifteen steam. He had investigated mainline electrification and estimated that there would a 30 per cent reduction in numbers of electric locomotives needed, instead of steam. He was optimistic that the necessary speed out of single-reduction gearing in electric motors was feasible. He felt that high speeds of eighty to eighty-five miles were unnecessary, but favoured a locomotive that could travel at an average of 60mph. He was confident in the future of the electric locomotive. He finally disagreed with the comment about symmetrical locomotives, saying that NER and other railways were building them. He saw that a lot of work on electric locomotives would have to be done by the contractors. This marked the end of the conference.

The technical information is essentially the same in the report as that in the address made by Raven as guest speaker to the North East Coast Institution of Engineers and Shipbuilders (NECIE&S) at the Literary and Philosophical Society of Newcastle-upon-Tyne in December 1921, entitled 'Railway Electrification', published in February 1922 and to the ICE conference, described in detail below, although each provides different perspectives. Those in attendance were:

2212, the 'Uniflow' *Atlantic*, the apparatus heavily disguised by prolonging leading bogie, which while distorting the front end, avoids the ugliness of calls 2, No.325.

Cyril Francis Bengough, NER
J Dalziel (electrical assistant EE – rolling stock for MR)
J.W. Hobson (locomotive boiler designer – Hawthorn's Newcastle)
C. Le Maistre CBE (secretary BESA – Raven was chairman)
F. Leigh Martineau (Still Engine Co.)
F. Mills, graduate
Sir William J. Noble, Lord Kirtley, Cairns Noble Co. (president of NECIE&S)
Sir Charles A. Parsons
Major S.G. Redman (for Merz and McLellan)
Roger T. Smith (EE to GWR)
Henry Angus Watson (general superintendent of NER)

The paper to NECIE&S given with lantern slides by way of illustration contrasted steam variability with electric reliability and of how average 'electric' speeds could be improved, not meaning their maximum ones, to the benefit of line occupation and traffic schedules.

The practice of 'double heading' with steam could be dispensed with, because the electric locomotives could be handled by a single crew. The support facilities for steam, i.e. coal pits, watering towers etc., ash pits and turntables were not necessary with electrics. Regenerative braking in the electrics would save energy. There would be increased comfort for the crew in the enclosed cabs. He could not, he said, give detailed comparisons of cost between the two, but was relying on his own careful scrutiny of capital costs for installing electrics and comparative running expenses between the two forms.

He thought that electrification would come by degrees, dependent on cheap power being available, even channelling waste heat for electricity generation. He felt that because of the better load factor available to electric generating companies, they were cheaper producers than railway companies (a point that Merz always made). He concluded with a description of No.13. He compared steam and electric locomotives, which could exert a tractive effort of 60,000lb, about twice that of current freight locomotives. An 0-6-6-0 electric locomotive could be kept within gauge and driven by one man, the equivalent steam locomotive would have to out of gauge and have a number of men to feed a 76ft grate. He also remarked that there would be a 60 per cent reduction in coal consumption. This was followed by a discussion, which asked him to look into the Garratt locomotive (which he would advocate later in his 1924 report on New Zealand Railways). Smith remarked that he agreed strongly with electrification and continued to do so as he made clear about eighteen months later when Raven spoke to the GWR Debating Society. C. Le Maistre (Secretary to British Engineering Standards Authority (BESA) Raven was its chairman), F. Mills, J.W. Hudson and Cyril Francis Bengough, NER's chief engineer agreed to send in their remarks and Raven promised to reply to the points that they raised. After that, there was the usual vote of thanks.

A footnote and a silent tribute to Wilson Worsdell, who died in 1919, was Raven's authorisation in 1921 of a further batch of William Worsdell's sturdy and useful class 'P3' 0-6-0s of 1906-1909 to be built at Darlington. Less surprisingly, this batch Raven duly fitted with larger boilers, superheaters and piston valves, all of which served to enhance the rather 'dumpy' look of the earlier batches.

1 National Archive RAIL 527/minute 12149 of NER Board of Directors meeting of 7 February 1919

2 Hennessey R.A.S., 1970, *The Electric Railway that never was*, Oriel Press, p.16-24

3 Bulleid, H.A.V., 1967, The Aspinall Era, Ian Allan Ltd, p.240

4 NER Board Minute 12181

5 NER Board Minute 12187

6 Burt Philip, 1926, *Control on the railways, a study in method*, Unwin Brothers Ltd, p.101-04

7 Grafton Peter, March 1971, *Edward Thompson of the LNER*, Kestrel Books, Knaresborough, Yorks, p.23

8 NER Board Minute 12207

9 Barnes Robin, 1985, *Locomotives that never were; Some 20th Century British Projects*, Jane's, p.36

10 Chicago, Milwaukee and St Paul (1909–1986) – a narrow, but long corridor across the north mid-west from Minneapolis on Lake Michigan, west to Tacoma and Seattle, across North and South Dakota, Montana, Idaho and Washington. Besides passenger traffic, its particular commodity for transport was originally wheat and then more industrial goods. In 1912, it started to electrify the line from South Dakota westwards

11 'Electric Locomotives', a paper by Raven given for IMechE in Paris in June 1922

12 Hughes Geoffrey, 1983, *The Gresley Influence*, Ian Allan Ltd, p.105

13 *Railway Engineer*, August 1922, p. 296-97, 313

14 Hennessey R A S, 1970, *The Electric Railway that never was*, Oriel Press, p.27

15 Bell R., 1951, *Twenty-five years of the North Eastern Railway*, Harrison and Sons Ltd, p.70

16 Hennessey R.A.S. , 1970, *The Electric Railway that never was*, Oriel Press, p.24-25

17 NER Board Minute 12238

18 NER Board Minute 12278

19 Hoole Ken, 1988, 'The Electric Locomotives of the North Eastern Railway', Locomotive Papers 167, Oakwood Press, p.19/25/28

20 Aves William A.T., 1998, 'North Eastern Eight-coupled Locomotives' (*Locomotives Illustrated* 123), RAS Publishing, p.7

21 Romans Mike, 1987, *North Eastern Railway 4-6-0s*, Ian Allan Ltd, p.6

22 Hughes Geoffrey, 1988, *LNER 4-6-0's at work*, Ian Allan Ltd, London, p.13

23 Allen Cecil J., 1964, *The North Eastern Railway*, Ian Allan Ltd, p.210

24 Hoole Ken, 1967, *North Road Locomotive Works 1863-1966*, Roundhouse Books, p.80

25 *NER Magazine*, 1922, vol.1, p.28

26 *NER Magazine*, 1922, vol.1, p.28

27 New York, New Haven & Hartford Railway (1872–1969), a compact passenger-carrying system of 1,800 miles, running along eastern seaboard from New York, north through Connecticut, Rhode

Island and eastern Massachussets to Boston. It used a high-voltage system for the first long-distance mainline electrification in USA

28 Norfolk & Western Railroad (1881–present), with only 2,100 miles of track, it was nevertheless a great coal transporting system from West Virginia to Norfolk, Virginia, out to Ohio and northwards to feed its ally, Pennysylvania Railroad

X

FAREWELL TO NER
(1922–1923)

R aven, during 1922, was still advocating mainline electrification based on the initial likelihood of it coming to pass. He gave NER the first British mainline electric locomotive and launched a massive new *Pacific*. Both of these enterprises meant that, at least on the engineering side, NER would go out with a blast rather than a whimper.

Nevertheless, despite all the lecturing and committee activity about electrification, the signs of valediction to the old NER were becoming increasingly obvious. Baister and Lockyear had already gone and key officers during 1922 would not be continuing as leading lights in future railway matters in the North East. On 24 February 1922, Raven was called to make a farewell presentation on the retirement of the NER general manager, Sir Alexander Kaye Butterworth, who, despite a rather ponderous approach to management when compared with Gibb, his predecessor, had been in post since 1906. Like Raven, he had received a knighthood for his war effort. Raven asked Sir Alexander to accept a loving cup wrought with old silver as a token of affection and good wishes. He said that it showed the trust, which had endeared him to the staff of all grades, was the human touch brought to bear on every problem. Despite his emphasis at the conferences and in addresses on rail electrification, Raven became involved in what became his 'swansong' for steam locomotives and his most controversial, the *Pacifics*.

The creation of NER *Pacifics* arose because the NER directors wanted to equal, if not surpass the two GNR *Pacifics* – No.1470, *Great Northern* and No.1471 *Sir Frederick Banbury*, the first two of the *Flying Scotsman* class which the GNR started to build in 1921 after a seven-year delay. Raven must have known something of Gresley's design, even if he was at that time more focussed on the idea of NER mainline electrification. Nevertheless, he wanted the new electric locomotives to have a similar tractive effort to the new *Pacific* so that they would to some extent be interchangeable. Despite, and probably because of, the Railways Act of 1921 and the forthcoming amalgamations, the first two locomotives were authorised on 30 March, a start being made as early as 3 March on design drawings by the Darlington team of draughtsmen, including C.A. King, James Maconchie, W.G. Amies, J. Baty and D.D. Gray.

All five of the class were built at Darlington, the largest locomotive built there up to that time. Two were authorised by Raven as CME and A. Pease as GM on 30 March 1922, namely Nos 2400 City of Newcastle and 2401 City of Kingston-upon-Hull, which were completed in December 1922, starting service in January 1923. Three more were authorised by the LNER on 24 February 1924, Nos 2402 *City of York*, 2403 *City of Durham* and 2404 *City of Ripon*, appearing in March 1924. They were at first unnamed as was usual with NER; the names were added from 1923 onward.[2]

There was an early Press release in the July 1922 edition of *The Railway Magazine* of an outline drawing and full dimensions, five months before its appearance. This caused a flurry of

The first NER
Pacific, Raven's
'swansong'
in steam,
magnificent if
flawed.

The complimentary mainline express duo. No.13, the quill drive express electric locomotive and
No.53 above, one of the class of five *Pacifics*, with a magnificently strong appearance, intended by
Raven to be interchangeable mainline express locomotives.

interest at its launch. The *NER Magazine* for December 1922 hailed the engines as 'the largest
passenger engine in Britain.'

Externally, the engines were impressive and were unmistakably both Raven and NER in
profile, like big sisters to earlier class Z/Z1 4-4-2s and S2 4-6-0s, but with larger cylinders, a larger
diameter boiler, a larger firebox and compared to the *Atlantic* another pair of coupled wheels, in
order to keep down the axle load to 20 tons. Unfortunately, possibly due to the pressure generated
by the rush to complete the enterprise before grouping got under way and so produce something
notable, Raven, for once, had not organised the design-and-build team to rethink what would be
necessary to help such a large locomotive function efficiently and economically, for a long time a
cry of his. He saw it as capable of working as a steam alternative to his electric mainline locomotive.
Like many of the more recent NER fleet, the new engine had to have three cylinders. They lay
in line with the piston valve chests. They would drive on to the leading pair of coupled wheels.
The locomotive needed a massive frame to support the longer boiler and smoke box. Raven,
according to the diary of Charles Innes, one of the draughtsmen, did not like it being pointed out
that this made a long engine have an even longer wheelbase (37ft 2in long when compared with
35ft 9in of GNR *Pacific*). Raven lost his temper, banged the table and shouted that he had always
driven on to the leading coupled axle and that he was going to do this with the *Pacific*. He failed
to appreciate that like his *Atlantics* six eccentrics and the middle big end had to be accommodated
on the crank axle – a difficult arrangement, known locally as 'fitter's nightmare'. This, coupled with
a comparatively narrow firebox for the size of boiler, meant that steaming as a result was not to be
so efficient. The very long boiler earned the class the nickname of 'Skittle Allies'.[3]

There was criticism that:

> ... the boiler was pretty ropy by the standards of the day. The sheer length of the barrel must
> have looked wrong on the drawing board, let alone on the shop floor, but it went ahead and it
> was a weak point before the first fire was lit.

Sir Alexander Kaye Butterworth, NER
general manager from 1906–1922.

Sir Ralph Wedgewood, general manager in
1922 for NER, then for LNER.

Perhaps if S. Woolford, the experienced chief boiler inspector at NER from 1883 to 1919 and Charlie Baister, as running superintendent, had both still been in post, they could have advised the planning team about developing the locomotives' capacity and mechanics as well as size. They were all scrapped in 1936–37.

When No.2400 was outshopped, Raven sent Tom Blades, doyen of Gateshead drivers, to Darlington to bring her to Gateshead. On arrival there, Raven fussed around what his team had created, enquiring of Blades what he thought of the locomotive. He was somewhat disgruntled when he received a less than enthusiastic reply. Blades told Raven in no uncertain Geordie terms that he would have trouble with the inside bearants (bearings) on the pony truck. Raven, obviously *au fait* with the Geordie twang (accent), enquired why this should be so. Blades replied, 'Why man, for wan thing them's tee near the fayah'. (They are too close to the firebox.) Blades proved to be right and three members of the class that were built in 1924 had the modification of Cartazzi sliding axle boxes fitted to the pony truck. Furthermore, the use of an elongated version of the Stephenson valve gear, which was so successful on class 'Z' *Atlantics* caused trouble, possibly through excessive side-thrust on to axle boxes. On the economic front, in use they were heavy coal users as was soon proved, but were regarded as better steamers than GNR locomotives.

In 1923, 2400, now named *City of Newcastle*, was given a fair comparative trial with GNR 1472 (now LNER 4472), *Flying Scotsman*. To emphasis the fairness of the trials, Gresley used the NER dynamometer car and crew and chose the hardest turns on the timetable at that time – the 10.51 a.m. Doncaster to Kings Cross and the return working at 5.40 p.m. The results seem to speak for themselves, despite having the redoubtable Tom Blades at the regulator of 2400 and fireman C. Fisher, but the results were not definitively conclusive. The tests were not, however, repeated, possibly in case they might be different.

Engines	Coal consumption	Water consumption	Drawbar hp
2400	58.7lb/mile	40.4 gals/mile	875
4472	52.6lb/mile	38.3 gals/mile	928

Furthermore, there were difficulties with early part of raising steam the Gresley engines being better in this respect.[4] Like their predecessor's class R1 4-4-0s, Raven's *Pacifics* were probably better machines than was reported at the time for long-distance heavy passenger haulage, even if heavier on coal and once the particular requirements to make them function well were known and nurtured. As Raven's engines no longer exist, it is difficult to appreciate their real worth, as they were scrapped prematurely before giving even 2 million route miles of service.

There was a lot of railway politicking at the LNER Board at the time, when so many decisions were being made. It is still thought in some quarters that the results were 'doctored' in favour of Gresley's engine. In some respects, GNR personnel were determined to dominate the future of LNER, a situation not helped locally as some of the difficulties with the Raven *Pacifics* were due to its drivers, who, apart from Jack Knight, did not make efforts to make the best running from them.[5] Aesthetically, the lines of the engine were uncluttered and massive, yet showed quite clearly the distinct Raven corporate style, seeming to underline how continuous NER's development had been from the beginning of the century. There was no attempt to anticipate future design, now beginning to move towards into an Art Deco future, of which Gresley's and Stanier's streamlined locomotives in the 1930s would become the most obvious mechanical symbol. While their machines were more dazzling to see and still continued to catch the public imagination, Raven's machines reflect his genuine efforts to move forward within an established tradition as did those of Churchward and Collett for GWR – hence the uncluttered lines and noble profiles of his designs.

Raven had himself to choose between retirement and going for the post of CME for new LNER. An indication that he was undecided in his thoughts about the future was his announcement to a large audience assembled on 3 April 1922 for the twenty-first AGM of the NER Assembly Rooms in Darlington that, after twenty-one years of association with it, he was retiring from its presidency. The faithful Stamer would take over from him as president.

Yet for the time being, as he probably valued the post, he allowed himself to be re-elected president of Gateshead NER Literary Institute at its sixty-fifth AGM on 12 May 1922. It is natural that Raven should consider his future and it is possible that Raven as early as April 1922 had considered whether he should stand as a candidate for the CME to the company soon to succeed NER, resign from the post of CME or find some alternative outlets for his energies.

Away from all the speculation over the grouping, electrification and the genesis of his *Pacifics*, Raven went on a 'busman's holiday' to the summer meeting of IMechE in mid-June, held in Paris and Liège. He was a guest speaker for la Societé des Ingénieurs Civiles de France (SICF). This was followed by attendance at the Conference and Exhibition, held by Association Belgique des Ingénieurs (ABI) in 1922. It turned out to be, in effect, a nine-day tour of Paris and Liège and places of interest around them.

In the early afternoon of Monday 12 June, the party of IMechE officials, consisting of the president Dr H.S. Hele-Shaw FRS, vice-chairmen Raven and Council members left London. They broke their journey at Amiens. On Tuesday 13, after lunch in Amiens, the party went on a circuitous ride through the war zone of the First World War, east of Amiens and south of Albert in the Somme valley (it was a repeat visit for Raven to the area where his son is likely to have been killed, and which he had visited before in March 1917):

> They proceeded by motor-cars to Compiègne travelling via Villers-Bretonnex, Warfusée-Abancourt, Proyart, Chuignolles, Chuignes, Rosières, Le Quesnol, Hangest-en-Santerre and Montdidier. A halt was made between Chuignolles and Chuignes to inspect the big gun captured by the Australians.

They had dinner and stopped overnight in Compiègne, travelling on to Paris, arriving at 11 a.m. Wednesday, where they were welcomed at the Hall of the SICF on the Rue Blanche by the SICF vice-president Professeur Léon Guillet DSc on behalf of the president M. Max Laubeuf. Among the distinguished guests was Hon. Life member, ninety-year-old Gustave Eiffel, who was given special recognition.

After this, as part of the morning session, Raven gave his paper on rail electrification, which he, with the help of Francis Lydall from Merz and McLennan had prepared for this conference. It covered much the same ground as his previous papers given in 1921, but expanded and refocussed its examples by referring, comparing and contrasting his own NER electric locomotives with those built for both US and Continental practice. Not only were large railroads like Baltimore & Ohio, Chicago, Milwaukee & St Paul, Great Northern, New York, New Haven and Hartford, Norfolk and Western, Pennsylvania referred to, but smaller ones with significant electrification schemes like Butte, Anaconda[6] and Pacific and Michigan Central.[7] Concerning rail electrification elsewhere, attention was drawn to practice on Italian State, Midi, Paulista (Brazil), Prussian State and Swiss Federal Railways. It provoked some discussion and support from the floor. He publicly thanked F. Lydall for the very valuable assistance he had given him in connection with this paper.

It is likely that he became an honorary Membre de la SICF as a result of giving his paper there.[8] (At home, more significantly for him and the British engineers who attended the conference, was the nearness of the date of the out-shopping of his mainline electric locomotive, the unlucky No.13. The future was in the balance, but was not rosy. He later replied in writing to items of discussion of this paper for the IMechE meeting on Friday 17 November.)

For Wednesday's lunch, they adjourned to Restaurant Garnier Perronell. This was followed by a choice of group visits either to the machine gun factory, Renault factory or Conservatoire

Institution of Mechanical Engineers, 1 Birdcage Walk, Westminster.

Nationale des Arts et metier, followed by a visit to Laboratoires d'Essais or individual visits to various workshops, including optical instruments, motor cars, boilers and the like. After a further lecture, members and ladies were received by the president and officers of the SICF in the Council Chamber.

During the course of Thursday, group visits were made to a construction factory and bus and train works. The ladies of the visiting party were shepherded by the La Bienvenue Française, a reception committee of French wives, whose husbands made up the Conference, and off they went to visit the Japanese garden at Boulogne-sur-Seine and the park at Bagette. In the evening, was the IMechE dinner in Hôtel Continental. Guests were received by the president of IMechE. The particular guests of the French SICF included, among others, Mr H.G.A. Mackie, CBE HBM Consul General; Max Laubeuf, Léon Guillet, Gustave Eiffel and M. le Conte de Dax. The British had in attendance members of the council, including the vice-presidents W. Patchell and Raven. The first toasts were to King George V and the President of the French Republic (Alexandre Millerand), then the Technical and Commercial Interests of France and Great Britain, one to the French delegation as our guests by president IMechE and finally the Institution of Mechanical Engineers, which was acknowledged by representatives of IMechE.

On Friday 16 November, there were excursions to Fontainebleau or the Union d'Éléctricité power station and the Paris water works. In the evening there was at the Association Amicale des Anciens Élèves de l'École Centrale des Arts et Manufactures, 8 Rue Jean Goujon.

On Saturday, before leaving for Liège by ordinary train, they went to lay a wreath at the tomb of the Unknown Soldier at the Arc de Triomphe in Paris.[9] On the Saturday afternoon, the party had arrived in Liège, to witness the well-loved Albert 1, King of the Belgians, open the Liège International Scientific Conference and Exhibition, held at the Palais (now Académie) des Beaux Arts, 21 Rue des Anglais, by ABI. The IMechE party was welcomed by the ABI president. In the evening, they had dinner at the Hall Renommée, welcomed by the ABI president, Gustave Trasenster. Sunday saw another visit to a First World War site, this time to Fort de Loncin, where its heroic resistance in 1914 was honoured under the guidance of M. Joseph Pasleau, secretary of the Liege branch of the Anglo-Belgian Union. Colonel Naessens, who had actually defended the fort, was present.

On Monday 19th, the Conference was opened by Prof. Herman Victor Hubert, CBE, president of Liège conference. Visits were available for various works of interest to the engineers, for instance steel factories, mining and machinery works etc., while the president's wife Mme Hubert went off to Spa. Monday evening was occupied by a reception in the Hôtel de Ville by Bourgmestre (Mayor), Digrelffe and his Échevins (Aldermen), followed by a special performance of Gounod's delightful Provençal opera, Mireille at the Jardin d'Acclimatation.

On Tuesday morning, there was a visit to Fabrique Nationale d'Armes de Guerre at Henstel. In the early afternoon of Tuesday 20 June, the president laid a wreath at the foot of the tablet erected in the house of the Liège Anglo-Belgian Association. In the afternoon, there was an official 'Farewell to the president and council of IMechE' by their Belgian counterparts. However, there was a last choice of visits, a reception at the Anglo-Belgian Union, another concert at the Jardin d'Acclimatation or a Revue in French at the Thèâtre de Gymnase. On Wednesday 21 June, the British party then left for London; no doubt the party had been glad that there had been opportunity to hear, see and visit so much of interest to different engineers and individuals.

During the latter part of 1922, frequent meetings were held between the locomotive engineers, chaired by Raven:

> not so much concerned with locomotive matters as with identifying topics, which needed inter-line standardisation, such as braking systems, corridor connections, and renumbering of rolling stock. One other subject was the ascertainment of the capability of several workshops of the new group for construction and repair of locomotives, coaches and wagons.

For instance, at the first meeting, he said that his general manager (Wedgwood, the chief GM designate) had asked him to call together the mechanical engineers.[10] Raven was accepted as chairman of the meetings without demur from the other CMEs attending. They all turned up for the meetings, except John G. Robinson (1856–1943, CME to GCR), who sent as his deputy R.A. Thom (assistant CME to GCR) with the instruction to the effect that 'the Great Central does it this way and there is no point in changing'.[11] They did achieve standardisation of brake and corridor connections.[12] There are two off-beat footnotes to all this development of steam and electric traction. First, there was the commissioning of a Leyland petrol bus giving it rail wheels. It provided a local service from Cawood, via Selby, through to York.

Even more significant when looking back on what has happened since was a drawing of 4-6-4 diesel locomotive made about this time; note the 'Baltic wheels again. This is remarkably like the outlines of class 56 and 58 diesels produced for British Rail in the 1960s, although they sport coupling rods to move the three driving wheels, linked to the horizontal engine and its rotating cam, which put it visually at the locomotive frame level still in the steam era. In this gearing and wheel arrangement, it of course shares some common ground with No.13 the 2-C-2 electric locomotive. It remains yet another prognostication of future development from Raven!

Raven was moving into a final post-war phase. He must have realised that his electrification scheme would not now be likely. Raven eventually indicated that he would support Gresley's candidature, thus probably easing the way for the Board eventually to appoint Gresley.

1 Bell R., 1951, *Twenty-five years of the North Eastern Railway*, Harrison & Sons Ltd, p.48

2 *NER Magazine* for August 1922

3 Middlemass Thomas, 1991, *Steam Locomotive Nicknames*, Silver Link Publishing Ltd, p.115

4 Armstrong Jim, 1974, *LNER Locomotive development between 1911 and 1947*, Peco Publications, p.28

5 Bell L.L., 'The North Eastern in 1919', *North East Express*, no.22, May 1966, p.22. Bell writes quite positively about the unrealised potential of the *Pacifics*

6 Butte Anaconda & Pacific Railway (1893-1895), opened to mine copper and electrified its sixty-nine miles of track in 1913

7 Michigan Central (1832-1931) served Ontario, Michigan and Indiana Illinois

8 Membership (probably honorary) of SICF is mentioned in several obituaries

9 Proceedings of IMechE, June 1922, p.697

10 Hughes Geoffrey, 1983, *The Gresley Influence*, Ian Allan Ltd, p.13

11 Hughes Geoffrey, 1983, *The Gresley Influence*, Ian Allan Ltd, p.14

12 Hughes Geoffrey, 1986, *LNER*, Ian Allan Ltd, p.87

XI

COMMISSIONS ROYAL
AND OTHERWISE
(1923–1924)

The Railways Act of 1921 began to have its effect on all levels of personnel, most markedly upon those in the most senior positions on the Board and in the Executive. Who would be in the chief positions in the new LNER became a matter for the usual wheeling and dealing of railway politics. Background to this were the difficulties with cash flow at this period, added to continuing tensions between management and labour. Geddes, the author of the act, would have been a most obvious and suitable candidate for general manager. He had been deputy GM to NER, the most powerful constituent of the LNER (for instance, it would contribute 2,001 locomotives to LNER stock, while GCR provided 1,361 and GNR 1,359).

Geddes, who was the Minister of Transport from January 1919, was the prime mover in the post-war period in securing the passage of the Railways Act 1921, which completed the ideas of grouping, to which the railways had been moving during the war. However, by moving to the Ministry of Transport, he had alienated the NER Board. Despite this, he was nevertheless granted £50,000 severance pay in lieu of completing his contract. They were therefore able to exclude him from running for GM of LNER and instead supported his erstwhile deputy chief GM Ralph Lewis Wedgwood. In 1921, Geddes moved on from the Ministry of Transport to become chairman of Imperial Airways.

During the latter part of 1922, frequent meetings were held between the locomotive engineers, chaired by Raven, not so much concerned with locomotive matters as with identifying topics, which needed inter-line standardisation, such as braking systems, corridor connections, and renumbering of rolling stock. One other subject was the ascertainment of the capability of several workshops of the new group for construction and repair of locomotives, coaches and wagons.

Raven, of course, was one of the three most powerful candidates for the post of CME to the LNER, when the 1923 grouping of UK railways in the four major companies – GWR, SR, LMSR and LNER – occurred. The other two candidates were Sir Nigel Gresley (CME – GNR) and John G. Robinson (CME – GCR). The Board with its powerful representation of NER interests favoured Raven, despite his being now over sixty-four years of age, but it was unlikely that another man from the dominant NER would be appointed.

One of the requirements was that it would be compulsory for the new CME to be based at King's Cross, as it happened in small offices, a considerable let down after the palatial 'Stooperdale' in Darlington.[4] This may have been a disappointment, but Raven was more likely disillusioned about the electrification, which was continually delayed and finally cancelled. He was easing the way for the Board to appoint Gresley. Whatever the truth of the matter, Raven retired on the last day of 1922.

However, Raven was far from being a spent force in other spheres of influence and had other irons in the fire around the time of his resignation from NER. He was the president of the Association of Locomotive Engineers at the August 1922 meeting in Scarborough.

On 1 January 1923, he joined the Board of Metropolitan-Vickers as a director. He already knew the firm and its chairman, Sir Philip Nash, as it had supplied the electrical equipment for his electric mainline locomotive. The original company had been formed in 1899 by an American, George Westinghouse (of brake fame) as a British subsidiary, called British Westinghouse. It combined with the Metropolitan Carriage, Wagon & Finance Co., which provided the capital for the merger. It then acquired Vickers Ltd, becoming a wholly British company under the name of Metropolitan-Vickers Electric Co. Ltd in 1919, based at Trafford Park, Manchester. As a result of all these mergers, the group thus formed was able to provide steel-making, rolling stock construction and electrical engineering on a significantly large scale.

The Metropolitan Railway had been able as part of its policy was to buy up and hold land in the London suburbs with a view to stimulating building of residential accommodation, and hence the transport services that new suburbia needed. Its first managing director was R.S. Hilton, with G.E. Bailey as works manager. Raven may have foreseen an alternate and appropriate outlet for his enthusiasm for railway electrification.

At the reception to bid him farewell as CME to NER, it was noted that Raven had spent the whole of his career, some forty-eight years, with the NER. On his retirement, he was leaving behind responsibility for 18,000 personnel. The faithful Stamer was destined to remain in Darlington to keep the ex-NER 'end' going as assistant CME to Gresley. On 8 January, Raven resigned from Gateshead NER Literary Institute as president and treasurer. It must have brought to mind former times on the occasion when the Worsdell brothers had retired.

Because the session had been booked before his retirement from NER, and still determined to pursue his *idée fixe*, electrification schemes, Raven gave yet another paper entitled 'The Advantages of Electric Traction on Railways' to the GWR (London Branch) Lecture and Debating Society on 4 January 1923 – a mere six weeks prior to the announcement of who would be CME for LNER. Raven now talked in a more generalised way about the benefits of electrification. The discussion that followed showed how impressed the listeners were with his ideas. For instance, Charles B. Collett, who had recently been elected member of the ARLE, asked why coal from South Wales could not be used to produce electricity that would be cheaper than that of Switzerland. He also stated that he would like to be relieved of the responsibility for high-pressure steam boilers, which electrification would cause to disappear. Then, Roger T. Smith (EE-GWR) compared the South Wales lines to Newport-Shildon, saying it would pay to electrify them. However, the CE emphasised how high the cost of conversion of electrification would be. Fred V. Russell, another contributor to the discussion, continued to advocate steam traction.

At this time it had not been officially confirmed who the new CME would be. Later that month, at a meeting of the ARLE at St Pancras Hotel on 19 January, there was a debate about revising the structure of ARLE in the light of the new Railway Act. Raven and Hughes had both made proposals. Gresley sent a letter dated 17 January, in which he made clear his preferences.

...the matter to be raised concerns the future of the Association and the amendment of the rules.

I have read through Mr Hughes suggestions, but I regret that I cannot agree to them. I much prefer the scheme which was outlined at the last meeting by Sir Vincent Raven, under which the Chief Mechanical Engineers of the four groups would have the final decision in all recommendations made by their principal Assistants, who would be members of the Association.

Hughes wanted all members to have equal voting rights – a seemingly more 'democratic' view than Raven's. Gresley threatened resignation, saying it could mean that the sssistants could outvote their CME's. His intervention won the day.[5] Regarding the post of CME to LNER, Gavin Henderson, first Lord Faringdon, formerly with CR, understandably favoured the powerful character of Robinson. Robinson now decided himself to back Gresley. The latter was of course the one who was eventually chosen by the Locomotive Committee for the post. On 22 February 1923 he was appointed with a salary of £4,500 p.a. – a decision ratified by the LNER Board of directors the next day. In fact, both Robinson and Raven would have to be replaced quite quickly. Although portrayed as mere caretakers, they both had the capacity and tenacity to produce surprises, if they came to power. In a typically gracious gesture, Gresley asked Oliver Bulleid to remain as his assistant as at GNR.

After this, Raven no longer pursued mainline rail electrification, but nothing daunted, entered into an Indian summer of activity, staying on with LNER as a technical advisor with his current salary of £4,000 p.a. for a further year. He was asked to do two reports, which were to be entitled, 'Organisation of Running Departments on the organisation and standards of running sheds for LNER'[6], and 'Utilisation of Workshops about organisation of maintenance workshops, for LNER.'[7]

His reports highlighted the need for raising the standards of the shops to an acceptable level. He commented on the number of overhauls being done, balancing up the need for having this done by workshops by the staff there or at workshops attached to the running sheds, which were smaller and less economic because they lacked the facilities of the larger workshops. He instanced that the ex-GER alone had 400 such shops.[8]

The topics mentioned above had previously been aired during discussions in 1922, and Raven quickly and, as usual, efficiently, compiled a report, which assessed clearly the position in each case. The previous CMEs had been responsible for running locomotive departments in NBR and the Southern Division of the NER; he also proposed CMEs should be relieved of such responsibility of locomotive running and that there should be locomotive running superintendents (LRS) who should be appointed to work under the GM. They should be qualified engineers, apprentice served in railway engineering workshops. They would have control of running staff and carrying out running repairs. They should work in close co-operation with traffic staff so that the most economical methods of working can be carried out. Other safeguards in practice were that there should be no alteration to designs and boiler inspectors work in the CME's department. Definition of what running repairs were to be done should be made between the CME and LRS and all failures should be made known to the CME.[9] Gorton was equipped to deal with twenty-seven locomotives, Stratford thirty: all in all it was not well equipped, despite higher pay at this workshop. There should an additional shop at Doncaster. Regarding locomotive castings Darlington bought in there at £17 per ton, Doncaster made their own at £11 25s per ton, although Raven astutely comments that castings rejected from contractors may be accepted by their own place of manufacture to their detriment.

He went on to comment that the number of locomotives on the books was 7,400. They had an average life of forty years, so that from Darlington and Doncaster the LNER would need 185 new engines per year. In practice, due to various economic stringencies as well as the effects of the Second World War and its effective railway nationalisation, less than 100 were built. There was some flaw in the arguments and numbers presented based on an assumption that pre-1914 rates still applied. At best, they could only be considered as indicators. Regarding carriages, it was recommended that brakes and corridor connections should be standardised. Nevertheless, the recommendations were mostly accepted, despite some misgivings from the staff of LNER CME's department. These themes had occurred in the past in his 1898 report to Cambrian Railways and would provide some of the substance for his reports for the Royal Commissions into New South Wales Government Railways (NSWGR) and New Zealand Railways (NZR) in the next year.

Raven had use of a small office in King's Cross Station during 1923, which he is likely to have used as a working base for doing these reports. He also had temporary secluded *pied-à-terre* at Abbey Gardens, Westminster, almost in the abbey close, just round the corner from the Institutions on Great George Street, which served as a useful place, between leaving Darlington and taking up residence in Hampshire. Sir Sam Fay, the ex-GM of GCR, had also been asked to remain for a year at the disposal of chief GM of LNER. He was a great gun man, and probably involved Raven in the sport. When asked his advice about men suitable for two Royal Commissions on the railways down under, LNER GM Ralph Wedgwood probably hit on the retired men as being suitable. Fay, therefore, came to travel with Raven in the next year, to the Antipodes.

Raven then examined proposals for the electrification of the ex-GN suburban system. This resulted in a committee being set up with him as chairman and with Gresley as one of the panel members of the Technical and Traffic Officers Committee, which first convened on 21 September 1923 at King's Cross. It proposed electrifying the line as far as Hitchin, using power compatible with the Metropolitan Railways, (650v dc), whereas from Potters Bar, 1,500v dc would be used (the rating used in Newport-Shildon system). Express passenger and fish trains would continue to be steam operated, but outer suburban, coal and goods would be hauled by electric traction, a changeover point being established at Hitchin. Provision was made for twenty 80-ton electric locomotives, designed for dual 650v/1,500v supply, which would replace an estimated sixty steam locomotives. The four articulated sets would have to be compatible with each system. Its last meeting was on 24 May 1925.

There was to be a three-man panel to discuss the technical side of this, Raven as technical advisor, Gresley and C.E. Fairburn, who represented the manufacturing firm, English Electric Co. Fairburn, as a twenty-five year old in 1912–1913, had been responsible for the overhead line system and for the electric locomotives for the Newport–Shildon electrification, so they would have known each other. This was the last public pronouncement on British rail electrification that Raven was involved with. He would then turn his attention abroad.

The Ravens had to leave Grantly as it was owned by the LNER. They moved in the autumn of 1923 to Nately Lodge, on the side of Scures Hill just west of Hook, Hampshire, on the A30. The house, similar in size to Grantly, stood in its own grounds.[10] The front had a southerly wooded aspect. Possibly he and Lady Raven decided to buy it earlier,[11] as it was similar in size to Grantly. Moreover, it was near enough to London for Raven still to use his 'golden pass' to attend business meetings and freelance projects more quickly and more easily, although it was further away from Connie and the grandchildren in Darlington and from Guen now back in Doncaster. Significantly, it was also near to Farnborough; granddaughter Mary Gifford went to Farnborough Hill School, the Catholic boarding school where from 1927 the sisters of the Institute of Christian Education had their private school. His resignation from the LNER consultancy post at the end of 1923 and the cessation of the presidency of ARLE on 10 December left him some time for other things. He had leisure time to go to the Wellington Club, as well as be a country gentleman, shooting, golfing and driving in his motorcar.

Besides activity within ICE and IMechE, Raven became a member of IEE in 1923, albeit rather belatedly considering the work he had done concerning electrification. He published a thirty-six-page report for the Metropolitan Vickers Electric Co. in 1924 concerning electrification and electric locomotives. This really marked the end of his push for electrification. His own Shildon–Newport line had begun to feel 'the pinch', due to trade depression in 1924. This particularly affected mining and the carriage of minerals, on which NER among all the British railways had invested its money and manpower and, as a consequence, relied on its existence for its prosperity. So it is all too easy to understand the LNER Board's thinking about further electrification proposals, shelving them during the General Strike and its aftermath in 1925. Despite a revival of interest in 1930, nothing further was done at the time. Raven's advocacy would have to wait another fifty years and more. Threats to and predictions concerning the diminishing supplies of coal and petroleum had to prevail, before the sense of what he was saying was examined once more and implemented.

Norman Raven and Edward Thompson enjoyed golfing and Sir Vincent enjoyed it, too. That there are two golf clubs, one established as long ago as 1851 in the Hook area, and the nearness of the New Forest, may have influenced the Raven's decision to move south. There he could also do some shooting, another interest of his.

Raven remained a Borough JP in Darlington until after 1925, not as onerous as it may sound, as it only required his attendance at the Quarter Sessions four times a year. The serious trade depression in the country during 1924 and 1925 now particularly affected the North East with its dependence on coal mining, engineering, shipbuilding and heavy industry. This together with increasing strife between men, management and Unions, meant that the loss of revenue, and the likelihood of further railway electrification, especially mainline, receded further into the background or distant future, depending on one's viewpoint.

With so little likelihood of his advocacy for rail electrification bearing fruit, it was not surprising that Raven had retired altogether from active railway service with LNER by 1924. Besides taking on honorary posts like president of IMechE, he now embarked on a 'St Martin's Summer' phase of travel to Australia, New Zealand and India on Commissions into their Railways, resulting in reports about them. It showed that he had not quite finished with railway affairs yet. There is no mention of wives being included on these travels. It is probable that Lady Raven went to stay with her daughters, Guen, now in York, and Constance, who still lived in Darlington. Here she could be with her family, especially the grandchildren.

The reason the New South Wales (NSW) Commission arose from its Parliament in 1923 was because there had been political pressure which had its leverage in upon more or less vague charges of incompetence and mismanagement levelled against the railway authority.'[12]

This resulted in the decision to have a Royal Commission to look into the NSW railways. It was announced on 23 December 1923 by NSW Premier, Sir George Fuller KCMG, that Raven and Sir Sam Fay had been appointed by the NSW Government with full powers as Members of the Royal Commission of Inquiry, which was to investigate and report on the state of the administration of NSW railways and tramways. On 13 February NSW Parliament was informed. Officially, there would be no limits as to what the Commission could choose to investigate within the field.

Sir Sam Fay will be the traffic expert on the commission, dealing with organisation, fares, permanent way &c, and Sir Vincent Raven the technical and locomotive expert. The desire of the Government is that at least six months, apart from travelling, should be spent by them in a close investigation of the whole of the railway system. They will be clothed with wide powers. Not merely will be they inspect the whole of the railway workings, and have access to all documents and other records, but they will be empowered to call upon all officers and other employees for any information or evidence which the experts may regard as desirable. The question of taking evidence from employees or from the public will be left to the discretion of the experts. Each will prepare his own special report, and they will afterwards collaborate in a general report.[13]

Raven's *pied-à-terre* at Abbey Gardens, Westminster, during 1923.

Sir Sam Fay, former general manager of GCR.

Major S.E. Fay.

Sir Sam Fay, quondam GM–GCR, had a lot of business connections. He was a director of Buenos Aires Great Southern and Buenos Aires Western Railways, president of the British Institute of Transport and chairman of Beyer Peacock Co. Earlier, as a clerk at the LSWR, he had written an early history of the company published in 1882. He moved to GCR as GM in 1902. He was publicly knighted by King George V at the opening of Immingham Docks on 12 July 1912, intended by GCR as an alternative to the monopoly on the north bank of the Humber exercised by NER and Hull & Barnsley Railway.

The other British members of the five-man Royal Commission were Mr Charles Travis as secretary to the Commission, former railway traffic manager – GCR, now editor of the British journals *The Railway Gazette* and *The Railway Engineer*, and Mr J.A. Warren King, head of the statistical section of the GM's office with the GWR. He was to act as secretary to Raven. Finally, there was Fay's youngest son, Major S.E. Fay, who had worked for GCR and with Brazilian and Canadian railways as assistant secretary.

R. M. S. - « ORVIETO »

Above: The Royal Mail Steamship, a former troopship, on which the Royal Commission party sailed in 1924 to Australia.

Oppposite: Government House, Macquarie Street, Sydney, where Fay and Raven conducted most of the Commission interviews.

To prepare themselves for this important task, the Commissioners are likely to have sent out a questionnaire as was done prior to the next Royal Commission, i.e. into New Zealand Railways. The reply would give detailed information about the system, which they could amplify and assess once for themselves when they arrived there.

Having left London on 29 March on board RMS *Orvieto*, a veteran of the First World War, having served as a troop carrier and minelayer, they stopped at Port Said on 9 April, arriving in Melbourne on 6 May, but docking at Sydney on 9 May. The Commission's terms of reference had been submitted to the State Cabinet of Sir George Warburton Fuller's Coalition Government of 1922–1925 by the Hon. Richard Thomas Ball, Minister for Railways, MP Corrowa and were approved on 23 April, after which the Attorney General, Thomas Rainsford Bavin, MP Ryde (and later in 1930 NSW Premier), agreed to have them drawn in a proper legal form. The party's official appointment as a Royal Commission was on 26 May, with the following terms of reference:

> ...the commission shall inquire into the management, equipment, and general working, including the finance, administration, control, and economy of the railway and tramway services, in New South Wales, and more particularly
>
> (1) The organisation and running of the passenger and goods traffic. The services rendered, the scales of fares and freights operating, and the financial returns.
>
> (2) Matters appertaining to the organisation and conduct of the mechanical section of the system in relation to the respective types of locomotives and rolling stock adopted, cost, economy of life and use, equipment, renewal, and maintenance charges.
>
> (3) Matters relating to the construction, renewal, and maintenance of the permanent way, including station equipment and the system of signalling and interlocking adopted.

They reported back well before the six-month period allotted to them. This meant that their recommendations were tabled in the Legislative assembly of NSW Government on 7 October 1924. What Fay and Raven contributed can be traced in the final 325 page report, company issues being the concern of Fay and the technical ones of Raven. In fact, Raven's contribution is strongly reminiscent of the themes he had already covered about locomotive management and maintenance in earlier reports for NER, Cambrian Railways and more recently for LNER.

There were 4,671 questions asked and recorded during the formal part of the Enquiry, based on comprehensive information provided by questionnaires and other sources, including manufacturing and agricultural representatives. The result was thirty-two individual recommendations, given under eight sections in the report. The first two sections probably had Sam Fay as author. The first section, 'Finance' (1-5), outlined a reform of the financial services of the state railway (and tramways), freeing it from political control and making the railway administration responsible for raising and balancing its own budget with yearly accountability to Parliament. The second section, 'Organisation' (6-10), outlined a simple hierarchical structure for new management, a chief railway commissioner, a Government appointment, who would appoint his own staff thereafter, viz. a financial assistant commissioner, a power assistant commissioner, a tramway assistant commissioner and three area assistant commissioners.

The third section was 'Construction' (11-12), and reads as if Raven was the author of this part of the report. Indeed, it is reminiscent of the Committee for Great Northern electrification scheme that Raven was still officially involved with at home in England. The NSWR system adopted 1,500v dc, the same as Raven's freight and mainline standard. Its first electric train started running in 1926. In the next section, 'Mechanical and electrical engineering' (13-26), Raven provided a detailed list of recommendations, which would streamline the provision for building and maintenance of locomotives and rolling stock, based at Eveleigh (Sydney), with new carriage workshops (eventually opened in 1937) and at Honeysuckle Point. He advocated standardising the Australian curse of mixed gauges, plus clearing away large numbers of old locomotive and coach stock and replacing them with standardised six passenger and four goods locomotive classes. The Area Commissioners should be based at Sydney for the metropolitan area, Newcastle and the south and Bathurst for Lithgow and rural west. The next section, 'Operation' (27-31) was to look at control systems for traffic and examine the passenger and freight facilities in Newcastle; and on rural branches, rail-motors should be introduced, and there should be adequate provision of rolling stock for carrying livestock. This section, 'Commercial' (32-4) dealt with fares, both for first and second class, suburban and rural, as well as rates for carrying fodder and provisions for drought. Linked with this was the next section, 'Stores', which should be under a specific official, called a Comptroller. They end with a last section called 'General', which really dealt with training issues, including a proper series of graduated in-service courses and internal placements for company officers in training and developing as well as sending officers to view the best contemporary practice elsewhere.

As can be seen, the report was both forward and backward looking, reliant as it was on the experience of both Fay and Raven. It has a political perspective, displaying in a rational set of proposals which aimed to reduce government interference as a subtext in the report as a whole. There is advocacy of a measure of freedom from the Treasury, letting responsibility for the whole running of the railway be invested its grades of Commissioner. This was an attempt to provide ten-year financial stability, e.g. by developing new lines, without the stop-go policies, dictated by changes of governmental mind. Raven and Fay could well be putting forward practical measures which they felt would work better than the systems they themselves had worked in. The Press welcomed the points leading to more independence, but were sceptical that that such change would happen. Nevertheless, the Government Railways (Amendment) Act of 1924 was passed, which appointed a chief railway commissioner for NSWR, with two assistants (all for a period of seven years) as well as four Area Commissioners. This organisational structure started on 1 January 1925.

The rationalisation of depots went ahead, although many (like Darlington North Road Works and Shildon back home) have now disappeared to become a technology/arts centre (Eveleigh) and a multi-purpose community centre (Honeysuckle Point). The Special Committee of Inquiry into Glenbrook Rail Accident in November 2000 hearkened back to this report, when considering management structures. Its Second Interim Report also pointed out that ignoring recommendations from the Fay–Raven report, especially No.37 about railway training and No.38 about educational visits to other railway systems, had resulted in a narrow view about what the best current practice could be. This Government Inquiry for once showed it had a long memory.[14] The Commission was given a farewell luncheon by the NSW Government at Parliament House, Macquarie Street, on 8 October before they departed for New Zealand the next day.

The party of five Commissioners from Britain now continued a further similar brief for New Zealand Government about its Railways (NZR). The New Zealand Government in its Annual Report of 1924 noted the presence of Fay and Raven in NSW. This made it decide that it would invite the Commissioners to undertake a similar task for NZR. So, Fay, Raven and their associates arrived in New Zealand after a three-day sailing, landing at Wellington South Island on 13 October. They had, prior to the visit:

> ... the advantage of previously perusing detailed information relative to railway practice in the Dominion, this being supplied in reply to a questionnaire of ninety-four items submitted by us from Sydney, through the (New Zealand) Minister of Railways (Hon. J.G. Coates).

Lord Jellicoe, Governor
General of New Zealand,
1920–1924.

They were then officially commissioned by the Rt-Hon. John Rushworth, Viscount Jellicoe, Governor General of New Zealand. He was famous as the Commander-in-Chief of the Grand Fleet at the Battle of Jutland during the First World War. The Commission, it was estimated, should last from two to three months. Fay, Raven and their team were provided on 18 October 1924 with the following terms of reference, similar in content, if rather more detailed than the NSW ones. It stated that:

> ... the commission shall inquire into and report as to the financial arrangements, management, equipment, and general working, including the administration, control, and economy of the railway services in New Zealand, and more particularly

(1) The organisation and running of the passenger and goods traffic, the services rendered, the scales of fares and freights operating, the finance and the financial returns.

(2) Matters appertaining to the organisation and conduct of the mechanical section of the system in relation to the respective types of locomotives and rolling stock adopted, cost, economy of life and use, equipment, renewal, and maintenance charges.

(3) Matters relating to the construction, renewal, and maintenance of the permanent way, including station equipment and the system of signalling and interlocking adopted.

(4) Improvements and new works that may be deemed essential to cope more economically with present and prospective traffic, including new station buildings, yards, deviations, &c., and the order in which such works should be carried out.

(5) Whether the present discretionary powers held by District Traffic Managers are sufficient under existing conditions, having regard to the increasing competition by road and sea. Whether more satisfactory and expeditious handling of traffic could by brought about by decentralisation.

(6) Delegating power to district Managers to enable them to make reduced quotations for traffic in exceptional cases to counteract competition or secure business.

(7) The general viewpoint of the staff in dealing with the Department's business.

(8) Whether the steps at present taken to secure excursion traffic in connection with big events is sufficient.

(9) Whether the present statistical data compiled by the Department is sufficient to enable transportation officers to accurately gauge the cost of services in dealing with general transportation matters.

(10) The policy of the Government in connection with the leasing and construction of private sidings.

(11) The use of rail motor-cars and the type suggested for New Zealand conditions.

(12) The construction of special rolling-stock, heavier or lighter, to meet special condition in various districts.

(13) The costing and statistical methods in the Maintenance, Workshops and other branches.

As before, they were given wide scope to conduct their enquiry as to the people and records from which they could gather evidence. They were required to report back no later than 31 January 1925.

We left Wellington on the 15th October to traverse the North Island system, and returned on the 24th October, after covering 2500 miles. We left Wellington again on the 27th October for the South island, and between that date and 15th November covered some 3200 miles. During the two tours we traversed 4850 miles by railway and 750 miles by motor, the latter being part to inspect projected connecting-links, and for the rest to reach isolated sections of the railway.

Besides the British party, which accompanied them, there was a group of five New Zealand Railway officials with them:

R.W. McVilly GM (current President of Institution of Professional Engineers, NZ),
F.J. Jones CE (future (1925-6) President of Institution of Professional Engineers, NZ),
E.E. Gillon CME,
H.J. Wynne, Signal and Electrical Engineer and
F.J. Murison Divisional Locomotive Engineer, plus
Frederick W. Fuckert, CE Public Works Department and Under-Secretary for Public Works, who had been included at the request of the Minister of Railways.

District officers joined the entourage, when it came into the boundaries of their jurisdiction.

Evidence was taken on twenty-six days, and in all thirty-two departmental officers and representatives of twenty-eight public bodies and associations were heard.

The report was dated 11 December 1924, a good seven weeks before the last day required and it has a very similar structure to that they had put before the NSW Government. Indeed, the first section on 'Finance' (1–7) with proposals that the railways became more autonomous by balancing expenditure and revenue, while still being accountable to Parliament, has sections with words identical to the NSWR report. In the section Organisation (8–13), there are more specific recommendations than for NSWR, and it details a Board, with chairman and two other members (7), the appointment of a CME, fully qualified and thoroughly conversant with up-to-date methods of railway working (10), General Superintendents, one for the North Island system with headquarters at Auckland (Petone), the other for the South Island system with headquarters at Christchurch (Addington) (12). There would be one Divisional Mechanical engineer for each island (13), each island having three traffic and civil engineering districts and other administrative personal, such as a secretary and finance officer. The 'Engineering' section looks at mainlines having rails of 70lb weight (14), with flying gangs for branch line maintenance (15).

However, the next section, 'Engineering' (17–37), which is clearly Raven's in style and content, is more radical for narrow gauge/Imperial gauge of 3ft 6in, NZR, than for 'standard-gauge' NSWR. It rationalises locomotive building and maintenance based at the two areas, where the divisional HQs would be, with other centres to close. The 3ft 6in gauge would be standard. He also advised a complete rationalisation of the number of locomotive classes. He detailed class by class those he opined should be scrapped, namely the older and more obsolete ones, and those to be retained as the best of the more modern locomotives. Others should be purchased from elsewhere as the current workshops are not adequate to build new ones at present. Maintenance should be improved, so that times out of shops be lengthened. As in the 1900s with NER, he advocated the 'rail-motor' idea, using some older locomotives as a way of reducing replacement costs for rural services. There is a similar requirement that coaching stock, brake vans and wagons should be replaced as soon as possible. He advocated the use of statistics for appraising costs (37). Other ways of boosting usage are discussed in 'Operation' (38–43) and 'Rates and Fares' (44–7), like revision of timetables, stimulating tourist and excursion trade encouraging freight pickup. The last section of the report, entitled 'General', concluded (51–3) with remarks about improving training.

Some time after that date, they had sailed back to Sydney, from where they sent a supplementary report about minor details, such as books detailing rates for charging of freight, whether local managers should have the authority to adjust rates and wharf charges at Westport. This was sent to the NZ Governor-General from Sydney, dated 25 December 1924.

The Commissioner's report[15] was tabled in the NZ Parliament and referred to in some detail in the 1925 Annual Report, tabled on 31 March 1925. The management structure was followed very much as in recommendations, with streamlining and condensation of management structures and workshops, for instance Addington became a major repair workshop, although Hillside, Dunedin South Island, became the site of locomotive manufacture until 1971.

Other effects of the report were as might be expected both immediate and long term, although it is difficult to know how much Fay and especially Raven understood about the workings of a 3ft 6in-gauge railway and a system split between two islands, in the main it was reasonable to simply rationalise operations and centres on each island. Raven was a 'standard gauge – big engine' man. Surprisingly, in the light of what he had so strongly advocated at home and again for a suburban system of NSWR, there was no mention of rail electrification.

The appointment of a CME for NZR was made quickly, the new CME entering into the post from 20 April 1925. Here, Sir Sam Fay's influence, an ex-GCR man, undoubtedly was evident, in the choice of Lt-Col. G.S. Hynde, a personal friend of the Fay family, having worked with Robinson and Fay at the GCR from 1909 as locomotive running superintendent at Gorton works. He had joined the City of London Royal Fusiliers, later transferring to the Railways Operating Division of the 'Sappers'. Like Raven's son Frederick Gifford, whom he may have known, he saw action in the Somme in 1917. He gained an OBE as well as his military rank as lieutenant colonel as a result of his work on the wartime railways in France, especially with GCR 0-6-0s and 0-8-0s.[16]

The appointment of Hynde was not a wholesale success. The connections with an 'old-boy' network, the fact that both Raven's and Fay's son had been in ROD of RE, the Fay's directorship at Garratt's, could well have influenced the decision by the New Zealand authorities to appoint Hynde. The advocacy by the Commission and eventual purchase of the Garratt locomotives was shown to be a mistake for NZR. The ones ordered were too massive and inflexible for a system notable for tight curves and gradients. To be fair, Hynde went on to prove an able CME in many other respects. They sailed home some time during the Christmas–New Year holiday and probably arrived in February–March 1925.

1 Hughes Geoffrey, 1986, *LNER*, Ian Allan Ltd, p.87

2 Hughes Geoffrey, 1983, *The Gresley Influence*, Ian Allan Ltd, p.14

3 Hughes Geoffrey, 1986, *LNER*, Ian Allan Ltd, p.87

4 Grafton Peter, March 1971, *Edward Thompson of the LNER*, Kestrel Books, Knaresborough, Yorks, p.24, where he says that Raven 'let it be known that he was not prepared to move – neither he nor Lady Raven had any wish to leave the North East'. I have not found any evidence of this apart from the statement in the book above. In fact, their move to Hampshire in the next year contradicts it. For more detail see note 11 below

5 Bulleid, HAV, 1983, *Master Builders of Steam*, 2nd edition, Ian Allan Ltd, p.55

6 National Archive, RAIL 390/293

7 National Archive, RAIL 390/319

8 Whitehouse Patrick & Thomas, David St John, 1980, *LNER 150: A Century and a Half of Progress*, p.129-30

9 *NER Magazine*, vol.12, no.6, p.223-24

10 Hughes Geoffrey, 1983, *The Gresley Influence*, Ian Allan Ltd, p.115

11 There is a link between Hampshire and Connie's children, which seems somehow significant but still is not clear. For instance, Mary Gifford Watson went to Farnborough Hill School. She married a friend of her brother Michael's, James Lascelles Iremonger, from a long-established Hampshire family. It was and still is a good place for golf and shooting, with Bisley nearby, and has good golf courses, which may have been another reason for Raven's choice

12 On a 1908 Ordnance Survey map of Hook and district in Hampshire County Library, there is an undated note that V.L. Raven owned this house. It is not clear whether he had it built as a holiday home/long-term investment, or whether he had bought or inherited it

13 *Sydney Morning Herald*, 9 October 1924, p.8. See also the author's fuller account in the paper for *The Bulletin of the Australian Railway History Society*, November 2005, 'Two British Knights come to Sydney – the 1924 Fay-Raven Royal Commission on New South Wales Railways', p.464-473

14 *Sydney Morning Herald*, 13 February 1924, p.12 and 6 May p.6

15 Special Committee of Inquiry into Glenbrook Rail disaster, November 2000, p.7-8 and its second Interim Report on Rail Safety History, p.36-37

16 Report of a Royal Commission of Inquiry into the Railway Service, 1925, published by the NZ Government. See also the author's fuller account in the paper for *The New Zealand Railway*

Observer, June-July 2005, 'Railway Knights in New Zealand – the 1924 Fay-Raven Report on New Zealand Railways', p.46-48

17 Jackson D., *JG Robinson – a lifetime's work*, Oakwood Press, p.189

XII

RAVEN'S LAST YEARS
(1925–1934)

Nominated at the meeting of the IMechE (always held at 6 p.m.) on 23 January 1925, Raven was elected president at the next meeting *in absentia*, as he was due to return two to three weeks later from his Antipodean visits. He did, indeed, return to preside at the next meeting held on 24 April 1925, where he delivered his first address. The constructive dismissal or forced resignation by the LMS Board of Colonel O'Brien, former assistant CME – L&YR, a friend of Gresley's, following his 1924 paper 'The Future of Main Line Electrification' (given at many locations while still involved officially with LMS) may have made Raven finally realise that the electrification issue was no longer worth pursuing as far as the power of his advocacy was concerned. Raven, of course, from the beginning of 1923, had been speaking as a freelance expert.

At the next IMechE meeting on Friday 8 May, Raven presided, when a report, from the quaintly named 'Steam Nozzles Research Committee', which was supported by IMechE, various Associations of Engineers, the Allied Industrial Research Association and Department of Science and Industrial Research, chaired by Captain H. Riall Sankey (the IMechE president before Raven) presented their current findings following a series of experiments. They had been working on it since 1923. At the extraordinary IMechE meeting on Friday 22 May at 6 p.m., Raven again presided, when new members and associates were put forward for approval. A paper was read on '2-stroke Cycle Oil engines' by Professor E.A. Allait, M.Sc., from Toronto University, Canada.[2]

On 2 July, with Gresley's typically gracious permission, one of Raven's *Pacifics*, 2404 *City of Newcastle*, led the cavalcade drawing the latest *Flying Scotsman* stock. Among those following among other old and new steam and electric locomotives, were NER 910, GWR replica of *North Star*, Hughes 4-6-0 pulling the latest LMS restaurant car, the LNER Garratt 2395 and Raven's unlucky NER No.13, all to celebrate the centenary of the opening of the Stockton & Darlington Railway, with their Highnesses the Duke and Duchess of York present to watch the cavalcade, with the LNER 'big-wigs' – William Whitelaw, chairman, Lord Faringdon, deputy chairman and Ralph Wedgwood, GM Raven, now out of the big picture, as it were, was noted among those watching the cavalcade.

At the opening of the summer event for the IMechE was a meeting in Newcastle on 7 July. Raven addressed those assembled with an historical survey about SDR and George Stephenson, the first president of IMechE, and he went on to mention how the early locomotives developed. He made an interestingly cogent comment by way of introducing Gresley's paper, '3-cylinder High Pressure Locomotives',[3] which was to follow. He said:

> The Railway Steam Locomotive had passed through many evolutions from the days of Stephenson to the present time owing to the careful study and research of many eminent

engineers. Its present power and speed are only limited by the road gauge and strength of the track and bridges over which it has to pass.

After a number of numerical details about carriage of goods and passengers, capital and mileage of track, he pays tribute to the pioneers:

> All this we owe to the little group of determined men who built the railway, whose centenary we celebrate this year and amongst these men we owe it chiefly to George Stephenson, the first President of the Institute of Mechanical Engineers.

A remarkable tribute from one man to another! Raven concluded with a vote of thanks, which merited applause.

This was followed by a programme full of activity with visits to engineering works at Darlington (to commemorate the centenary of SDR) and excursions to the river Tyne, Durham Cathedral, Rothbury and Cragside and the Roman Wall. On 8 July there followed a Civic Reception in the beautiful eighteenth-century Grand Assembly Rooms on Westgate Road given by The Lord Mayor of Newcastle and Lady Mayoress on behalf of the City Council. Raven and his wife were both present at this function. Another reception and dinner was given by the Newcastle Reception Committee in Armstrong College. Raven was also given the title of an Honorary Life-long President of the Gateshead LNER (formerly NER) Literary Institute, 'Charlie' Baister being now its president.[4]

Raven was asked during 1925 to fulfil a Commission advising on some Indian rail workshops, their manning and organisation. This involved four Indian railway companies, recently put under state control, namely East Bengal Railway (EBR), Great Indian Peninsular Railway (GIPR), the North Western Railway (NWR) and East Indian Railway (EIR), all of which had a long and venerable history. There is a feeling of 'old-boys' network' being again in operation concerning how Raven became involved with the Commission. Over and above his reputation for meticulous reports arising from his previous Commissions over the years from the time of his appointment as CME, Raven had met a number of British men involved with Indian railway affairs, either as engineers or Board members of industrial concerns with railway or other professional connections, at meetings of IMechE, ICE or IEE with people like Rendell, Palmer and Tritton, who were advisors and suppliers to the various Indian Railways. He was, from 1921, chairman of the British Engineering Standards Association, which brought about much standardisation of locomotives, especially in its recommendation of eight classes of locomotives for India. He was also a director on the Board of Metro-Vick, which had recently provided a massive 1500v dc electric locomotive for the GIPR in the Bombay region. He is likely to have known, or at least have been known to, Sir Clement Hindley, president of the Institution of Professional Engineers and Chief Commissioner of Railways, whose office was at Dalziel Simla. He is likely to have been influential in choosing Raven and the more local Commission members. Another reason for Raven's willingness to travel to India, besides financial and continuing to work on railway matters, may have been sentimental journey to visit where Frederick, his son, had worked at Multan on NWR.

Raven travelled out to India, possibly on the P&O mail service SS *Rawalpindi*, leaving London in mid-December 1925, travelling via Gibraltar and the Suez Canal to Bombay, to take up his position as Commission chairman. He was to be assisted by three experienced men. Two were British-born officials working for various Indian Railways, John Mervyn Dallas Wrench, CME to GIPR, and R. McChesney, assistant to CME of NWR, who acted as secretary to the Commission; the other was an Indian, Kalyan C. Srinivasan, FCS, deputy auditor–in–charge at the Audit and Account Service as well as workshop auditor for EBR (he was to act as the Commission's finance assistant).

This four-man Commission assembled at Bombay (now Mumbai) on 4 January, quickly followed up two questionnaires about the running and administration of the workshops, sent out to each of the four companies earlier, with two shorter ones about such matters as manpower supervision and transportation.

Their report was entitled 'Report of the State Railway Workshop Commission', appointed to inquire into matters connected with mechanical departments of the State Railways of India. Raven made ingenuous comments in the report's preface, where it will be seen that the number of men employed and the size of the shops in India is very much in excess of those in England. However, he failed to acknowledge the differences which broad (1,676mm, the so-called 'Indian' gauge), metre (1,000mm) and narrow gauges (610mm and 762mm) and the more generous loading gauge even on narrow-gauge lines could make on the railways they visited. Nor does he look at the socio-economic effects of the vast amount of cheap labour available to the local rail companies:

> The most striking features of the shops, when considered with those in England are their size and the strength of labour they employ, in consideration of the volume of work turned out. While aware of the disabilities that have to be contended against with respect to the climatic conditions, the low efficiency of the average Indian Workmen, the difficulty of obtaining suitable supervising staff and the need for the provision of longer leave, I was not altogether prepared for the marked differences that exist between Indian and English workshops. I have attempted to bring these out in the following table:

Railway	Authorised stock on 1 April 1925	Total Tractive effort on 1 April 1925 (000)	Annual cost
	No.	lbs	No.
Eastern Bengal Broad gauge	293	5,391	}
Narrow gauge (610mm)	11	40	}1,665
Metre gauge	241	3,271	
East Indian	1,349	25,866	906
Oudh and Rohilkhund	316	5,746	1,799
Great Indian Peninsula	1,281	29,234	8,776
North Western Broad gauge	1,554	34,486	}
Narrow gauge (762mm)	99	1,320	}
	Surplus Broad Gauge 53		}12,169
	Surplus Narrow. Gauge. 1		]

Facts and figures from the 1925 Indian Railways Commission.

		Indian State Railways	London and North Eastern Group of Railways
Locomotives	No.	5,144	7,143
Coaching vehicles (bogies)	No.	9,698	20,275
Goods vehicles (4-wheelers)	No.	12,7076	30,1354
Men in locomotive shops	No.	31,860	12,079
Do. To carry out same volume of work as in the L&NER Shops	No.	46,000	
Area of locomotive shops	sq ft	2,569,286	1,928,370
Men in Carriage and Wagon shops	No.	34,943	11,795
Do. To carry out same volume of work as in the L&NER Shops	No.	82,000	
Area of Carriage and Wagon shops	sq ft	3,498,300	2,460,259

Manpower differences between Indian Railways and the LNER.

He went on to quote the numbers of locomotives currently in use on state railways and included the Oudh and Rohilkhand Railway (where Geddes had worked over twenty years before) in an attempt to cost them, but it really is not relevant to most of the recommendations.

As in previous reports, he looked intently at centralising workshops in key areas and sought to avoid duplication of facilities. He remarked on some of the sites about local subsidiary factories to supply workshops. He was, of course, keen to point out what he saw as a lack of planning, of smooth running and supervision.[5]

The Commission travelled 7,500 miles in all, visiting, inspecting and reporting on the four railways and some other railway installations, starting out from Bombay where the GIPR had its HQ. Incorporated in 1849 and opened in 1853, it covered what is now north-west and central India. Its locomotive works were in Parel, north of Bombay, which Raven found commendable, but was concerned by the cost and instability of the labour force. He remarked, somewhat nostalgically, that the recent introduction of electric locomotives in Bombay meant less need for steam engine 'pits' (452a). The GIPR carriage and wagon works in Matunga were more modern, but poorly equipped, organised and expensive in terms of workforce (432); they should increase their productivity (447a & b).

Going almost due north to the NWR and Lahore in the north Punjab, the Commission visited its HQ there and the Moghulpura (Lahore) locomotive workshops which Raven praised for being 'modern, well-laid out and excellently equipped', but castigated for the lack of planning and supervision, then recommended that it should have a well-equipped wagon repair workshop (445c). He found the railway's subsidiary workshops unsatisfactory (429). The running sheds at Rawalpindi were visited, where he recommended closure of its locomotive (441 a) and carriage workshops (445a), but praised its well-equipped wagon works repair shops. At Sukkur in the south east, he recommended rebuilding locomotive workshops (441b) and updating carriage repair shops and wagon repair workshops, but closure of the locomotive (441a) and carriage (445a) workshops, with a rebuild of the wagon repair workshops in Karachi on the coast.

Then moving east, the Commission visited the EBR and EIR, which both radiated from Calcutta. The EBR opened in 1857 covered what is now called Bangladesh and the adjacent parts of West Bengal (now in present-day India). They went on to locomotive workshops near Calcutta at Kanchapara, recommending that they should be remodelled (444) and the size of its carriage and wagon repair works should be increased so as to take up more work. They also visited the Standard Wagon Co.'s works at Asansol, West Bengal. East at Saidpur, there was a metre gauge locomotive, carriage and wagon workshops, which were 'old and badly laid out', 'it should be rebuilt' (448c).

EIR formed in 1847 and opened in 1855, and covered the northern Indian plains below the Nepal in the Himalyas in a north-westerly direction from Calcutta to Lucknow. The Commission visited Jamalpur locomotive works, which Raven found old, badly planned and greatly congested (430) and needing remodelling (442). At Lilooah north of Calcutta, there should be carriage construction, rather than merely repair (446a), but a 50 per cent increase in wagon repair (446b).

In addition, the party visited three other works around Calcutta, which serviced the rail industry: west to Messrs Tata Iron & Steel Co.'s work at Jamshedpur and nearby the Peninsular Locomotive Works at Tatanagar and then WSW to Khargpur for the Locomotive and Carriage shops of the Bengal-Nagpur railway (running south-west from Calcutta to mid-northern India).

Then going north-west into GIPR territory again, they visited Jhansi in Uttar Pradesh to see both locomotive works, whose workforce, working in less favourable circumstances than at Parel, he found worthy of special mention, but the works would need rebuilding (452b). Wagon and carriage repair work there should be increased (447b & d) at Jhansi (increased wagon repair also at Bhusawai) and running sheds at both Jhansi and Agra.

They travelled on north-east to EIR locomotive, carriage and wagon works and running sheds at Lucknow. He recommended expansion of the wagon repair shops there or at Ondal. Also there he saw those of ORR, whose locomotive shops he found well-equipped not the carriage and wagon shops (431). They also visited the running sheds at Lucknow.

The report was published on 8 April 1926 at Bombay. Its style of presentation is rather rambling, darting from one railway to another, rather than dealing with matters in general, then focussing on each railway in particular. Much of what he wrote in conjunction with the other committee members, especially Wrench, its other signatory, gives a clear enough picture and no doubt gave the railway companies and their boards the material they wanted to see. Over-manning and haphazard administration and updating were endemic in India for different socio-ethnic, geographic and climatic reasons to those in Britain. Raven, with the typical Imperial attitudes of the time, took British standards to be the main criteria, by which he made his judgments about the Indian railways, which he had seen on the whistle-stop tour. Nevertheless, unlike NSW and New Zealand, whose railway infra-structure has followed retraction and privatisation like much of the rest of the Western world, many Indian centres noted in the report have continued to function to the present day.

Raven probably arrived back in England towards the close of May. It was remarked at the end of his term as president that he had not attended many meetings, which was perhaps a good thing as a sign of his trust in the ability of Council members. While Raven was absent, Mr Patchell provided cover for the first half of the year, and Sir Henry Fowler for the second half. He was then added to the list of past-presidents, while remaining a member of the Council. It is likely that he then quietly gave up various posts he had as director or chairman, only appearing for IMechE annual dinner.

The same year, 1926, the IMechE changed the timing of the Annual Institution Dinner, separating it from the summer event as a separate function to be held later in the year. Raven was present at many of these dinners (seemingly all-male occasions) held on a Thursday at 7 p.m. in one of the London hotels, usually the Connaught Rooms, Great Queen Street, Covent Garden. The ritual consisted of a dinner, often with a member of the Royal Family present, for notables mainly of scientific background and the main senior officials of the IMechE. This was followed by loyal toasts to the King, Queen and Prince of Wales and to other Royal Family members and then other appropriate toasts before and between the after-dinner speakers, who usually nicely rounded the evening off. For instance, at the dinner of 9 December 1926 at the Connaught Rooms, after the loyal toasts, the Progress of Engineering, Our Institution and the Visitors were proposed and toasted.

In 1927 Raven was not included in the Formation of the Railway Electrification Committee, under Colonel Sir J.W. Pringle, although both Gresley and Merz were. Thus it probably signalled that he had effectively retired from public life. Nevertheless, on 15 December 1927 he attended the dinner, which was again held at the Connaught Rooms. After the loyal toasts, 'Our Institution, His Majesty's Ministers and Our Visitors' were this time proposed and toasted. He attended the next year on 18 October 1928, when the dinner changed to the May Fair Hotel, Berkeley Square, with 377 guests present. Now after the loyal toasts, the other toasts were to 'His Majesty's Ministers, Our Institution and Science and Industry'. The next year, the dinner returned to the Connaught Rooms on 17 October 1929, and after the loyal toast, the other toasts were to 'Royal Air Force, Our Institution and Our Guests'.

A clear sign Raven was thinking of what would happen after his death was the will he had drawn up on 29 May 1931, with his wife and son Norman, and Leslie Pearkes, his solicitor, as trustees. He made detailed arrangements with provision for both his wife in an immediate cash payment of £100 on his demise and in a trust fund for her while she lived.

Finally, at the first 1932 meeting at IMechE HQ in London, it was proposed and agreed that Raven, together with Sir Henry Fowler, be appointed Honorary Life Members of the IMechE on 29 January 1932. Raven's last attendance, when he was aged nearly seventy-three, was at the annual dinner was on 21 October 1932, again at the Connaught Rooms, where 400 guests were present. The toasts this time were for the 'Institution and its Charter and Our Guests'.

The Ravens' Golden Wedding took place on 15 February 1933. In late 1933, Raven went to Felixstowe for a winter holiday with Lady Raven. During early December he had some heart trouble. In early February, Raven became increasingly ill, sinking into unconsciousness a few days before he died in Felixstowe on 14 February 1934, the day before his fifty-first wedding anniversary. In marking his decease, two days later, Dr Hele Shaw, at the eighty-seventh AGM of the IMechE, expressed much of the admiration of those present for the past-president and what he had done, recalling that he had a charming manner.

As in 1918, 1934 saw the loss of yet another Raven brother, Frederick Rainbow, who had immigrated to the USA and married Minnie Taylor, the daughter of a Lancashire emigrant. He was a civil engineer on Long Island and died in August, about five months after his wife died.

Following the formation of the LNER, Edward Thompson became an area workshop manager and in 1930 he became a mechanical engineer at Stratford Works, where he rebuilt ex-GCR 4-6-0s and 4-4-0s. Thompson returned to Darlington in 1934, to succeed

Old Hall, Hurworth, bought by the Thompsons and where Lady Raven came after Raven's death.

A.C. Stamer as assistant chief mechanical engineer for the north-eastern area of LNER. It is likely that he would have succeeded Stamer at Darlington if there had been no grouping. The Thompsons first lived at Elton Parade briefly, quite close to the Watson's on Coniscliffe Road, but they moved in 1936 to an elegant early eighteenth-century red-brick house Old Hall, Hurworth, a charming riverside village on the north bank of the Tees. Strangely enough for the time, the house was in Guen's name and not her husband's.

Lady Raven had moved back to the North East from Hampshire after Sir Vincent's death, to spend the last three years of her life with Guen and Thompson and with Norman, whose address was now at 169 George Street WI. It meant that she would also have been near Constance, George and the grandchildren in Darlington. Lady Raven, like her husband, had been involved with social matters as a member of the local Women's Institute. Later she became president of Darlington North End Townswomen's Guild, founded in 1931, presumably after this return to the North East in 1934–1935. Probably while she was staying with Norman, she fell ill. After she had spent three weeks in a London nursing home on Devonshire Street WI (significantly close to Harley Street), she died on 2 August 1937. Her death was registered as a result in Marylebone.

Guen did not long outlive her father or mother. She had contracted scarlet fever in 1937, which may have resulted in the then frequently encountered complication of damage to her mitral valves of the heart. In addition, grieving for her mother could well have aggravated the underlying condition. Despite making an apparent recovery, she died quite suddenly on 22 May 1938, during preparations for her husband's move to Doncaster as assistant chief mechanical engineer (LNER). Following her death, Thompson moved quickly to Doncaster, as planned, in about a month after her funeral. While still trying to come to terms with his wife's death, to whom he was devoted, he went off on holiday with his brother-in-law, Norman Raven, to Corsica.[6]

Thompson went on to become CME to LNER in 1941, following Gresley's sudden death. He retired in 1946, spending a lot of time with a few close friends, and was really rather lonely after Guen died. Constance and George, with their two children Michael and Mary Gifford, moved from Polam Road to three further addresses in the Coniscliffe Road areas into terraced houses, 8 Fife Road, in 1924–1925, 5 West Terrace in 1925 and 47 Coniscliffe Road in 1927–1932. George continued to practise in Darlington for forty years, working as clerk to Durham County Council, as well as for the Lunacy Act and the Commissioner of Taxes. He was a somewhat restless character and, besides changing house, George moved his place of worship to St Mary's, Cockerton Green, in the west of the town and later went to St Hilda's, Parkgate, in the town centre. Finally, George Herbert left the Church of England altogether and converted to the Roman Catholic Church, where he eventually became a member of the Catenians, a Catholic men's society similar to the Rotarians.

Connie became a founder member of the Darlington North End Townswomen's Guild, serving on the first committee on 23 February 1932, being on the Committee in 1934, president in 1938 and chairman in 1939. The Guild met at the Darlington LNER Institute on Monday evenings. She died on 20 September 1946 after a short illness. A funeral service was held at All Saints C/E church at Blackwell, followed by interment at the West Cemetery. A memorial, a seat for the blind, dedicated to Mrs George H. Watson in thanksgiving for her work with them, was placed by Darlington Townswomen's Guild in 1946 in North Lodge Park (this lies behind the former Technical College building on Northgate).

George Herbert retired in 1947 and lived at Nateby Lodge, Abbey Road, close to the town centre. He survived his wife by a period of about three years, dying on 10 August 1949. On 12 August, a Requiem Mass was said for him at St Augustine's Roman Catholic church on Coniscliffe Road, celebrated by Revd J.P. Whelan, the curate to Revd J.J. Wilkinson as Parish priest. The chief mourners were his daughter and sister-in-law. Captain A. Thomas and the lonely Edward Thompson were there, as were a host of civic and religious dignitaries. They are buried side by side in West Cemetery.[7]

Michael Litchfield, their son, followed his grandfather's career in transport, albeit in a more modern form – aeroplanes. Sadly, like his uncle Frederick, he would lose his life in another global conflict. He joined the RAF as personnel No.33337, and rose to Squadron Leader in the 82nd Squadron under Wing Commander Atkinson. The Squadron flew Bristol Blenheims Mark IV after the Battle of Britain in 1941 on bombing missions out of RAF Watton or its nearby overflow airport at Bodney, near Thetford, Norfolk, ironically a few miles south of Great Fransham his grandfather's birthplace. During mid-May 1941, Watson's squadron was posted to Luqa in Malta to increase the aerial harassment of Italian convoys, sailing back and forth from Naples to Tripoli. He and his nine-man crew in Blenheim Bristol Z6426 died in action on Wednesday 11 June 1941 over the Aegean Sea in over Lampedusa in Pelagian Islands. He is commemorated on the Runnemede Memorial. He left a wife behind called Mary; she came from Farnborough, Kent. Mary Gifford married James Lascelles Iremonger, a friend of her brother's from his University days. They had a son, Peter, born in 1941.

Belatedly, on 3 August 1950, one of the Peppercorn 'A1' class *Pacifics*, British Railways No.60126, was named *Sir Vincent Raven* at a naming ceremony in Darlington. The locomotive's name was officially put in place by Councillor G Dougill, with M. Lyonette in attendance. More significantly, among those present at the naming were Raven's granddaughter, Mrs Mary Iremonger, and her nine-year-old son Peter, his great-grandson.

1 For full details of the Committee's paper, see Proceedings of IMechE, January–June 1925, p.747-831
2 For full details of Professor Allait's paper, see Proceedings of IMechE, January–June 1925, p.849-912
3 For full details of Gresley's paper, see Proceedings of IMechE, June–December 1925, p.927-967

4 Minutes of 31 March 1927, Gateshead LNER (formerly NER) Literary Institute

5 1925 Report of the State Railway Workshop Commission appointed to inquire into matters connected with mechanical departments of the State railways of India, published on 8 April 1926 in Bombay. Numbers in brackets refer to report's sections. It is not nearly so tightly structured as the earlier reports. The text keeps to the itinerary rather than the work reported upon

6 Grafton Peter, March 1971, *Edward Thompson of the LNER*, Kestrel Books, Knaresborough, Yorks, p.40

7 Their grave numbers are section F/F12 for George for Herbert and F/F 13 for Connie, respectively

EVALUATION OF RAVEN'S ACHIEVEMENTS

One of the obituaries commemorating Raven comments on his firm character and strong personality.[1] He lived at Grantly for about ten years and I picture Raven as a railway engineer version of Anthony Trollope's Archdeacon Grantly, knowledgeable, organising and controlling those under him, yes, mildly pompous, even brusque at times, yet overall well-meaning and kindly at heart. Indeed, he could be quite dogged in pursuit of what he perceived to be the goals of his craft, either through professional means within NER and elsewhere, or via exerting influence in more social spheres, such as by participating in a number of committees, conferences and other meetings with his peers.[2]

A later evaluation also opined that his strength was not in his designs for locomotives. This is not a universal opinion and subsequent writers have noted their smoothly harmonious lines, their sturdy practicality as well as their distinct NER company identity. It is, of course, difficult to know how much Raven contributed to the build-and-design team for NER locomotives both before and after his time as CME over the years 1893–1922, but he came to wield an increasing influence over their well-worked-out, virile designs and their efficient functioning. As a group, with Wilson Worsdell and then Raven at the 'helm', as it were, they welded functionality with noble simplicity of design. Raven preferred to work out how beneficial new developments from a variety of sources would be. In the early days, he reported on 'Compounding' and this was eventually was replaced in future designs. He tested out 'superheating' for himself and experimented with the 'Uniflow' system, with both axle and quill drives in his electric locomotives and looked into petrol and diesel engines as alternative means of providing propulsion. He provided carriage and wagons of various kinds for the system and beyond. He investigated and built electric cranes, and developed fog signalling.

Less spectacularly, he was an oustanding department administrator, as is shown not only at NER in Gateshead and Darlington, but at Woolwich Arsenal and the Admiralty with an ability to organise his area of work and to marshall the workforce towards greater productivity and cost-effectiveness, despite difficulties at times with industrial action.

He was a largely self-taught, but able engineer. He introduced the 'Miniblock' casting of cylinders at Darlington for class 'Z' 4-4-2s and those later locomotives that followed. Indeed, these *Atlantics* were among the best of their kind during the 1910s and continued to give sterling service on secondary routes in their later life, some lasting until after the Second World War. Even more useful and just as handsome were the mixed goods 4-6-0 locomotives of class 'S3', the product of working out improvements through two decades of a design started in 1899.

The sturdy, if not so elegant, design of class 'T2' locomotives, combined with rugged practicality, made them the very backbone of ex-NER lines until steam was phased out. Even

Raven in later life.

more impressive was the development of this class as 'T3'. Both of these developments of well-tried types, the mixed traffic working in all kinds of faster traffic, and the mineral/goods serving collieries, would give 40-50 service until steam was dispensed with altogether in the 1960s. They were able to continue to perform their work, despite the poor maintenance given during the Second World War, when more famous locomotives needed more cosseting.

Raven has had to take some of the blame for his *Pacifics'* comparative failure, although opinion is still divided about this class. They were amazing in their size and design and represented all that had been learned by Raven and his team until then about combining economy and power, but they were not altogether successful. More rigorous testing over a longer period would have produced suitable modifications, rather than the recurrent replacement of bearings made to them (always excepting Gresley's reboilering of 2404). Some of their ultimate rejection was as much due to the strange undercurrents of railway politics at the time as any lack on the design-and-build team's part. His mechanical fog signalling always merits a footnote in rail safety history and he was interested in applications of electricity to railway usage; witness his electric fog signalling, his hydro-electric cranes and espousal of rail electrification.

With today's more ecological frame of mind, his use and advocacy of electric traction as the motive power for future express and heavy goods haulage made him a visionary figure, a Cassandra figure with the ears of those in political power deaf to his pleading. It was his most genuinely innovative contribution to railway development, sadly destined only to happen in the future, because it was so ahead of its time and thus not implemented. Over the years his reports influenced policy on manning maintenance departments (Cambrian Railways and LNER); for NER, the use of compounding and superheating; he was a constant advocate for professional education for engineers, both locally and nationally through the institutions; and lastly, his mid–1920s reports helped to shape some of the railway history of the countries visited and is still remembered in NSW.

1 Obituary, 1934, *The Engineer*, v.157, p.211
2 This much later article by Hughes G.J., June 1983, 'Sir Vincent Raven', *The Railway Magazine*, vol.129, no.986, p.226-28, disappointingly does not value Raven's contribution to railways much. It damns his locomotives with faint praise and soon gets side-tracked with detail instead of attempting a balanced appreciation of his work

APPENDIX I

CHRONOLOGY

1859	3 December	Raven born at Great Fransham Rectory (third of ten children, seven boys, three girls)
1860s (later)		boarding school in Brighton.
1872–1875		pupil at Aldenham School, Herts
1875	May	'Premium' apprentice engineer with Fletcher at NER, Gateshead
1880		qualifies as engineer
1881–1886		became fireman, then foreman for firemen, lastly inspector, investigates braking.
1883	15 February	married Gifford Allan Crichton, his father Revd Vincent Raven performs the ceremony in St Stephens, Low Elswick, Newcastle
	20 March	passed for 1427 Percy (Freemason) Lodge, Neville Hall, Newcastle, raised, 17 April, balloted, 5 May Fellow, 13 June Master of Percy Lodge, 2 August signed Grand Lodge Certificate
	late autumn	Constance Gifford Raven born at 20 Heaton Road, Newcastle
Late 1884		Edith Guendolen Raven born at Hope Villa, Low Fell, Gateshead
	14 April 1886	Norman Vincent born at Hope Villa, Low Fell, Gateshead
	July 1887	Annie born
1888		promoted to sssistant locomotive superintendent (Northern Division).
	16 April	
	7 May	meetings
	2 July	
		30 July special meeting, 9 September meeting, 22 October special meeting, 26 November meeting of Gateshead NER Literary Institute
	3 December	elected to Gateshead NER Literary Institute Committee
1889		Frederick Gifford born at Mardale Parade, Bensham, Gateshead

1890		4 March, meeting, 1 April meeting, 23 April half yearly meeting, 8 August meeting, 9 August meeting, 9 September meeting/opening of Billiard Room at Gateshead NER Literary Institute, 19 September special meeting about opening celebrations of New NER Literary Institute Buildings in Hudson Street, Gateshead, 7 October meeting, 22 October opening of new buildings
1890		October promoted to chief assistant locomotive superintendent, 20 November special meeting, 2 December special meeting of Gateshead NER Literary Institute
c.1890		moved to Cambridge Terrace, Gateshead
1891	3 February	at meeting of Gateshead NER Literary Institute
1893	1 August	became member of Institution of Mechanical Engineers (MIMechE) in Middlesbrough
	October	promoted to chief assistant locomotive superintendent, report requested by Wilson Worsdell on 'compounding'
	November	report on 'compounding' done by Raven and Ramsey Kendall, transferred to Darlington North Road works
	Late 1893	moved to Whessoe Street, Darlington
	1 December	joined Freemason 1379 Marquess of Ripon Lodge, Darlington
1894		becomes involved with Darlington NER Literary Institute with Ramsay Kendall, 4 May to 1 June attended (always on Friday) Freemason's Lodge meeting as visitor, 2 November attended Lodge as a joining member
	November	designed mechanical fog signal with Charlie Baister
1895	21 August	rode on the footplate of locomotives 1621 and 1420 in Great Railway Race to the North
	21 October	present at opening of Wear Valley Extension Railway
1896		6 March, 3 April, 5 June 1896, 6 November attended Marquess of Ripon Lodge, 27 November gave paper on 'Mechanical fog signalling' to ARLE
1897	8 January	5 March, 5 November attended Marquess of Ripon Lodge
1898	10 February	elected, 5 April 1898 officially becomes Associate member of Institution of Civil Engineers (ICE)
	Autumn	report on Cambrian Railway's workshops
1899	6 January	
	3 February	
	3 March	
	1 December	attended Marquess of Ripon Lodge
1900	17 February	involved in consultation for North Tyneside electrification
	October	first fact-finding journey to USA, promoted as assistant CME to Wilson Worsdell, becomes involved with East Coast Joint Stock, working with Gresley until 1922, beginning of their co-operative friendship
	29 August	reviews new electric cars for North Tyneside electrification

1903		Raven's brother, Charlton Cuthbert Raven, gets married at Brentford
1904	4 March	
	1 April	attended Marquess of Ripon Lodge
	31 May to	
	3 June	IMechE/American Institution of Civil Engineers Conference in Chicago, 2 June, paper given for IMechE in Chicago on hydro-electric cranes
	4 November	attended Lodge
1905	6 January	
	3 February	attended Marquess of Ripon Lodge as junior warden
	7 April	
	9 May	letter to Thornberrow about ECJS carriages
	3 November	attended Marquess of Ripon Lodge as junior warden
1906	2 March	
	6 April	attended Marquess of Ripon Lodge as senior warden. After April 1906 he stopped attending any future Lodge meetings, despite being proposed as future Master
1907	late May	travels to Edinburgh to start acting as consultant to North British Railway (NBR) regarding improving their *Atlantics*, electric signalling trials start
	10–12 June	further visit to NBR, travels behind *Waverley*, 10 July 1907 monitoring changes at NBR he had recommended
1908	15 February	Silver Wedding Anniversary
1909–13		becomes involved with amalgamation of Scarborough, Driffield and West Yorkshire Junction Railway with NER
1910	1 June	became CME – NER
	18 July	railway strike begins at Park Lane, Gateshead
	November	Constance marries George Herbert Watson, a Darlington solicitor. They have two children
1911	11 January	becomes MICE
	24 November	becomes Member of ARLE
1911–13		first phase of new locomotives, both steam and electric
1912		moved into NER Engineering HQ to new offices at Stooperdale, Darlington, moves into Grantly, Carmel Road, Darlington, begins superheating scheme for many older and new NER steam locomotives
	12 July	sent letter to ARLE about footplate staff wearing protective glasses
	9 August	attends banquet given by Iron and Steel institute in London
1913		travels to USA with Charles Merz
	9 April	gives an address on engineering education to students at Darlington Technical College
	6 June	inauguration of electrification of Newport (Middlesbrough)–Shildon freight line, following advice from Merz to Raven
	7 June	opening of Darlington NER Athletic Club, with Raven as president

	25 June	Guen marries Edward Thompson, future CME of LNER
	15 October	Mary Gifford Watson born, *d.*1982 (she had three sons, two living, one with children and grandchildren)
	14 November	ARLE meeting at Midland Hotel, St Pancras, Norman Vincent becomes AMIEE
1915	April	elected local councillor for West Ward, Darlington Borough Council
	September	goes to Ministry of Munitions, Council Member of IMechE
1917	January	knighted and received KBE. Transfers to Admiralty
	24 March	younger son, Frederick Gifford, in Railway Operating Division, Royal Engineers, dies at Le Havre of blood poisoning after being wounded. Raven becomes JP in Darlington
1918	8 March	Michael Litchfield *d.*1941 (he had one daughter living, who has a daughter with grandchildren)
	August	Hubert, his brother, dies, probably in Princetown, NJ
	22 November	ARLE meeting at Midland Hotel, St Pancras
	23 November	Ernest Woodhouse his brother dies Returns to NER. With Merz promotes further electrification of NER mainlines.
	28 November	elected vice-president of ARLE at at Midland Hotel, St Pancras
1919-22		second phase of locomotive building (committed to 3-cylinder locomotives) also includes planning and building new *Pacifics* and electric express locomotive. Norman, now Lt, gains MBE. Working for Merz, he assists with father's new mainline electric express locomotive
1920	13 February	ARLE meeting at Midland Hotel, St Pancras, travels to USA with representative of Merz and McLellan and reports
	21 January	ARLE meeting at Midland Hotel, St Pancras
	22 April	ARLE meeting at Midland Hotel, St Pancras
	June	papers at IMechE and ICE meetings and conferences. Elected as vice-president of IMechE chairman of BESA
	28 October	ARLE meeting at Railway Engineers' Association at Euston
	December	talk on 'Electrification to North East Coast Institution of Engineers and Shipbuilders'
1922	27 January	elected president of ARLE
	4 April	accepts presidency of NER Pupils' Association
	27 April	ARLE meeting at Midland Hotel, St Pancras
	14 June	travels to Paris for IMechE Summer Conference, actively pursues advocacy of electrification of railways
	16 June	travels to Liege for Engineering Conference
	23 June	ARLE meeting at ARLE Scarborough Conference
	14 July	ARLE meeting at Felixstowe
	27 October	ARLE meeting at City & Guilds Engineering College, London

	17 November	IMechE meeting to discuss Paris paper, resigns as CME – NER
1923	1 January	a director of Metropolitan Vickers Co. Board continues to work as consultant to LNER during its first year, writes two reports for it
	19 January	ARLE meeting at Midland Hotel, St Pancras
	6 February	ARLE meeting at Midland Hotel, St Pancras
	17 April	ARLE meeting at Midland Hotel, St Pancras
	June	becomes Member of Institution of Electrical Engineers
	11 November	president of ARLE
	10 December	ARLE meeting at Midland Hotel, St Pancras
late 1923		moves to Nately Lodge, Hook, Hampshire
1924	18 January	ARLE meeting at Midland Hotel, St Pancras
	13 February	announcement of Royal Commission of Inquiry on its railways by New South Wales Government
	29 March	sails with Sir Sam Fay and Commission support staff on RMS *Orvieto* to New South Wales
	6 May	boat docks in Melbourne
	9 May	lands in Sydney
	13 May	start of Commission work
	7 October	report published in Sydney
	8 October	farewell dinner for them
	9 October	sets sail for New Zealand
	7 December	Royal Commission of Inquiry reports back to New Zealand Government
1925	23 January	nominated as president of IMechE
	March	returns to Britain
	24 April	delivers first presidential address at IMechE
	22 May	attends IMechE meeting
	7 July	in Newcastle for IMechE Summer Conference and gives an address on S&DR Centenary
	23 October	attends IMechE meeting in London, gives a long travelogue on his Australian and New Zealand visits
	20 November	presides at IMechE meeting on Ground Gears
	11 December	presides at IMechE meeting. Mid-December travels to India
1926	6 April	reports back to Indian Railways Commissioner
	9 December 1926, 5 December 1927, 18 October 1928, 17 October	
	1929	attends annual dinners of IMechE
1932	29 January	became Honorary Life Member of IMechE
	21 October	attends annual dinner of IMechE
1933	15 February	Golden Wedding Anniversary
	winter after October	goes to Felixstowe for holiday with Lady Raven. Has heart trouble
1934	14 February	dies after a few days of unconsciousness at Felixstowe. Lady Raven moves back to Darlington to live with Guen and Thompson at Hurworth Old Hall
	August	Raven's brother Frederic Rainbow dies in Long Island, USA
1937	early August	Lady Raven dies in a Marylebone nursing home
1938	22 May	Guen Thompson dies suddenly

APPENDIX II

TWO TABLES FOR COMPARISON OF NER LOCOMOTIVES

Table 1   Wilson Wordell from 1899-1910

CLASS Wheel	S	S1	P1	P2/3	T	T1	4CC	R	R1	V	V/09	X
	4-6-0 super heated from 1914-24	4-6-0 super	0-6-0 super	0-6-0 super heated	0-8-0 super heated	0-8-0 super heated	4-4-2 super heated in 1914 design by WM Smith	4-4-0 super heated	4-4-0 super heated	4-4-2 super	4-4-2 super heated from 1914-20	4-8-0T super heated rebuilt as 4-8-2
Dates	1899	1900-1		1918-23	1901	1902	1906	1899	1908-9	1903	1907	1909-10
Numbers built	40	5	120	50/80	10	40	2	60	10	10/		10x
Cylinders in inches	2 x (20 x 26)	2x 20 x 26	2 x (18½ x 26)	2 x (18½ x 26)	2 x (20 x 26)	2 x (20x 26)	2 x (14 ¾ x 26)	2 x (19 x 26)	2 x (19 x 26)	2 x (20x 28)/	2 x (19½ x 28)	(19 x 26) x 3 Cylinders and steam chest in one casing
Motion - Stephenson, unless otherwise stated	with slide valves	With 8½in piston valves	with 7½in slide valves	With slide valves/ with 7½in piston valves	With segmental ring piston valves	10 with	with 10in piston valves	With 8½in piston valves	with 10in piston valves	with 10in piston valves	with Walschaerts gear	with 8½in piston valves

Tractive effort @ 85% in pounds	24,136	22,069	21,904	24,042	28,100	28,100	18,387	15,567	17,026	20,350	19,350	24,080
Boiler												
Pressure in pounds per sq in	Saturated 200	175	160	180	175	175	200	160	175	175	200	175
Maximum diameter outside	4ft, 9in	4ft, 9in	4ft, 8in	5ft, 6in	4ft 7½in	5ft 6in	5ft	4ft 9in	5ft 6in.	5ft 6in	5ft 6in	4ft 9 x in
Barrel length	15ft	15ft 10½in	10ft 7in	10 ft 7in	17ft 4¾in	17ft 4¾in	16ft 8in	11ft 6in	11ft 6in.	16ft 8in	16ft 8 in	11ft
Firebox length outside	8ft	8ft	6ft	7ft	7ft 6in	7ft 6in	9ft.	7ft	9ft.	9ft	9ft	8ft.
Heating surface in square feet:												
Tubes	883	935 sq ft	480 sq ft	1,453	1,496	1,906	974	683.7ft	529	763.9	763.9	1,169
Flues	379	401.5	270	360	-	-	371 .	292	371	534	534	-
Firebox	120	120	108	7ft	130	144	180	139	158	185	185	141
Total evaporative in sq ft	1,383	1,456	1,133		1,626	2,050	1,525	1,114.7	1,058	1,483.4	1,483.4	1,295
Superheater	276	294	183.5	247	-	-	271	204	27 1	392	392	

SIR VINCENT RAVEN

Grate area	23	23	17.2	20.3 /20ft	21ft	21ft	29	20	1,316	27	27	23
Length												
Over buffers	61ft ¾in	61ft 11¼in	51ft in	51ft 11in	58ft	58ft	63ft 6¾in	56ft 7¼in	58ft 8¼in	62ft 8¾in	62ft 8¾	42ft 1in
Coupled wheels	(6ft 1¾in) x 6	(6ft 8¾in) x 6	4ft 7¼in x 6	4ft 7¼in x 6	7ft 1¾in x 6	7ft 1¾in X 6	7ft 1¾in x 4	6ft 10 in x 4	23ft 9in	6ft 10in	6ft 10in	4ft 7¼in x 4
Leading wheels	3ft 7¼in	3ft 7¼in					3ft x 4	4 ft	3ft 7¼in x 4	3ft 7¼in x 4	3ft 7¼in x 4	3ft 1¼in
Trailing wheels	–	–	–	–		–	4ft X 2	–	–	4ft x 2	4ft x 2	
Tender			–	–	–							–
Weight	43 tons, 10 cwt	43 tons, 10 cwt	36 tons, 6 cwt	37 tons, 12 cwt	40 tons, 18 cwt	40 tons, 18 cwt	45 tons, 6 cwt	41 tons, 4 cwt	41 tons, 4 cwt	45 tons, 6 cwt	45 tons, 6 cwt	85 tons, 8 cwt
Engine	64 tons, 6 cwt	67 tons, 2 cwt	41 tons, 14 cwt	46 tons, 16 cwt	61 tons, 2 cwt	61 tons, 2 cwt	73 tons, 4 cwt.	54 tons, 2 cwt	59 ton	76 tons, 4 cwt	76 tons, 4 cwt	85 tons, 8 cwt
Maximum axle load	19 tons, 14 cwt	19 tons, 10 cwt	15 tons, 16 cwt	16 tons, 14 cwt	16 tons, 18 cwt	16 tons, 18 cwt	19 tons, 18 cwt	19 tons, 16 cwt	20 tons, 6 cwt	20 tons, 4 cwt	20 tons, 4 cwt	18 ton
Coal capacity	5 tons	5 tons	5 ton	5 ton	5 ton	5 ton	5 ton	5 ton	5 tons, 10 cwt	5 tons	5 tons	4 tons, 5 cwt
Water Capacity in gallons	3,940	3,940	3,038	4,125	41,253	41,253	3,800	3,537	4,125	4,125	4,125	2,500

Table II Raven from 1910–1922

CLASS Wheel	Y 4-6-2T	Z 4-4-2 Atlantic	Z1 4-4-2	S2 4-6-0 (825 - Uniflow - 1913 Second nos)	T2 0-8-0	T3 0-8-0	D 4-4-4T	S3 4-6-0	Pacific 4-6-2
Dates	1910–11	1911/ 1914–18	1912	1912	1911–21	1919/1924	1913–14/ 1920–22	1919–24	1922–24
Numbers built	20	40	10	20	70	15	40	70	5
Cylinders in inches	(15½ x 26) x 3 / (16½ x 26) x 3	(15½ x 26) x 3	(16½ x 26) X 3	(20 x 26) x 2	(20 x 26) X 2	(18½ x 26) x 3	(16½ x 26) x 2	(18½ x 26) x 3	(19 x 26) x 3
Motion – Stephenson, unless otherwise stated	with 7½in piston valves	with 7½in piston valves	with 7½in piston valves	825 – with Walschaerts	With 8½in piston valves	with 8½in piston valves	with 7½in piston valves	with 8½in piston valves	With 8 19/32in piston valves
Tractive effort @ 85% in lb	29,403/ 26140	19,300	19,300	21,155	28,800	36,963	22,940	30,030	29,9180
Boiler									
Pressure in pounds per sq in	1,80/160	180	160	180/160	180	180	160	180	200
Maximum diameter outside	5ft 6in	5ft 6in	5ft 6in	5ft 6in	5ft 6in	5ft 6in	4ft 9in	5ft 6in	6ft (plus 3in cladding)
Barrel length	15ft 10½in	15ft 10½in	15ft 10½in	15ft 6in	15ft 7½in	15ft 7½in	11ft	16ft 8½in	26ft

Firebox length outside	9ft	9ft	9ft	8ft	8ft	9ft	8ft	9ft	9ft
Tubes	1,507/534	763.9	763.9	2,153/1,677	723	1,129	624.24 sq ft	866 sq in	1,472
Flues	186	2,160	2,329	-	506	534	208.6 sq ft	534 sq in	24 – 962.7ft
Firebox		185	185	144	140	166		166	200
Total evaporative		1,485.4	1,485.4	1,730	1,369	1,829	1,331.8	1,566	2,374.6
Superheater	258.3	392	392	504	361	392	194	392	509.9
Grate area	23	27	27	23	23	27	23	27	412
Length									
Over buffers	42ft 10in.	63ft 3in	63ft 3in	61ft	59ft 3in	60ft 10in	42ft 10in	62ft 6in	72ft 4in
Coupled wheels	(4ft 7¼in) x 6 – rigid wheel base	(6ft 10in) x 4	(6ft 10in) x 4	6ft 1¾in	(5ft 7in) x 8	(4ft 7¾in) x 8	(5ft 9in) x 4	(5ft 8in) x 6	(6ft 8in) x 6
Leading wheels	(3ft 3¼in) x 4	3ft 7¼in x 4	3ft 7¼in x 4	3ft 7½in	-		(3ft 3¼in) x 4	(3ft 1in) x 4	(3ft 1in) x 4
Trailing wheels	(3ft 9¾in) x 2	(4ft) x 2	-	-	-	-	(3ft 3¼in) x 4		(63ft 9in) x 2
Tender	-	12ft 8in	12ft 8in	12ft 8in	12ft 8in	12ft 8in	-	12ft 8in	12ft 8in – 6 -wheeled
Weight									
Engine	87 tons, 8 cwt	76 tons, 15 cwt	77 tons, 2 cwt	71 tons, 2 cwt./ 71 tons, 15 cwt	65 tons, 18 cwt	71 tons, 12 cwt	84 tons, 15 cwt	77 tons, 14cwt	101 tons, 10 cwt

Maximum axle load	19 tons, 10 cwt	20 tons, 16 cwt	20 tons, 18 cwt	19 tons, 8 cwt	17 tons, 12 cwt	19 ton	19 ton 19½ cwt	20 tons, 6 cwt	20 ton
Tender		44 tons, 2 cwt	46 tons, 12 cwt	44 tons, 2 cwt	110 tons	44 tons, 2 cwt	–	40 tons, 12 cwt	46 tons, 12 cwt
Coal capacity	5 tons	5 tons, 10 cwt	5 tons, 10 cwt	5 tons	5 tons, 10 cwt	5 tons, 10 cwt	4 tons	5 tons, 10 cwt	60 tons
Water Capacity in gallons	2,300	4,125	4,125	3,940	4,125	4,125	2,000	4,125	4,125 (self-trimming)

BIBLIOGRAPHY

RAVEN'S OWN WRITINGS, REPORTS AND CONFERENCE MATERIAL (IN CHRONOLOGICAL ORDER)

1893 'Report with reference to the Working of Compound Engines compared with Working of other Classes of Engines on the North Eastern Railway' (with Ramsey Kendall) for the NER Locomotive and Stores Committee

1896 'Report on Fog Signalling' for ARLE on 27 November

1898 'Report on the state of Cambrian Railways' for Cambrian Railways Board

1904 'Middlesborough Docks Electrical and Hydraulic Power Plant', given on 2 June 1904, at American Society of Mechanical Engineers Congress with IMechE in Chicago

1909 'North Eastern Railway Hours and Report', 258-page document on wages and working conditions of drivers and firemen and inspectors

1909-1913 Evidence to proceedings in dispute between Scarborough, Bridlington and West Riding Junction Railway Co. and NER Co. (PRO RAIL 527/1027)

1913 Paper given at prize-giving at Darlington Technical College on engineering education, superheating and proposed electrification, given on 9 April 1913

1914 'Superheating Steam in Locomotives', paper

1914 'Electrical System of Cab Signalling', for IMechE, 18 December 1914

1919 Paper on York to Newcastle electrification in February 1919 to IEE

1919 Report on 'Proposed Electrification of NER Main Line York to Newcastle, with intermediary feeders' (with Henry Angus Watson, the superintendent of the Line), dated October 1919 (PRO Rail 527/286)

1920 Report about visit to USA (and its electrified railways) (with F. Lydall), October 1920

1921 'The Advantages of Electric Traction on Railways', a paper given to the York Railway and Lecture Debating Society on 25 January 1921

1921, 'Mechanical Advantages of Electric Locomotives compared with Steam', a paper given at 1921 ICE Conference

1922 'Electric Locomotives', a paper given for IMechE in Paris in June 1922

1923 'The Advantages of Electric Traction on Railways' paper given to the GWR (London Branch) Lecture and Debating Society on 4 January 1923

1923/24 Report 'Organisation of Running Departments' on the organisation and standards of running sheds for LNER (PRO RAIL 390/293)

1923/24 Report 'Utilisation of Workshops' about organisation of maintenance workshops, for LNER (PRO RAIL 390/319)

1924 A thirty-six-page report in 1924 for the Metropolitan Vickers Electric Co. concerning electrification and electric locomotives

7 October 1924 Report of Royal Commission of Inquiry into New South Wales Railways (with Sir Sam Fay)

11 December 1924 Report of Royal Commission of Inquiry into New Zealand Railways (with Sir Sam Fay)

1925 As president, IMechE, opening speech reflecting centenary of SDR, with later contributions to discussion at Summer Meeting of IMechE in Newcastle, following Gresley paper, 'Three-Cylinder high Pressure Locomotives'

23 October 1925 Speech about Australia and New Zealand following Commission visits

7 April 1926 Report on rail workshops and their organisation in India, February 1926

BOOKS

General Reference

Ahrons Ernest Leopold, 1927 (reprint 1969), *The British Steam Railway Locomotive 1825-1925 Volume 1*, Ian Allan Publishing

Appleby K.C., 1990, *Shildon-Newport Retrospective: the forerunner of mainline electrification*, The Railway Correspondence and Travel Society

Briggs Asa, 1968, *Victorian Cities*, Penguin Books, especially Chapter 6 'Middlesbrough'

Burt Philip, 1926, *Control on the Railways, a study in method*, Unwin Brothers Ltd

Christiansen Rex, Miller R.W., 1967, *The Cambrian Railways: Volume I 1852-1888* and *Volume 2: 1889-1968*, David & Charles, Newton Abbott

Clarke J.F., 1984, *A Century of Service to Engineering and Shipbuilding A Centenary history of the North East Coast Institution of Engineers and Shipbuilders 1884-1984*, North East Coast Institution of Engineers and Shipbuilders

Drury George H., 1985, *The Historical Guide to North American Railroads*, Kalmbach Books

Freeman Michael, 1999, *Railways and the Victorian Imagination*, Yale University Press, New Haven and London

Green C.C., 1977, *Cambrian Railways Album*, Ian Allan Publishing

Green C.C., 1981, *Cambrian Railways Album -2*, Ian Allan Publishing

Griffiths Denis, 1987, *Locomotive Engineers of the GWR*, Patrick Stepheens, Wellingborough, Northamptonshire

Hughes Geoffrey, 2001, *Sir Nigel Gresley: The Engineer and his family*, Oakwood Press

Hughes Hugh, 1990, *Indian Locomotives: Part 1 - Broad Gauge 1851-1940*, The Continental Railway Circle

Parris Henry, 1965, *Government and the Railways in Nineteenth Century Britain*, Routledge, Kegan & Paul, London

Pevsner Nikolaus, 1972, *Yorkshire: York and the East Riding*, Penguin Books

Rounthwaite T.E., 1965, *The Railways of Weardale*, The Railway Correspondence & Travel Society

Rowland John, 1960, *Progress in power: The contribution of Charles Merz and his associates to sixty years of electrical development 1899-1959*, Newman Neame for Merz & McClellan

Schafer Mike & Solomon Brain, 1997, *Pennysylvania Railroad*, Motorbooks International

Sherrington C.E.R., 1928, *The Economics of Rail Transport in Great Britain*, Edward Arnold & Co.

Simmons Jack & Biddle Gordon (editors), 1997, *The Oxford Companion to British Railway History*, Oxford University Press

Thomson David, 1950, *England in the Nineteenth Century*, Penguin Books

Whiteley J.S. & Morrison J.W., 1984, *The Power of A1's, A2's, and A3's (Power Series)*, Oxford Rail Publishing Co., section on Raven LNER 'A2' class

Young John N., 1977, *GN Suburban*, David & Charles

Specific references in text:

Alderman Geoffrey, 1973, *The Railway Interest*, Leicester University Press

Ambler R.W. (editor), 1999, *The History and Practice of Britain's Railway, A New Research Agenda*, Ashgate

Armstrong Jim, 1974, *LNER Locomotive development between 1911 and 1947*, Peco Publications

Bagwell Philip S., 1963, *The History of National Union of Railwaymen*, George Allen & Unwin Ltd

Barnes Robin, 1985, *Locomotives that never were; Some Twentieth Century British Projects*, Jane's

Bell R., 1951, *Twenty-five Years of the North Eastern Railway*, Harrison and Sons Ltd

Biddle Gordon, 1990, *The Railway Surveyors*, Ian Allan Ltd

Bonavia Michael R., 1981, *Railway Policy between the Wars*, Manchester University Press

Bradley Roger P., 1988, *LNER 4-6-0's*, David & Charles

Bulleid, H.A.V., 1967, *The Aspinall Era*, Ian Allan Ltd

Bulleid, H.A.V., 1983, *Master Builders of Steam*, second edition, Ian Allan Ltd

Campling Nick, 1997, *Historic Carriage Drawings - Volume 1 LNER and Constituents*, The Pendragon Partnership

Christiansen Rex and Miller R.W, *1968, Volume 2: 1889-1968*, David and Charles, Newtown Abbott

Dawson John B., Forster, Colin, Mallon John F, Prattley Ron, Williamson Claire and David, 1994, *North Eastern Record Vol.2*, North Eastern Railway Association

Evans R.J., *The History of Aldenham School 1599-1969*, Old Aldenhamian Society

Everett Andrew, June-July 2005, 'Railway Knights in New Zealand – The 1924 Fay-Raven Royal Commission of New Zealand Railways', *The Bulletin of Australian Railway History Society*, p.46-48

Everett Andrew, November 2005, 'Two British Knights Come to Sydney – the 1924 Fay-Raven Royal Commission of New South Wales Government Railways', *The Bulletin of the Australian Railway History Society*, p.464-73

Everett Andrew, May 2006, 'The July Strike on the North Eastern Railway', *North Eastern Express*, vol.45, no.182, 57-70

Fleming M.J., 2000, *North Eastern Record, vol.3, A Survey of Locomotives of the North Eastern Railway*, Historical Model Railway Society

Fryer Charles, 1990, *Experiments with Steam: Landmarks in unusual British Locomotive design 1846-1959*, Patrick Stephens Ltd

Grafton Peter, March 1971, *Edward Thompson of the LNER*, Kestrel Books Knaresborough, Yorks

Grafton Peter, March 2005, *Sir Vincent Raven and the North Eastern Railway*, Oakwood Press

Grieves Keith, 1989, *Sir Eric Geddes: Business and government in war and peace*, Manchester University Press

Gresley Herbert Nigel, *Letter to George Jackson Churchward*, 7 April 1914, Boxtest/test 4, NRM, York

Groundwater Ken, 1998, *Newcastle's Railways: a View from the Past*, Ian Allan Publishing

Gourvich Terence Richard, 1980, *Railways and the British Economy 1830-1914*, Studies in Economic and Social History, Macmillan Press

Harris Michael, 1973, *Gresley's Coaches: coaches built for the GNR, ECJS and LNER 1905-53*, David St. John Thomas Newton Abbott

Harris Michael, 1995, *Great Northern Railway and East Coast Joint Carriages from 1905*, Oakwood Press

Harris Michael, 1994, *LNER Carriages*, David St John Thomas

Hennessey Roger A.S., 1970, *The Electric Railway that never was*, Oriel Press

Hill Geoffrey, February 1991, *The Worsdells: a Quaker Engineering Dynasty*, The Transport Publishing Co.

Hoole Ken, 1967, *North Road Locomotive Works 1863-1966*, Roundhouse Books

Hoole Ken, 1969, *NER Buses, Lorries and Autocars*, Nidd Valley NGR Ltd., Knaresborough.

Hoole Ken, 1967 reprint by Augustus M. Kelley, New York, 1967 of Tomlinson William Weaver, 1914, *North Eastern Railway: its rise and development*, with new notes, corrections and updating by K. Hoole

Hoole Ken, 1986, third edition, *The North East, volume 4 – A Regional History of the Railways of Great Britain*, David St John Charles; David & Charles

Hoole Ken, 1987, *The North Eastern Electrics: the History of the Tyneside Electric Passenger Services (1904-1967)*, Locomotion Papers 165, The Oakwood Press

Hoole Ken, 1988, *The Electric Locomotives of the North Eastern Railway*, Locomotive Papers 167, Oakwood Press

Hughes Geoffrey, 1983, *The Gresley Influence*, Ian Allan Ltd, London

Hughes Geoffrey, 1986, *LNER*, Guild Publishing

Hughes Geoffrey, 1988, *LNER 4-6-0's at work*, Ian Allan Ltd, London

Irving R.J., 1976, *The North Eastern Railway Company 1870-1914: an economic history*, Leicester University Press

Jackson D., *J G Robinson – a lifetime's work*, Oakwood Press

Jenkinson David, 1988, *British Railway Carriages of the Twentieth Century Volume 1: the end of an era 1901-22*, Patrick Stephens

Kelly's Directory for Durham, 1868, 1871–1872 and 1873

Kitchenside Geoffrey & Williams Alan, 1998, *Two Centuries of Railway Signalling*, Oxford Publishing Co.

Larkin Edgar J. & John G., 1988, *The Railway Workshops of Britain 1823-1986*, Macmillan Press

Maclean, *The locomotives of the North Eastern Railway, 1854-1903*

Manders, F.W.D., 1973 (second impression with amendments), *A History of Gateshead*, Gateshead Corporation

Middlemiss Thomas, 1991, *Steam Locomotive Nicknames*, Silver Link Publishing Ltd

Mulligan Fergus, 1990, *One Hundred and Fifty Years of Irish Railways*, Appletree Press

Nock Oswald S., 1954, *The Locomotives of the North Eastern Railway*, Ian Allan Ltd, London

Nock Oswald S., 1983, *British Locomotives of the Twentieth Century; vol.1 1900–1930*, Patrick Stephens

Pevsner Nikolaus, 1985 (second reprint with corrections by Elizabeth Williamson), *Durham*, Penguin Books

Pevsner Nikolaus, 1962, *The Buildings of England: North-West and South Norfolk*, Penguin Books

Pratt Edwin A., 1912, *A History of Inland Transport and Communication in England*, Kegan Paul, Trench, Trübner & Co. Ltd

Pratt, Edwin A., 1921, *British Railways and the Great War*, Blount Odhams

Rounthwaite T.E., 1965, *The Railways of Weardale*, The Railway Correspondence and Travel Society

Semmens Peter William Brett, 1991, *Electrifying the East Coast Route: the making of the first 140mph railway*, Patrick Stephens

Simmons Jack, 1991, *The Victorian Railway*, Thomas & Hudson

Straddon S.A. et al, 1978, *Horse Tram to Metro: One Hundred Years of Local Public Transport in Tyne and Wear*, Tyne and Wear Transport Executive

Thomas John, 1972, *North British Atlantics*, David Charles, Newton Abbot

Vaughan, Adrian 1997, *Railwaymen, Politics & Money*, John Murray

White Francis, *History, Gazetteer and Directory of Norfolk*, 1854

Whitehouse Patrick & Thomas David St John, 1980, *LNER 150: A Century and a Half of Progress*

Westwood J.N., 1977, *Locomotive Designers in the Age of Steam*, Sedgewick and Jackson

Wilson C. David, 1995, *Racing Trains, the 1895 Railway Races to the North*, Alan Sutton Publishing Ltd

NEWSPAPERS AND MAGAZINES

General references

Boyle David, June 2003, *The man who made us work like this....*, BBC History Magazine, vol.4, no.6, p.42-44

Darlington and Stockton Times, 1894–1952

Daily Chronicle, August 1910

Hughes G.J., June 1983, 'Sir Vincent Raven', *Railway Magazine*, vol.129, no. 986, p.226-28

Laybourn Mike, May 2000, 'Strike' (*BBC History Magazine*), BBC Worldwide Ltd, p.20-24

Stanier Mike, March 2002, 'Traction Electrical Engineering', *Entrain*, p.26-30

Northern Despatch 1894–1952

Northern Echo 1894–1952

Northern Express, vol. 1 to present
Sydney Morning Herald, 1924
Teesdale Mercury, 2 June 1917

Specific references in text:

Atkins Philip, August 2000, '4-cylinder Compounds of the North Eastern Railway', *Back Track*
Atkins Philip, September 2000, 'Career Moves – George Heppel', *Back Track*
Aves William A.T., 1998, 'North Eastern Eight-coupled Locomotives: Locomotives Illustrated'
    123, RAS Publishing
Bell T.M. Dr, August 2002, 'Railways Planned and Built – the North Pennines', *North Eastern
    Express*, vol. 41. no. 167   .
Drew Paul, 1975, 'The North Eastern Railway' (*Trains Illustrated* 15), Ian Allen
Dodd's Darlington Annual, 1912, *North Eastern Railway New Offices in Darlington*
Drew Paul, 1975, *The North Eastern Railway* (Trains Illustrated 15), Ian Allen
The Engineer, 1934, v.157
Hughes Geoffrey, 2001, 'Raven, Collett, Gresley and Electrification', *Back Track* Special Issue 2 –
    'LNER', edited by Michael Blakemore, published by Atlantic Publishers
Hughes J.G., June 1983, 'Sir Vincent Raven', *Railway Magazine*, vol.129, no.986, p.226-28
NER Magazine, 1911-1922
Newman Aubrey, April 2000, 'Trains and Shelters and Ships', paper presented at a seminar under
    the auspices of the Jewish Genealogical Society of Great Britain
Railway Engineer, August 1922
Romans Mike, 1987, 'North Eastern Railway 4-6-0's' (*Locomotives Illustrated* 57), Ian Allan Ltd
Romans Mike, 1994, 'North Eastern Atlantics and Pacifics' (*Locomotives Illustrated* 93), RAS
    Publishing
Russell Patrick, 1994, 'The LNER 4-6-2 Tank Locomotives' (*Locomotives Illustrated* 98), RAS
    Publishing
Semmens Peter William Brett, 'Tyneside Electrics Then and Now', August 2000, *The Railway
    Magazine*
The Stephenson Locomotive Society, Jubilee (1959) Volume 1909–1959 – LNER section – The
    North Eastern Railway
Teasdale John G., February 2002, 'Transatlantic traffic: being a consideration upon how American
    Railway Practices Influenced those of the North Eastern Railway', *The North Eastern Express*,
    vol.41, no.165

PROCEEDINGS ETC.
ICE Proceedings
IMechE, Proceedings 1886–1934
NER Board minutes 1854–1922
NER Literary Institute, Minutes, 1889–1890, 1904, 1911, 1915–1916, 1927

INDEX